Urgency in the Anthropocene

Urgency in the Anthropocene

Amanda H. Lynch and Siri Veland

The MIT Press
Cambridge, Massachusetts
London, England

This book was set in ITC Stone Sans Std and ITC Stone Serif Std by Toppan Best-set Premedia Limited. Printed and bound in the United States of America.

Library of Congress Cataloging-in-Publication Data

Names: Lynch, Amanda H., author. | Veland, Siri, author.
Title: Urgency in the anthropocene / Amanda H. Lynch and Siri Veland.
Description: Cambridge, MA : MIT Press, [2018] | Includes bibliographical references and index.
Identifiers: LCCN 2018007476| ISBN 9780262038706 (hardcover : alk. paper) | ISBN 9780262535762 (pbk. : alk. paper)
Subjects: LCSH: Human ecology. | Nature--Effect of human beings on. | Global environmental change.
Classification: LCC GF21 .L96 2018 | DDC 304.2--dc23 LC record available at https://lccn.loc.gov/2018007476

10 9 8 7 6 5 4 3 2 1

For Nikolai, Brigitte, and Johanna

Contents

Preface

Since Maarten Hajer observed that the ways we name crisis can prevent us from imagining solutions, since Paul Crutzen proposed that humans have become a geological force of nature, since Bruno Latour suggested that naming the age of humankind was decisive to understanding it, the Anthropocene has emerged as a productive, and sometimes divisive, narrative. This geological neologism, defined where human activities have left ubiquitous signals in the earth's sediments, has come to symbolize a domain of urgency. Why? The ability to detect the human fingerprint in earth system processes is evolving into an ability to predict extreme, unprecedented, and catastrophic events. Furthermore, the attribution of these events to human activities, whether scientifically or in the popular discourse, raises the specter of apocalypse, wrought by our own hands.

The need to respond to crisis and disaster is challenging human values. Systems of sovereignty and law are being stretched in an attempt to meet the onrushing challenges. This discourse of urgency emboldens impulsive policy and governance responses. The once unacceptable, such as geoengineering solutions or totalitarian governance, have become anticipated and even demanded.

But the ages of humans in the world have unfolded as nuanced and multifaceted journeys of many millennia. The Anthropocene offers one framing of the world among many in which human agency prevents, prepares for, and responds to change, even catastrophic change. Stories of being, becoming, and ending in the world are innumerable, and each serves to define a rationale for human agency, in nature or apart from it. In the urgency to respond according to any one framing of the changing world, other framings may be overlooked, limiting the possibilities we are able to envision and accept.

In this book, we examine the interplay between this new and ostensibly global state of urgency, and the means by which this urgency is identified and addressed. We invite a sense of commonality in a shared world undergoing rapid change: our aim is to pose the questions that Anthropocene urgency is raising among those who see themselves as promoters of the Anthropocene schema and those who may not. This invitation is also a challenge[1]—to find new epistemologies for coexistence in this age of humans.

We organize our enquiry around the central theme of myth—that is, the underlying narrative by which we make sense of the world, setting our frameworks for expectations, demands, and actions. In our analysis, myths are not construed as false or factual: in either case, myths materially affect the achievement of human dignity and environmental sustainability. The Anthropocene as myth emerged from earth system science. Now, it is being narrated variously as the new normal, a state of exception, an apocalypse, or a coming techno-utopia. Many narratives of the human period—the Everywhen of Australian Indigenous peoples, piloting Spaceship Earth in the modern era, the Wilderness Myth of the environmental movement, and the Age of Enlightenment myth of scientific progress—influence the ways in which the myths of the Anthropocene are evolving.

We explore the three pillars of Anthropocene manifestations of urgency—phenomenology, policy, and governance—through a case-based approach. Attending to the particularities of cases builds upon the insight that "men are apt to deceive themselves upon general matters, but not so much when they come to particulars" and, further, that "to look at things only in a general way deceives."[2] By offering an examination of a diverse array of case studies, we both invite reflection and offer alternatives.

Chapter 1 presents the Anthropocene epoch and its protagonists, and introduces the theoretical underpinning and practical implications of understanding the Anthropocene as a coupled problem of phenomenon and discourse. We introduce examples of Anthropocene phenomena, policy, and governance: weather disasters, species extinction, and authoritarian environmentalism. We define the elements of myth as an analytic framework and illustrate the flexibility of this framework for understanding the foundations of geological sciences, Australian Indigenous cosmologies, and the establishment of the European Union. Finally, we provide a context for the emerging Anthropocene myth by briefly presenting other examples—historic and coexisting—of myths of humans and nature. These include the myths of the Mayacene, the Australian Everywhen, the Epic of Gilgamesh, and the Greek myth of the world-for-us.

Chapter 2 examines three recent weather disasters that illuminate the intersections of phenomenon and urgency. We begin with the provenance of organized disaster response in the Battle of Solferino, revisiting Henri Dunant as a protagonist in setting the standards of humanitarianism. We investigate the interplay between the ability to detect or anticipate an event and the propensity to act on a sense of urgency commensurate with the scale of the disaster. We look back on the preparedness, response, and aftermath of Typhoon Haiyan in the Philippines; revisit the geophysical parameters and socioeconomic drivers of the 2011–2016 Californian drought; and explore the lessons of the 2003 European heat wave. Although science treats the attribution of extreme weather to anthropogenic climate change as ambiguous, public discourse often treats it as unequivocal, and hence these disasters reveal patterns of expectations regarding the scale and frequency of extreme events and the appropriate responses to them.

Chapter 3 considers the ways in which urgency is both narrowing our policy options and broadening the arenas of the acceptable. We introduce this topic by considering the role of "safe limits" in United States clean air policies and in global proposals of planetary limits. We examine policies of decoupling at national and international scales, policies implied by the Sustainable Development Goals, and the innovative policy implicit in the Sendai Framework for Disaster Risk Reduction. We address the short time scale of disasters and the longer time scale of sustainability, along with the different lenses on urgency they represent. In particular, the foreshortening of time and the compression of space leads to serious questions of justice and equity in finding strategies for a sustainable future.

Chapter 4 explores encounters with urgent governance, beginning with the case of the Haida Gwaii and its implications for unilateral geoengineering experiments. The task of democratic modes of governance to rise to the challenge of urgency has been a particular focus in the literature. We explore this through the lenses of international climate change agreements and national approaches to environmental governance, before introducing the particular insights that can be gained through a serious consideration of Indigenous governance. In the increasingly polarized arena of global change, the world needs an alternative approach that leaves incompatibilities unresolved, reciprocity and opposition coexisting, seeking the logic of the included middle. Coexistence, however, is a fragile geography; contemporaneity is imposed rather than chosen and competing myths cannot be settled. Many of these contexts are legacies of a colonial past or an unjust present.

Finally, chapter 5 addresses the profound dilemmas that coexistence presents by framing competing interests as fostering the resilience needed to follow paths of development in which redundancy and complexity are encouraged rather than resolved. We make a normative commitment to the dual goals of human dignity and environmental sustainability. We renarrate the Anthropocene as an epoch of actual and emerging coexistence with earth system variability—in cultural, political, and economic systems, as well as in the patterns of climatic, ecological, and geological systems. Our proposition is that the commons is not a tragedy, but rather the opportunity for coexistence. In this way, we may map a path through the fragmentation that Anthropocene urgency invites, to invoke a sense of commonality in purpose. Rather than stake a course, we conclude with an urgency for unprecedented listening—to think together with greater imagination and across a broader range of possibilities.

Acknowledgments

We'd like to give special thanks to those who made this book possible: to Beth Clevenger at the MIT Press for encouraging the effort, to Bill Ascher for his enthusiastic support, and to our reviewers for helping us to improve the argument. Thank you to Carolina Adler, Zac Bischoff-Mattson, Emma Calgaro, Jerome Zayas, and Leyla Craig, scholars all. Meghan Blanchette helped to streamline the narrative, and Keren Alfred kept the references in line. Any and all mistakes are our own. We tried the patience of our two families, and we are more thankful than they realize for their abiding support. Thanks also to Askvoll for being a great host. We offer our deepest gratitude to Ron Brunner and Richie Howitt for their steadfast mentorship, challenge, and insight.

1 Whose Anthropocene?

We pile the long stakes at the breaches and cast precious jades into the river.
The Lord of the River hears our plea
But there is not enough brushwood.
There is not enough brushwood—
—Wu Di (156–87 BC)

Introduction: A Geology of Humankind

As if you could kill time without injuring eternity.
—Henri David Thoreau[1]

Urgency and Insecurity

Humans are causation machines—the foundation of our ability to make meaning is built through telling valid stories of causality. Although these stories need not be empirically verifiable, an internal logic must be observed. The sense of validity is supported by events in the world, from weather to war, unfolding according to our expectations. Validity leads to a sense of ontological security, an ability to anticipate responses and relationships in the context of a relevant worldview.

When the world violates our expectations, it threatens our ontological security. Ulrich Beck speaks of the "abyss" as three pillars of ontological security crumble, in which "the state, science and the economy are failing to provide security."[2] Add to these pillars the natural world we expect to support and sustain us. The ontological security provided by the natural world reasserts the material consequences of our stories, our values, and our expectations, providing the coordinates by which we navigate the tumultuous world-for-us.[3]

The threats of exceeding planetary boundaries present an unprecedented ontological risk for contemporary thinkers. For others, the ending of the world has happened again and again. From the catastrophic ending of the Inca Empire to white sails on the horizons of the Americas, from Christian eschatology to the atrocities of World War II, apocalypse is ever the companion of human sociality.[4] Indeed, as Haraway points out, "Surely, to say 'unprecedented' in view of the realities of the last centuries is to say something almost unimaginable."[5] How will the particular insecurities of the Anthropocene compel us to act, and are there alternatives?

There is, at present, an emerging discourse of anthropogenic planetary emergency that is manifest in a hermeneutic temporal compression—that is, a sense of urgency. An empirically verifiable causal connection between experienced changes—hurricane intensity, ice sheet collapse, drought frequency, or habitat loss—and anthropogenic forces is not necessary in this compression process. It is sufficient that anthropogenic symbols are invoked.

We argue that our narration of causation and expectation fundamentally determines the preparation for, response to, and recovery from each perceived manifestation of anthropogenic global change. Maarten Hajer has argued that the discourse that permitted discovering the environmental crisis is simultaneously preventing us from imagining solutions.[6] In ontological terms, what we understand as the building blocks and connections of reality have been found wanting, but they are also all we have to build upon. This, then, is indicative of ontological risk, where the world, the world-for-us, changes "surreptitiously and unplanned."[7] It is this world, changing apace in unforeseen ways, that many have come to narrate as the Anthropocene.

A Force of Nature

Determining onset of the Anthropocene has been proposed in several ways: the spread of humans across the continents, the expansion of agriculture in the Neolithic, the detectable increase in species extinctions starting around 1500, the Industrial Revolution, the invention of plastics, the atomic era. In all of these definitions, the Anthropocene belongs to a modern European mythology about the linear nature of time. Its very recognition owes to the development of the modern science of geology. This science can be traced back to Nicolas Steno (1638–1686) and James Hutton (1726–1797) and their descriptions of the processes that have shaped the surface of the earth. Most critically, these processes were inferred from direct observations of the earth and its stratigraphy.

William Smith (1769–1839), a surveyor, observed a pattern in the fossils occupying the layers of rock in mines near Somerset in England. Continuing his observations as he traveled the country, surveying canals, Smith in 1815 published the first national geologic map[8] displaying the large-scale geologic strata of the United Kingdom. These efforts earned him the nickname "Strata" Smith, the founder of stratigraphy. Stratigraphy would lead to discoveries such as continental drift, ice ages, and geological chronologies. Today, geological time periods constitute demarcations agreed upon through the International Commission on Stratigraphy, using defined biogeochemical markers and radiometric dating. Geological strata are delineated on the basis of stability and distribution and are designated via a start point.

Paul Crutzen and Eugene Stoermer[9] used stratigraphy to conceive the Anthropocene, with the proposition that anthropogenic traces can be detected and made to correspond in geological strata across the world. "The global effects of human activities have become clearly noticeable," Crutzen and Stoermer wrote in 2000, and proposed that we have been in the Anthropocene since the late nineteenth century. The neologism gave rise to a "geology of mankind,"[10] with specified anthropogenic signals manifest in geologic strata. Through the Working Group on the Anthropocene of the International Commission on Stratigraphy, the science of stratigraphy has permitted debate on when the Anthropocene epoch commenced—as well as whether such an epoch can be delineated at all.[11] In this way, the idea of an Anthropocene has already taken hold as a concept by which epistemic communities can debate meaning and purpose.[12]

Evidence in the stratigraphic record has since suggested that broad-scale and high-impact human activities such as agriculture, fossil fuel use, and nuclear fission technologies signify a geological force in their own right, a signature of global change in the earth system itself.[13] A common thread in these Anthropocene framings is characterizing humans as "one of the great forces of nature"—a framing that is often intertwined with concerns around global environmental crises.[14] Detecting the signals of these crises is, therefore, not only a matter of biophysical empiricism; it also demands attention to the entanglement between earth system phenomena and those of social dynamics. In this way, anthropogenic global change has come to be understood as the quintessential "wicked" problem[15]—that is, a problem in which natural and social processes are inextricably coupled in multiple, dynamic, and irreducibly complex ways. Indeed, Zalasiewicz and colleagues suggest that "this phenomenon is now arguably the most important question of our age—scientifically, socially and politically. We cannot think of a greater or more urgent challenge."[16] But any discourse of urgency has the potential to both expand and limit the perceived range of alternative responses.

Locating the Anthropocene in Time

Consider the implications of characterizing the modern era as a start point, a midpoint, or an end point of an Anthropocene epoch.[17] As a start point, the anthropogenic strata exemplify "the new normal." Earth systems prior to this point in time are designated as natural, not manipulated by human activities, and, typically, superior. The wilderness, a pure, primeval place, is defined by the absence of human beings. Whichever signal is selected as the start point, from agriculture to atoms, the time period following is considered to be inferior, degraded. The Anthropocene as a start point embodies the cumulative understanding of earth systems that has permitted a recognition of our profound (negative) influence on geological timescales.

Alternatively, the present as the end point of the Anthropocene symbolizes apocalypse, "the noose around the neck of the earth."[18] In this perspective, "current trends of habitat loss and overexploitation, if maintained, would push Earth into the sixth mass extinction event (with ~75% of species extinct) in the next few centuries. … Not only would this represent the first instance of a new epoch having been witnessed firsthand by advanced human societies, it would be one stemming from the consequences of their own doing."[19] Apocalyptic anxiety is a common thread throughout human history, together with the storying of human causation and themes of divine retribution.[20]

Alternatively, when the modern era is seen as the midpoint of the Anthropocene, the current state symbolizes "a state of exception" emerging from a linear human history. This progression develops from original human cultures, through the current nadir of human-environment interactions, and into a developed future in which our "environmental" problems have been overcome. In this more optimistic view, the future is characterized as moving beyond apocalyptic orientations to see environmental problems as challenges for social, technical and economic reform, rather than as the existential consequences of industrialization.

Finally, when the current era is seen as a moment of transformation, of tipping points, or of coming-into-being, this opens the possibilities we might be able to imagine. This delineation would recognize the role of human thought and ingenuity as suggested by the work of geochemist Vladimir Vernadsky. In 1938, Vernadsky suggested that the *noösphere*, or the sphere of human thought, was as significant in the history of the planet as the geosphere and the biosphere: "Although [hu]man, Homo sapiens is a surface phenomenon in one of the envelopes of the Earth's crust, namely in the biosphere, a new geological factor—the reason—introduced by the appearance of man into the history of the planet is so great as to its consequences and chances given by it that, as it seems to me, one may not object against taking this factor into account for geological division together with the stratigraphic and tectonic factors. The scope of the changes in these cases is comparable."[21] In this sense, it is the development and transmission of human thought that delineates the Anthropocene.

Using this latter framing, the present moment permits capturing how the breadth of human epistemic communities and cosmologies both drive environmental crises (Mayan Civilization, Industrial Revolution, etc.) and offer domains of ingenuity and agency for devising sustainability in challenging environments (e.g., Australian Indigenous and Arctic Inuit peoples). This refutes the assertion that our enlightenment is necessarily accompanied by our ruin. In this context, transformative human knowledge can emerge from many different directions, toward an imperative to protect each other and other life forms. With attention to the coupled goals of human dignity[22] and environmental stewardship,[23] what lies ahead in this Anthropocene may be human societies integrated with nature, transformed and resilient.

This constructively fuzzy framing intersects with a different kind of optimism, in which many timelines, many spaces, many systems, *coexist* in the Anthropocene (box 1.1). The idea of the anthropogenic stratigraphic layers symbolizing coexistence is congruent with, for example, Indigenous Australian conceptions of space-time as a state of emergence and co-becoming, in which there are no noumena, only radically contextual[24] and emergent phenomena. It is also congruent with the conceptualization of linear change customary in European and East Asian traditions. This,

Box 1.1
Coexistence

The recognition of coexistence acknowledges different—inconsistent, incompatible, irreconcilable—doctrines to persist side by side as policies and modes of governance are explored. In this definition, coexistence does not imply a proposition or probability of consensus, win-win outcomes, or resolution of conflict. Rather, it admits that reconciliation may not be possible but that multiple strategies to achieve preferred outcomes can nevertheless proceed. The practice of coexistence maintains questions of justice and human dignity in tension with pragmatic decision processes.

then, is a relational story that does not make prior ontological separation between humans and nature. The Anthropocene becomes a framework for narrating coexistence, contextualizing our responses at a crossway among numerous urgent story lines, and toward transformed understandings of human-environment relations.

Three Pillars of Anthropocene Urgency

Can we imagine the huge conversion of fossil fuels into carbon dioxide as literally turning rocks into air on a planetary scale, because that is what we are in fact doing? —Simon Dalby[25]

The three pillars of Anthropocene urgency—phenomenology, policy, and governance—and the concerns to which they give rise, form the core structure of this volume. Here, we offer an introduction as they relate to global change.

Phenomenology of Urgency

Extremes of weather and climate represent the front line of Anthropocene symbols for urgency. Each new extreme weather event—from Hurricane Katrina of 2005 to Typhoon Haiyan of 2013, from the European heat wave of 2003 to the 2008 Afghanistan blizzard, from the Black Saturday fires of 2009 to the Pakistan flood of 2010—contributes to the mounting insecurity that perhaps not just our human vulnerabilities but also the geophysical events themselves are self-inflicted. In the Anthropocene, the connection has become more pressing: Is each event an act of god, a statistical quirk in a world-for-us, or a direct result of our past actions? If an act of god, is it a sanction for some human failing or transgression? If it is a direct result of our past actions, how does this insight impel us to act now?

If we were to ascribe causation to humans directly or indirectly, each storm, fire, flood, or heat wave identified with the Anthropocene would motivate action beyond immediate humanitarian relief. If a direct link can be argued, extreme phenomena provide a window of opportunity to increase our material security,[26] because "in effect nature penalizes with severe sanctions past policies, including inaction, that have allowed significant losses from an extreme weather event to occur."[27] In this role, the extreme phenomenon can serve as a surrogate for social processes that enable policies and governance to change, thereby preventing the compounding of vulnerability. Why has this not occurred more widely?

One reason is that an Anthropocene attribution introduces ambiguity by crossing policy realms. Not all extreme phenomena present a hazard,[28] but even when actionable losses of life and property emerge and disasters result, those responsible for detecting extreme events, those responding with humanitarian aid, and those responsible for building resilience inhabit vastly different policy arenas. Anthropocene extreme events include weather and climate disasters within the realm of human experience, extreme events with no past analog, and slow changes that push natural and human systems beyond their coping ranges. As a result, hurricane and drought, crop failure and sea level rise, all can be attributed (or not) to the Anthropocene, prompting urgent action in one or several sectors. Further, minimizing vulnerability to any extreme phenomenon, even if linked symbolically to the Anthropocene, is only one of many interests to be pursued by human societies. As a result, "the declaration of an emergency situation is ultimately a political act, and thus will inevitably be used for political purposes."[29]

A second factor that prevents a positive impact of disasters on building resilience lies in the consequences of extreme events being unevenly distributed. The worst human catastrophes tend to occur in the developing world, but even when they do not, asymmetries in impact are typical. In all countries, impoverished people are less able to mitigate hazards, lack access to insurance, and are less able to relocate from hazard-exposed areas. Nevertheless, by their very lack of resources, impoverished populations are often considered capable of absorbing environmental damage more readily than those with a lot to lose. Although the proportion of the world's population living in extreme poverty has more than halved over recent decades, the absolute number of the poor is increasing with global population growth. This compounds the challenge of efforts to plan for and respond to disasters.

A third factor inhibiting policy reform is the fact that extreme events are rare by definition. Formalizations of *rare* vary, but these events typically are defined as the tenth or ninetieth percentile of the observed probability density function for that phenomenon—if, indeed, such a distribution can be measured by available data. Furthermore, the characteristics of what is understood as rare varies from place to place: a heat wave in Boston leading to significant morbidity and mortality might be a typical summer week in Miami.

A fourth factor that prevents a positive impact of disasters on building resilience is that extreme events rarely present themselves passively to the human imagination. Every culture provides ontological security and its allied perception of risk, which has been identified as a stronger predictor of behavior than any objective measurement of risk.[30] For climate change, the time scales involved and the scale of investment required often exceed individual capacity to imagine, leading to paralysis.[31] For some, the rationales for climate change causality themselves violate ontological security, leading to active antagonism.[32] For others, competing demands direct priorities away from Anthropocene urgencies, leading to inattention or maladaptations that surreptitiously increase vulnerability.[33]

As a result, extreme events may or may not violate expectations; they may be single events or slow-moving disasters; they may or may not motivate humanitarian relief and rebuilding efforts. All such events, particularly when they are attributed to the Anthropocene, allow us to explore the phenomenology of urgency in the Anthropocene.

Urgency in Policy Making

The Conference of the Parties to the UN Framework Convention on Climate Change negotiated the Kyoto Protocol in 1997, prescribing national targets and timetables for reductions in greenhouse gas emissions, and entering into force in 2005. The Doha Amendment of 2012 extended reduction targets to 2020, and the Paris Agreement of 2015 governs the period after 2020. The proposal leading to the adoption of the Paris Agreement formally recognizes that "climate change represents an urgent and potentially irreversible threat to human societies and the planet and thus requires the widest possible cooperation by all countries, and their participation in an effective and appropriate international response, with a view to accelerating the reduction of global greenhouse gas emissions."[34] The Paris Agreement goes on to cite the urgency of the problem a further five times, including twice in the agreement itself. The term *urgent* is not mentioned once in the Kyoto Protocol, nor in the Doha Amendment. The foreshortening of the time scale from Kyoto to Paris confronts the growing sense that that critical "planetary boundaries"[35] are being exceeded, at a rate that defies the capacities of our international institutions to respond.

A potent representation of this urgency is the accelerating extinction of species,[36] symbolized by charismatic megafauna at risk, such as the polar bear, the panda, and the tiger. The resilience of many species, and the ecosystems of which they are a part, is being exceeded by a combination of changes in climate, concomitant changes in other systems, such as increasing parasite ranges and ocean acidification, and other Anthropocene drivers, such as land-use change, pollution, landscape fragmentation, and overexploitation of resources. The International Union for Conservation of Nature and Natural Resources (IUCN) observes, however, that the risk of extinction has been systematically evaluated for less than 5 percent of the world's described species. In 2016, the IUCN has established 860 species as likely to be extinct but acknowledges this is certainly an underestimate. The Millennium Ecosystem Assessment frames this with urgency: "The rate of known extinctions of species in the past century is roughly 50–500 times greater than the extinction rate calculated from the fossil record of 0.1–1 extinctions per 1,000 species per 1,000 years. The rate is up to 1,000 times higher than the background extinction rates if possibly extinct species are included."[37] This framing gets parsed as substantial losses at global and local scales.[38] In this "Anthropocene defaunation ... of a conservatively estimated 5 million to 9 million animal species on the planet, we are likely losing ~11,000 to 58,000 species annually."[39] In this way, the "sixth mass extinction" has become a potent symbol for the Anthropocene.

Without doubt, the threat to ecosystems is real and present. The significance of this circumstance made global goes beyond the deeply human questions of our place in nature to question the international institutions we shape to cope with urgency. And yet, our very conceptions of humans of or apart from nature have a profound and lasting impact on the policies we can envision in facing an unprecedented future.

Challenges to Governance

In 1922, Walter Lippman famously noted: "When quick results are imperative, the manipulation of masses through symbols may be the only quick
way of having a critical thing done. It is often more important to act than
to understand. It is sometimes true that action would fail if everyone understood it."[40] In the face of the imperative for urgent action, it has been suggested that "it is not entirely clear that democracy is up to the challenge."[41]
Authoritarian approaches have been proposed as a solution. Bruce Gilley
defined the ideal of authoritarian environmentalism as "a public policy
model that concentrates authority in a few executive agencies manned by
capable and uncorrupt elites seeking to improve environmental outcomes."[42]

Authoritarian policy making has been identified as an approach that
may be desirable even in liberal democracies.[43] In practice, all regimes
embody mixtures of centralized and participatory processes; however, significant challenges face authoritarian decisions in democratic systems. For
example, having failed to make progress on strategies to address carbon
dioxide emissions in legislation, in 2014 President Barack Obama took an
executive action to set a national standard for emissions from power plants.
The Clean Power Plan was subsequently challenged in court, with implementation delayed until 2016. In 2017, President Donald Trump similarly
used executive orders to initiate the rescinding of the Clean Power Plan, an
action that was also challenged in court and remains unresolved at the time
of writing. In practice, all regimes embody some combination of representative, centralized, and participatory processes.

The relative effectiveness of authoritarian and democratic modes of
governance in addressing the urgencies of the Anthropocene is an open
question. We will argue, however, that a normative commitment to participatory governance and a practice of coexistence combine to suggest that
the spread and enhancement of democratic regimes are a preferred developmental construct.[44]

A Path Forward

How can valid and appropriate interests be integrated to mobilize support
for democratically legitimate decisions that advance responses to urgency
in the Anthropocene? John Dryzek suggests two important requirements.
The first is the support of satisficing compromises and consensus-building
approaches facilitated by the processes of deliberative democracy.[45] But the

second is permitting, even encouraging, contestation. We view this second provision as a critical criterion. Close proximity between the state and civil society, Dryzek suggests, tends to thwart radical critique. Furthermore, human dignity demands that some wrongs cannot be righted, particularly those associated with the legacies of colonialism and war. If we accept that addressing the urgent manifestations of the Anthropocene requires thinking beyond dualisms, the Anthropocene must take account of a more complete narrative that accepts multiplicity and simultaneity—that is, coexistence.

It is therefore not enough to insist that our existing worldviews, policies and institutions are wrong, or insufficient, and therefore in need of rejection. Developing new symbols and designing robust policies that contribute to a sense of ontological as well as material security require explicit linkages to an acceptable way of directing human agency. At present, alternative stories of the Anthropocene either urge the "end of man" or reject any notion of crisis. We simultaneously have innumerable ways of storying extremes while also lacking the stories needed to cope with the unimaginable future of Anthropocene urgency. Our proposition in this book is that a redirection of societies to sustainably just pathways requires an epistemic transformation of science, policy, and governance—a transformation that is open to the coexistence of many, sometimes incompatible, doctrines. This proposition first demands attention to the relationship between observable or experienced phenomena and the discourse that allows us to make sense of them. To this conjunction, the following section turns.

A Coupled Problem of Phenomenon and Discourse

There is greater attention to fewer symbols in periods of prolonged tension.
—Daniel Lerner, Ithiel de Sola Pool, and Harold D. Lasswell[46]

Incipient manifestations of global change in extreme meteorological events, declarations of states of emergency, deployment of plan and response: these expressions of urgency bring into sharp relief the conjunction between the phenomenon itself and the human discourses that render them knowable and accessible to human agency. Global change, even with successful policies, promises a future unlike any humans have experienced in the past. We cannot confront that which we cannot imagine. To resolve global environmental crises, we argue, the emergent Anthropocene discourse must be grounded in this conjunction.

Consider the nature of this relationship and how it has changed over time and varied in space. In Western scholarly traditions, theorizing the interactions between the material world and human thought emerged most strongly over the last century, in parallel with modern epistemologies. For example, John Dewey extended the ideas of pragmatism to propose that though thought is indeed a response to changing phenomena, thoughts also transform relationships with the environment and, further, the structure of the environment itself.[47] Alfred North Whitehead similarly rejected Descartes's real distinction between the material and the mind.[48] Building on new advances in physics, Niels Bohr argued for the principle of *complementarity*, whereby "any observation of atomic phenomena will involve an interaction with the agency of observation not to be neglected. Accordingly, an independent reality in the ordinary physical sense can neither be ascribed to the phenomena nor to the agencies of observation."[49] He extended this idea beyond the angstrom scale, going on to suggest that "the nature of our consciousness brings about a complementarity, in all domains of knowledge, between the analysis of a concept and its immediate application."[50] This thread of interplay between environment and thought continue to be invoked, most recently as a way of interpreting the Anthropocene. As Simon Dalby writes, "On all scales the human presence in nature changes it as it changes humans. ... How all this might change our understandings of the appropriate governance structures for humanity is only beginning to be considered. To facilitate such understandings the term Anthropocene may be helpful."[51]

Formalizing the influence of thought on what can be observed, Kurt Gödel demonstrated that there are true statements in any unambiguous epistemology that cannot be proven within that system.[52] Michel Foucault took this on, arguing for discourse as both an enabling and restricting element that determines how we are able to think and talk about the phenomenological world.[53] In turn, Maarten Hajer drew Foucault's insights into the context of environmental discourse, proposing that the discourse that caused environmental problems may fundamentally prevent us from imagining solutions to those same problems.[54] We may not in fact possess the concepts required to solve the kinds of problems presented by the identification of the Anthropocene. Nevertheless, there are alternative discourses that may reframe this observation as a need for an epistemic opening. Our limitations emerge most clearly in risk-perception research.[55] Indeed, if "reality itself is multiple" and robbed "of its alleged stable, given, universal character,"[56] then humanity is already engaged in a plurality of options for human-shaped futures. As a result, "discussion has turned around the question of how this diversity must—or might—be valued."[57]

Some traditions do not have demands for ontological resolution between human and nature in any case, and freely accommodate coexistent but apparently discordant explanations for how particular earth formations came into being.[58] For example, there are many coexisting creation stories (Dreamings) that constitute Uluru (formerly known to Europeans as Ayers Rock) in central Australia. Accounts of causality offered by different Dreamings overlap in place but do not require resolution among them. Each Dreaming offers an origin story and account of causality that enables particular agencies in and on the world.[59] In another example, the Hindu tradition of Advaita Vedanta understands that subjective experience creates an illusion of duality, although this interpretation appears to have evolved over time.[60] In this and many other ways, multiple threads of epistemological thought have taken issue with a clockwork, material earth, *out there*, separate from the world of human thought.

The coupled problem of phenomenon and discourse is nowhere more apparent than in the influence of the dominant understanding of human-environmental relationships on responses to climate change. Karen O'Brien and colleagues demonstrated how different formulations of the environmental change discourse influence outcomes. "They influence interpretations of what certain phrases mean and control how they are used, prioritize the questions that are asked and answered, and influence the solutions that are prescribed."[61] And as observed by Neil Adger and colleagues, "Climate change narratives often interact with other beliefs to motivate responses, which in some cases may not be consistent with the 'rational' responses."[62] Anthropogenic climate change is an emblematic example of a phenomenon constructed through the interaction of three trends—a material change in environmental conditions, a heightened ecological consciousness affecting public values, and the growing institutional managerialism of capitalist economies. The different ways in which this construction takes place lead almost inevitably to conflict in the high-stakes Anthropocene.[63]

Myth as Analytic Framework

The schemes that permit observing, interpreting, ordering, and communicating the meaning of phenomena can be thought of as discourses, narratives, traditions, paradigms, or *myths*. Myth has been characterized as "frozen meaning"[64]—a metaphor that "emphasizes the stability of the pattern." As such, "myths shape the entire perceptual field for humans as people make meaning for themselves" through "the stories we tell ourselves (often subconsciously) about life and its purposes."[65] But myth is rarely asserted explicitly; it is inferred, rather, from oral, representational, behavioral, or textual evidence. Nor should the stability of myth be mistaken as static—any individual myth may take on emergent and dynamic character over time and space.

Myths perform an epistemic role in shaping the interpretative framework for changes in the world: as the world changes, myths change. This process is also reversed: as myths change, new possibilities for effecting change emerge. As such, there is no implication that a myth is *necessarily* either false or factual in an empirical sense. Rather, myth sets the social framework for acting in the face of social and environmental changes by carrying the values—patterns of demands, expectations, and identifications—most widely shared among a group of people. Further, myths serve to justify and explain the possession and use of values in communities—for example, political communities (the possession and use of power), scientific communities (the possession and use of enlightenment), business communities (of wealth), environmental communities (of well-being), and so forth. Other terms that might be used equivalently include vision, world view, social contract, frame, and lens. Shared expectations can be obscured by such differences in vocabulary and indeed by the fact that their functions are best served when they are taken for granted.

The metaphysical or cosmological myth is particularly powerful in shaping enduring values shared widely across a diversity of communities, through addressing the nature of creation (the *world-in-itself*) or existence (the *world-for-us*).[66] Importantly, the cosmological myth further provides the interpretive scheme for new or unencountered events, as it is the ordered scheme of the universe that "restrains the aberrations of the mere undisciplined imagination."[67] It is the purpose of a cosmology to be sufficient. "For this reason, a cosmology must consider those factors which have not been adequately embraced in some science."[68] Within it should be found the totality of real and observable elements and relations, and removed from it should be those concepts that have been found wrong and misleading.[69]

The political myth is important for understanding the role of power relationships in response to crises and challenges. This pattern has a bearing on the intrinsic constitutive structure, as well as any particular power relationship or practice. Plato's Republic is the foundational source of political myth in the tradition of Western political thought.[70] Plato presented what is often termed the *noble lie* (γεννᾷον ψεῦδος, *gennaion pseudos*) in a fictional tale, wherein Socrates proposes that if the people believed "this myth … [it] would have a good effect, making them more inclined to care for the state and one another." That said, Gaetano Mosca suggests that political myths are not "mere quackeries invented to trick the masses into obedience." Indeed, "They answer a real need in man's social nature; and this need, so universally felt, of knowing that one so governed not on the basis of mere material or intellectual force, but on the basis of a moral principle, has beyond any doubt a practical and real importance."[71] Harold Lasswell and colleagues concur, using the interpretation "metaphorical allusion" rather than "noble lie," and noting that Plato "spoke of the desirability of having the guardians as well as the people accept the myth."[72] This also aligns with Desmond Lee, who translates *gennaion pseudos* in Plato as *magnificent myth* and similarly notes that it is intended to be accepted by both rulers and ruled.[73] These interpretations focus on the primary function of a political myth: to justify and explain the possession and use of power in a political community or institution.

An important normative element in these conceptions of power and the political myth is the inadequacy of coercion as a tool to establish an enduring sovereignty. For example, Ibn Khaldūn, in his formative study of nomadic North Africans in 1377,[74] diagnosed "solidarity of sentiment" (*asabiyyah*) as decisive for successful regimes. Similarly, writing in the 1830s, de Tocqueville argued that the founding generation of the United States had developed a resilient political system, characterized by "repairable mistakes," wherein the public interest could overcome parochial concerns.

Myths—scientific, cosmological, and political—provide in this book the analytic framework for the observable anthropogenic traces in earth strata and our discourse about them. The Anthropocene can be conceived thereby as a coupled phenomenon of manifest and discursive elements—that is, the delineation of detectable and attributable change and the way in which that delineation is asserted. In the remainder of this section, we clarify the elements that comprise myth by providing some disparate examples from the science of geology, the European Union, and Indigenous Australian cosmologies.

Elements of Myth

Every myth embodies innate, strategic, and asserting roles, which we iden-tify in this book as doctrine, formula, and symbol.[75] The *doctrine* affirms the stable perspectives, axioms, or philosophies of the group. The *formula* develops these stable perspectives into prescriptions, norms, or policies. *Symbols* communicate and share those norms. Our thesis is that the myths of the Anthropocene essentially and sometimes surreptitiously constrain the policy and governance responses that can be entertained.

The doctrine is the basic premise or underlying philosophy of a myth. This conventional wisdom is so obvious to the holders of that myth that, though it formulates expectations and demands, it is very often unques-tioned and almost always uncontroversial. Scientific doctrines are most usefully underpinned by a conception of causality. Political doctrines typically assume that territory and government are one, even if acquired illegitimately. Cosmological doctrines are often based on the idea that an explanation for creation and (perhaps) an eschatology are necessary.

Although doctrines are needed to underpin a functioning myth, the for-mula is the manifestation of those doctrines in practice. The formula can be both prescriptive—requiring conformity to expectations through threat of sanctions—and descriptive—in the routine acceptance of practice or the development of norms of behavior. As a result, formulae are not always expressed as unambiguous prescriptions, policies, or laws. In the case of the political formula, we include both the body of legislation and regulation and the exercise of these by appropriately constituted agencies. As noted by Harold Laski, "The will of the state is in its laws; but it is the government which gives substance and effect to their content."[76]

Symbols are the powerful expression of myth in a way that simplifies the complexity and ambiguity of reality.[77] Symbols function as a tool for educa-tion, a means of generating solidarity, an instrument to identify outsiders, and a way to arouse sentiment. Walter Lippmann illustrated the power of symbols vividly: "The question of a proper fare on a municipal subway is symbolized as an issue between the People and the Interests, and then the People is inserted in the symbol American, so that finally in the heat of the campaign, an eight cent fare becomes un-American. The Revolutionary fathers died to prevent it. Lincoln suffered that it might not come to pass, resistance to it was implied by the death of those who sleep in France."[78] Although symbols act to confer legitimacy, it should not be understood that all symbols are propaganda. That is, the unifying role of the symbol is not limited to the institutions of power. Nevertheless, symbols are always more than they appear: Edward Sapir notes that "all symbolism implies meanings which cannot be derived directly from the contexts of experience. ... [The symbol] expresses a condensation of energy, its actual significance being out of all proportion to the apparent triviality of meaning suggested by its mere form."[79] Symbols, then, situate people in spaces and times of meaning and provide a sense of the predictability and interpretability of reality.

To ground these definitions in practice and to illustrate the flexibility of the analytic framework, we provide three diverse examples of myth. Here we outline a key doctrine, a formula, and a symbol of the science of geology, the European Union regime, and Australian Indigenous Dreamings (see table 1.1 for a summary).

Table 1.1
Examples of doctrine, formula, and symbol for a scientific, a political, and a cosmological myth

	Doctrine	Formula	Symbol
Geology	The same laws of physics operate at all places and in all times.	Hypothetico-deductive and empirico-inductive scientific methods.	Holocene, Anthropocene, the "hockey stick."*
European Union	Federation underpins the values of human rights and the rule of law.	The (much debated) principle of subsidiarity, generally intended to balance a norm of noninterference with a desire for social unity.	Treaty of Lisbon (2009), allowing member states prior scrutiny of proposed EU legislation.
Dreamings	Continuous creation of people and country, indivisible and bound by Law.	Caring for people and (on, in, with) country is a fundamental obligation.	The Rainbow Serpent or Serpents, in their various incarnations.

*See the original so-called hockey stick graph in figure 3a in Mann, Bradley, and Hughes, "Northern Hemisphere Temperatures," 761.

Note: This summary, even more than the text that accompanies it, is necessarily a highly simplified and truncated representation, for the purposes of illustration only.

The Geology Myth

The doctrine of geology rests on a key first principle: uniformitarianism. In 1785, based on extensive empirical observation, James Hutton proposed the idea that geological strata were formed through an infinite series of cycles that followed the natural laws of physics: "But from this view of things, there is no reason to suppose that there is any other system in nature besides that which has been now exposed; a system in which the old continents are wearing away, and new continents forming at the bottom of the sea; and a system in which the subterranean power of fire, or heat, co-operates with the action of water upon the Surface of the Earth."[80] This was refined in the nineteenth century by geologist Charles Lyell into a series of axioms that came to be collectively termed the *principle of uniformitarianism*. Lyell assumed that the same laws of physics operate at all places and in all times. He also assumed that change is both gradual and evenly distributed. These latter ideas were not unanimously accepted at the time and are now considered irrelevant to the modern science of geology. The first axiom, however—that the laws of physics do not change—cannot be tested empirically in the manner of a hypothesis, as famously observed by Stephen Jay Gould.[81] For this reason, it must be understood as doctrine—and indeed it is necessary for progress in scientific understanding of the natural world. As a result, this doctrine is fundamental to all modern Western science but is associated particularly with the science of geology.

In the practice of geology, as with other natural sciences, the "scientific method" is often taken to be the most critical statement of the formula that is underpinned by the doctrine that physical laws do not change. When this formula is invoked, what often is being described is the hypothetico-deductive model. In this model, an experiment or observation is designed to invalidate a logical consequence of a hypothesis. If the consequence is not invalidated, the experiment or observation must be replicable to the extent that it can be shown that the consequence did not occur by chance. There remain philosophical problems with this model,[82] but the most important problem from the standpoint of geology is the difficulty of designing experiments that can—as a practical matter—isolate the phenomenon of interest.

For this reason, the practice of geology includes both deductive and inductive formulae. *Induction* is the procedure of generalizing from specific examples and was the method by which James Hutton was able to propose his theory of the earth. Indeed, because the phenomena in which Hutton was most interested occur so slowly that they may not be observed directly, it was direct observations of strata in Scotland, France, and Spain, and comparisons with the observations of other natural philosophers, that allowed Hutton to gather evidence to support the mechanisms he proposed. Confirmation of hypotheses is inherently partial using an empirico-inductive formula, but the convergence of multiple streams of evidence increases the confidence of conclusions over time.

The Holocene epoch is a symbol of the power of glacial cycles to re-form the earth, over and again. The Holocene is the name proposed by Charles Lyell in 1833 to denote the 11,700 years since the last ice age. However, as early as 1873, human activities were starting to be compared to terrestrial geologic forces.[83] As human activities threaten to compete in magnitude and global extent with the impacts of these forces, the Anthropocene has become a symbol of the coming epoch (figure 1.1). More proximately, symbols range from the clearing of forests to the rerouting of rivers, from the release of toxic pollutants to the mining of resources.[84] But climate has emerged as a powerful element of this symbol as human civilization developed within a narrow window of temperature variations. Mike Hulme observed: "Climate is frequently bound up in notions of personal or national identity ... and in the idea of social memory ... while climatic fluctuations are adopted as anchors for personal memory."[85]

Australian Indigenous Myths

In Indigenous Australia, the doctrine of unceasing genesis of the universe is embodied by people and country, indivisible.[86] As Deborah Bird Rose translates this: "The term 'Dreaming' connotes both creation and connection. It refers to the beings who made the world, and it further refers to the continuing process of life's coming forth in the world, thus referencing both original and on-going creation."[87] The consequences of this cosmological myth-making are far reaching, not least of which is the doctrine that the source of Law is, quoting Rose again, "the logic of country"—the web of obligations, identities, and relationships that arise uniquely from and are literally embodied by place. This doctrine establishes a country as unequivocally as a constitution: "A country is small enough to accommodate face-to-face groups of people, and large enough to sustain their lives; it is politically autonomous in respect of other, structurally equivalent

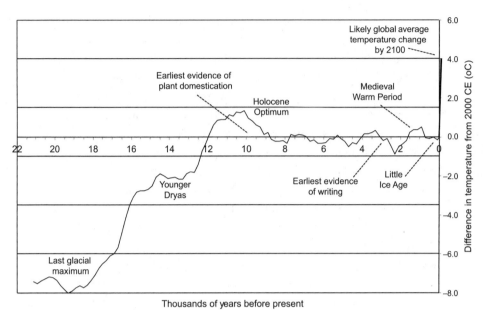

Figure 1.1

Temperature reconstruction based on oxygen isotope ratios in an ice core recovered at Dome Fuji in Antarctica, shown here for the Late Quaternary period since the Last Glacial Maximum. The bold black line represents an estimate of global average temperature change if emissions continue largely unabated. An estimate of future temperature localized to Dome Fuji is difficult as the stability of the ice sheet in future scenarios is not well understood at present. The Younger Dryas was a period during which the transition from glacial to interglacial conditions reversed for a short period of time due to internal feedback processes. Note that the Holocene Optimum (the warmest period) was not synchronized between the Northern and Southern Hemispheres.

Source: Uemura et al., "Ranges of Moisture-Source Temperature."

countries, and at the same time is interdependent with other countries."[88] In this way, the relationship among Dreamings, Law, and Country is both the cosmological and political doctrine upon which Indigenous Australian societies are founded.

Indigenous Australian formulae converge in the obligation to live according to Dreaming. Consider Aboriginal elder Mussolini Harvey's explanation to John Bradley: "The Dreamings made our Law or *narnu-Yuwa*. This Law is the way we live, our rules. This Law is our ceremonies, our songs, our stories; all of these things came from the Dreaming."[89] A distributive norm arises in the formulae of many peoples across Australia; this norm is understood, if accompanied by appropriate etiquette, to be in the context of reciprocal expectations. That said, this formula does not eliminate the fundamental responsibility accruing to all of caring for country: "Social relations cross-cut the boundaries of rights and responsibilities without obliterating or undermining them. On the one hand, countries were under the control of the people who belonged there and who, through creation, bore responsibility for the country and its living things, including water. People protected their own country from strangers out of necessity as well as love of country. Their ongoing subsistence depended on control of resources, and this is a matter of life and death."[90]

The Rainbow Serpent is an important symbol of Dreamings where there is permanent surface water in Indigenous Australia. Indeed, it is likely to be one of the oldest continually held cosmological symbols in the world.[91] In the country of the Ngiyampaa people, Steve Meredith spoke about Wawi: "*Wawi* the Rainbow Serpent came up through the springs, he came from Nakabo springs, Ngilyitri country. Wherever he travelled he left ochre to show where he had been. The springs were entry and exit points. He came out of the earth, travelled along its surface, and then went back to the earth. Wawi travels, and is still there. We know he's still there."[92] The Rainbow Serpent is known by different names in different Aboriginal cultures, and though the symbol shares some common attributes, the English translation was coined by English anthropologist Alfred Radcliffe-Brown in the early twentieth century. A symbol translated roughly as the Rainbow Serpent (or Rainbow Serpents if there are more than one) is known as *Goorialla* by the Lardil people, *Numereji* by the Kakadu, *Witij* by the Yolngu, and many other names. The Rainbow Serpent can be male, female, hermaphrodite, or no gender at all. It may have hair. It may represent blood, healing, or creation. The Rainbow Serpent symbol always represents a connection to water and the lawful use of water. Ever adaptable, the Rainbow Serpent was adopted as a symbol for an anti-uranium-mining campaign in far northern Australia.

The European Union Myth

"Ever closer union": this phrase is found in the Preamble to the 1957 Treaty of Rome to create a European Economic Community. As with many political myths, the doctrines of the European Union (EU) are laid out in the preambles of its constitutive documents, which include the Treaty of Rome and the Maastricht Treaty (1992), among others. The ultimate aim of "ever closer union" was held to be a de facto federation. But the European Union has struggled with many aspects of its founding myth for decades. The economic crises of the last decade have, for good or ill, "highlighted not only the power of EU institutions to transform seemingly domestic economic and political issues into 'all-European' matters, but have also resulted in a wholesale remaking of a distinct 'European' political space, not just within but also vis-a-vis its putative 'outside.'"[93] At the same time, concerns about the erosion of national cultures and an emergent identity politics—evident in, for example, the Brexit vote of 2016—were predicted right from the beginning.[94] Paradoxically, the inherent ambiguity of the nature of the European Union has demonstrated the fundamental acceptance of key doctrines. These key doctrines included, for example, human rights and the rule of law: "The Union shall respect fundamental rights, as guaranteed by the European Convention for the Protection of Human Rights and Fundamental Freedoms signed in Rome on 4 November 1950 and as they result from the constitutional traditions common to the Member States, as general principles of Community law."[95] These general principles, or doctrines, have continued to be maintained explicitly, so that the consolidated Treaty for the Functioning of the European Union of 2007 declared that on principle the Maastricht Treaty continued to hold the same legal value as subsequent treaties.

Prominent elements of formulae in the European Union are the prescriptions associated with subsidiarity,[96] which seeks to resolve the tension between deepening the solidarity among European peoples and respecting their diverse histories, cultures, and traditions. This principle, as promoted by the Assembly of European Regions,[97] holds that government should undertake only those initiatives that exceed the capacity of individuals or communities acting independently. Chantal Millon-Delsol traces the principle back to the classical Greek supposition that each human person has innate worth, but is also inherently social, and this aspect also carries worth.[98] As a result, legislation and regulation by the European Union is required to balance a norm of noninterference with a desire for social unity: "The principle of subsidiarity reunites these antitheses, and affirms them jointly. Subsidiarity is the locus of a paradox that it takes up in a specific way. It exists only because this paradox exists."[99]

There are many competing interpretations of the term *subsidiarity*, some of which carry a strong ideology concerning what the idea of subsidiarity performs:[100] "Some may reasonably wonder whether subsidiarity can really support [State-based] forms of sovereignty, since subsidiarity seems to imply a challenge to such centralized powers. Yet many commentators—politicians and academics—have maintained … that subsidiarity stands as the great limiting principle that will defend national sovereignty against incursion by the ever-expanding Brussels bureaucracy."[101] Thus, the understanding of the impact of subsidiarity has evolved over time. Nevertheless, doctrine becomes formula in the Maastricht Treaty in Article 3b, which states: "In areas which do not fall within its exclusive competence, the Community shall take action, in accordance with the principle of subsidiarity, only if and in so far as the objectives of the proposed action cannot be sufficiently achieved by the Member states and can therefore, by reason of the scale or effects of the proposed action, be better achieved by the Community. Any action by the Community shall not go beyond what is necessary to achieve the objectives of this Treaty."

A key symbol of the role of subsidiarity in the European Union is the Treaty of Lisbon (2007, which amended the 1992 Maastricht Treaty, and entered into force in 2009). The Treaty of Lisbon, itself a statement of formula, expanded the role of member states' parliaments in the legislative processes of the EU by giving them a prior scrutiny of legislative proposals before the Council and the Parliament can take a position. The Treaty of Lisbon provides for national parliaments "to contribute to the good functioning of the Union" through receiving draft EU legislation, creating the important symbol that the formula for subsidiarity is explicitly respected. Swedish Minister of European Affairs, and later EU Commissioner, Cecilia Malmström, spelled out the significance of the Treaty of Lisbon as a symbol in the Riksdag in 2008: "Democracy is also strengthened. The competences of the EU are defined in a clearer way. The Treaty states that both in the Member States as well as in the Treaty it is defined how much power the EU should have. The Riksdag and other national parliaments get a strengthened role. No legislation will come from the EU without it having been checked by national parliaments. If a sufficient number of national parliaments think a proposal for legislation shouldn't be formulated at EU level it can be completely stopped."[102]

These three very disparate examples demonstrate the ways in which the construction of myth as doctrine, formula, and symbol can help to elucidate the ways in which human beings shape and share values. Importantly, the myths we operate within are epistemic in shaping the kinds of questions, methodologies, and conclusions with which we are able to effect change. This proves particularly significant in understanding relationships between humans and the environment and how it might be possible to narrate the world-for-us to achieve human dignity and environmental sustainability.

Historical Framings of Humans and Nature

The true use of history is that we extract from it general principles as to the discipline of practice and the discipline of speculation. The object of this discipline is not stability, but progress.
—Alfred North Whitehead[103]

This initial exploration of doctrines, formulae, and symbols raises what Rogow and Lasswell termed the "historical question."[104] Namely, how do we explain the course of events in relation to the realization of human aspirations over time? To answer this question, it is important to place the Anthropocene in a broad historical context. Histories exist through their use by people now living, not by virtue of having an actual existence in an actual past that one could visit. Similarly, the Anthropocene is not a period that has existence independent of human epistemologies. Shaping a narrative for the Anthropocene is "not discovering an epoch 'out there,' but seeking narratives that will prove equal to the challenge of solving global environmental crises."[105]

We recognize that though "people in different times and cultures have lived, and live, in different conceptual worlds,"[106] the barriers between them are not impervious. Further, while translation of myths is necessarily incomplete, we agree with Mark Elvin that "there is no necessity for evidence from another time or culture to be flawed by ... otherness to the point of being unusable by us."[107] Indeed, this very otherness presents a compelling argument to improve cross-cultural communication as we seek to imagine alternatives to current trajectories of change. The exploration of relevant pasts offered in the passages ahead cannot, of course, be exhaustive, but merely indicative of the potential of these explorations.

The Everywhen

We begin with a return to the question of time in Indigenous Australian cosmologies, acknowledging that these are among the most ancient surviving cultures. By some estimates, Indigenous Australian myths have been passed through generations for sixty-five thousand years or more, and as such may be the oldest surviving myths about the world-for-us. Indigenous Australian myths normalize the human-nature relationship and introduce us to the idea that the world-in-itself is not beyond our reach. Furthermore, this cosmology accounts for the relationship between people and their environment that in many ways most radically differs from European historicity. Indeed, these, our oldest stories of human-environment interactions, are not historical in a conventional sense. There is no arrow of time pointing from creation, through the present, and into a distant future. Creating is an ever-unfolding emergence of being, enacted through Dreaming. It is important to note that the cosmological myths of Indigenous Australia are not alternative accounts of what is, *in fact*, our shared world-for-us. Rather, they account for spatial-temporal systems of origins, of phenomena, and of the place and agency of humans in a profoundly distinctive way.

A host of translational concepts have been mobilized to acquaint the European world to the nature of Indigenous Australian myths.[108] For instance, the terms Dreaming, Animism, and Country have been invoked as rough English equivalents of Indigenous discourses for the world we inhabit. Yet translating the experience of being human in such cosmologies continues to prove challenging, with arguments for their value often resorting to hyphenated attempts to combine or oppose seemingly ontologically separate categories, such as the "every-when." Moreover, as Kate Rigby notes: "Non-dualistic and anti-colonial talk of nature can be strategically valuable in defending the agency and interests of the other-than-human."[109] Living through Indigenous cosmologies can be understood as never having separated such categories and therefore not requiring their recombination to conceptualize, for example, "environmental impacts."

Another translational tool is to fix Dreaming to a linear timeline that correlates the flick of a serpent's tail, for example, with a dated geological record of fault uplift. Such translational accounts are not without value within any given Indigenous cosmology. Many Indigenous cosmologies do not require resolution among apparently conflicting accounts for causality, and express an accommodation for difference that is not permissible in European traditions of thought. Rose shows that "virtually anything *can* be accommodated … from tin cans to Toyotas, but everything *must* be accommodated according to the logic of country."[110] Indeed, the Christian story of Christ and the story of Captain Cook have been accommodated in some Indigenous societies according to such logics.[111] As such, "Aboriginal people moved 'not in a landscape, but in a humanized realm saturated with significations.'"[112] This is a place that cannot, by definition, exclude the active presence of humanity, physically, culturally, and spiritually. This is a time that cannot, by definition, be interrogated with "when did this really happen?"[113]

These myths prefigure a fundamental perspective of the Anthropocene, that of the role of humans in the environment. The lesson for the Anthropocene, however, may be that it is the historical sense of human progress that inculcates a sense of urgency—be it catastrophe or opportunity. What we consider the human era is one story within a vast realm of every-when; thus, policies and governance built for the urgent "now" constructed from that perspective will always come up short. What is suggested is not so much a "long view" or "perspective" as a more deeply profound form of sustainability: a planning for all time, not this time.

The Mayacene

An epochal shift in humanity's relationship with the earth attended the creation of towns in the major agrarian civilizations of the ancient world, first appearing in Mesopotamia around 3500 BCE, then around 3000 BCE in Egypt, 2600 BCE in the Indus Valley, 1600 BCE in China, and 500 BCE in Mesoamerica (see also figure 1.1). The Postclassic Quiché kingdom of the Mayas (900–1500 CE) in Guatemala's western highlands was one such civilization. Because the Maya were a rainfall-dependent agricultural society, the passage of time was fundamental to their doctrine. Seasonal variability had a major bearing on their decision making, diachronically and synchronically. Water and agricultural land availability impacted how people lived, built, and moved across the landscape. The calendar was law, was formula.

The *Popol Vuh* (modern Quiché: *Poopol Wuuj*) is one example of the Mayan myths, and like many Indigenous Australian Dreamings, there is no distinction made among cosmological, political, and scientific myths. The survival of this text is attributable to the Spanish Dominican friar Francisco Ximénez, who transcribed and translated a phonetic manuscript (now lost) in the early eighteenth century. The doctrine it describes was one in which the gods wanted to create human beings with hearts and minds who could keep the days.[114] The first humans of earth and mud soak up water and dissolve. The second humans are created from wood, but they did not have souls. The third "true" humans are made from yellow and white corn gathered by animals, and could speak the language of the gods. These first humans could see to the limits of space and time. But the gods had not intended that they have the potential to become equals of gods and so limited their sight to what was obvious and nearby. The book, the *Popul Vuh*, became their *ilb'al*, or instrument for seeing. The book was not regarded as sacred or authoritative itself, but rather as an important record of religious rituals and knowledge and, more specifically, the keeping of the calendar.

The history of the Mayan civilization, its rapid growth and catastrophic decline, has provided a model for thinking about the Anthropocene.[115] Indeed, the many parallels have led to the coining of the term the "Mayacene." The thriving of Mayan culture was sustained by the surpluses of highly productive corn farmers,[116] which in turn depended on a sophisticated and attentive use of the calendar, with rules and practices maintained over long periods of time. "They altered ecosystems with vast urban and rural infrastructure that included thousands of reservoirs, wetland fields and canals, terraces, field ridges, and temples. ... Existing forests are still influenced by ancient Maya forest gardening, particularly by the large expanses of ancient stone structures, terraces, and wetland fields that form their substrates."[117] This complex system, while founded on a doctrine of the world-for-us, was completely dependent upon the reliable annual return of rain, an expectation that was violated by a two-hundred-year drought from 800 CE to 1000 CE.

But as with other challenges of the Anthropocene, climate alone cannot explain the decline of Mayan societies. Also implicated have been the loss of trade routes due to regional wars, European invasion and the attendant communicable diseases, and the consequences of deforestation, including soil exhaustion and erosion. And yet the Mayan civilization flourished in the most unlikely of terrains—a mountainous tropical rainforest that functioned as a seasonal desert. Mayan societies retreated but continued to develop in many ways until at least 1700 CE, and the Maya people have retained a cohesive culture in the Yucatán Peninsula. The lesson for the Anthropocene is perhaps less associated with the hubris of overdevelopment or the bad fortune of climate variability, and more associated with the need for reserves and redundancies even in highly successful systems, a robust planning for every-when.

Early Western Myths

In the West, the human-environment relationship was documented systematically coincident with urbanization in centers of power such as Mesopotamia. This is the beginning of the doctrine whereby production and
habitation are separated from "the wild." One vivid example of the earliest
forms of this doctrine is the *Epic of Gilgamesh*, which dates from the Sumerian empire during the third dynasty of the city of Ur (around 2100 BCE). In
the various versions of this myth, a dominant symbol is the defeat and subjection of the wild as a necessary precursor to the triumph of culture and
civilization. The story follows the exploits of King Gilgamesh, part god and
part man, who oppresses his people. The gods heed the pleading of his people and create the wild, primitive Enkidu to end the tyranny. Instead, Gilgamesh overcomes and tames Enkidu, and together they slay the guardian
Huwawa of the forest of Lebanon and lay waste to the forest.[118]. The Gods
punish Gilgamesh by slaying Enkidu, driving Gilgamesh to seek, in vain,
the help of the only man known to have conquered death—Utnapishtim—
who had built an arc to survive the great flood. As noted by Rigby, "The separation of the truly human and his works from other-than-human spaces
and entities is already implicit here."[119] The doctrine of coercive subjection
seems entrenched, applied both to nature and some classes of human. But
later in the epic poem, the goddess Ishtar unleashes Gugalanna, the Bull of
Heaven, on Gilgamesh's city, causing widespread devastation, lowering the
level of the Euphrates River, and drying up the marshes. The consequence
of divine retribution for mistreating nature is manifest.

Analysis of the marks left by grain stored in Sumerian pots indicates
that from about 3500 BCE, the proportion of wheat declines in favor of
barley, a more salt-tolerant crop. By 1700 BCE, wheat has disappeared
entirely.[120]. Eisenberg suggests that salinization might have been a major
factor in the gradual shift of power and population upriver: from Sumer
to Akkad to Ur to Babylon to Nineveh. Recognition "that their greatest
triumph, irrigation, was bringing about their greatest disaster, salinization"[121] is symbolized in the Akkadian *Atra-Hasis* epic, which recounts how
the gods punished humans for making too much of a racket by causing
the salty sea below to rise up through the earth: "During the nights the
fields turned white. The broad plain brought forth salt crystals, so that
no plant came forth, no grain sprouted."[122] The doctrine continued to

enshrine dominion over the earth, but symbols consistently evoked the consequences of unchecked exploitation.

This doctrine has underpinned the myth that passes from ancient Mesopotamian cultures through to the present day in Western cultures. The mixed blessing of the world-for-us is perhaps the oldest continuous myth in the Western world, illustrated systematically in Hesiod's epic poem *Works and Days*. Hesiod recounts the Greek cosmological myth that traces the Golden, Silver, Bronze, and Heroic Ages to the present age, the Iron Age. The humans of these earlier ages were made by the god Zeus. After the destruction of the Heroic Henisthoi in the great wars of Greek legend, Zeus created a fifth race of humans. With this fifth race came the Iron Age: virtues began to disappear, evil was created, and the gods abandoned the earth. It is understood by the end of the poem that Zeus will destroy this race at some point. This myth, as the *Epic of Gilgamesh*, embodies consequences in the gods.

However, as Greek civilization evolved, so did the underlying doctrine, and formulae that included punishment for exploitation and the virtue of limits became less prominent. By the time of Socrates, the dominant doctrine was underpinned by a belief that nature is ordered for the benefit of and use by humans. The world was storied as actually "for us." Xenophon reported: "Socrates observed that there is a light for everyday tasks but dark which is needed for rest. The seasons and earth are created so as to provide man with a continuous supply of food. Fire is created as a defense against cold and dark. Animals, too, are produced for the sake of man, who gains more advantages from the animals than from the fruits of the earth."[123] Aristotle went further, postulating that human techne was "said to 'imitate' nature (physis), while simultaneously accomplishing 'what physis is incapable of effecting,' by creating something that does not develop and reproduce itself according to its own indwelling principle, but instead has a determinate form imposed upon it from outside by its human maker."[124] This doctrine of dominion continued to be characterized by formulae that privileged entitlements over responsibilities. The common threads that run through Western civilization are the shared symbols that serve to communicate the doctrine: "Not only was the creation of nature orderly, but man, as the last of God's creation, was given dominion over it."[125]

The Enlightenment

The modern era dawned with the coincident and somewhat codependent Age of Enlightenment scientific revolution[126] and European colonial period. This phase of Western civilization, lasting from the sixteenth century to the mid-twentieth century, developed a profoundly optimistic myth in which humans could make nature better than it could make itself. Cartesian dualism, Linnean classification, Smith's political economy, Kant's noumena, Darwinian natural selection: each emerged as the myth developed. An early embodiment was found in Francis Bacon: "The new man of science must not think that the 'inquisition of nature is in any part interdicted or forbidden.' Nature must be 'bound into service' and made a 'slave,' put 'in constraint' and 'molded' by the mechanical arts."[127]

In many ways, the cementing of separation from and dominion over nature had its roots in the mercantilism of this period. Michel Foucault and Ulrich Beck write of the emerging role of quantification as a means to comprehend and hence control the territory, drawing on the work of Blaise Pascal[128] and the emerging science of probability.[129] James Scott observes, "Much of early modern European statecraft seemed ... devoted to rationalizing and standardizing what was a social hieroglyph into a legible and administratively more convenient format."[130] In this way, the Enlightenment serves to deepen the conceptual rift between "human" and "nature" and gives rise to an idea of progress as an unequivocal good that, in turn, becomes a validating basis for the expansion of empire. These ideas enabled colonial expansion through classification and quantification, making nature abstract and generalizable, but also making it auditable.[131] In this myth, nature becomes a standing reserve, awaiting extraction, manipulation, and commodification. John Locke made the primacy of human agency explicit: "It is labour indeed that puts the difference of value on everything. ... If we will rightly estimate things as they come to our use and cast up the several expenses about them—what in them is purely owing to Nature and what to labour—we shall find that in most of them ninety-nine hundredths are wholly to be put on the account of labour."[132]

Despite many alternative myths arising in the ensuing centuries, the fundamental doctrine that nature is a fungible good only realized by human agency has proved remarkably tenacious. As a result, subsequent thinkers continued to build on this edifice: "Let us have a new class of students, suitably prepared, whose business it shall be to take the respective sciences as they are, determine the spirit of each, ascertain their relations and mutual connection, and reduce their respective principles to the smallest number of general principles, in conformity with the fundamental rules of the Positive method."[133] The "Positive method" was used, of course, in the new science of geology. This thinking actually culminates in the valuation of ecosystem services—though in the present discourse not to tax them, but to set thresholds for the cost of protecting them.[134]

An alternative doctrine that provided a seed for the Romantic myth of the late eighteenth and early nineteenth centuries was the idea that creative artists, particularly poets, were the guardians and defenders of nature. Friedrich Schiller was one writer who planted this seed through his interpretation of Kantian ideas of genius; for Schiller, the artist's genius for the creation of beauty was innate. It followed then that the nature of the artist was of a piece with nature itself. Kate Rigby explored Schiller's thinking further: "Whereas ancient poets such as Homer paid little heed to the beauties of the natural world because their culture was still largely integrated into it, Schiller argued, later writers waxed increasingly lyrical about such things as ... wild landscapes, in proportion to the disappearance of nature and naturalness from human life. Nature, that is to say, becomes thematic in literature only when it becomes problematic in reality."[135] This myth seems a reassertion of the world-in-itself. However, as Rigby astutely observes, "what looks like a defense of writing in the service of nature actually turns out to be an argument for the subordination of nature to art."

Natural philosophers of the Romantic era understood that change was an intrinsic part of the natural world, an understanding that was as one with Lyell's uniformitarianism and Darwin's natural selection. And yet new ideas of nature also gave rise to an important new wilderness aesthetic—the idea of the sublime. This idea evolved into the wilderness myth embodied by Henry David Thoreau, John Muir, and Aldo Leopold. It is worth considering these three towering figures because their experiences, perspectives, and contributions were strongly embedded in this evolution as the modernists of the twentieth century carried the torch of the Enlightenment forward (see chapter 3).

Nevertheless, the nineteenth and twentieth centuries deepened the entrenchment of the scientific revolution in partnership with new perspectives on efficient management arising from the Industrial Revolution: "One major characteristic of the modern era is the embrace of science and the scientific method. The rise of science as a cultural force marked a revolution in humankind's understanding of environment. It served to deepen the rift between man and nature and gave rise to an idea of progress as an unequivocal good that, in turn, became a validating basis for the expansion of human empire into nature."[136] The world-for-us reasserts itself.

The myth of technological mastery over the natural world arose from converging streams of scientific management[137] and technological optimism. "Scientific management aspired to rise above politics, relying on science as the foundation for efficient policies made through a single central authority—a bureaucratic structure with the appropriate mandate, jurisdiction, and expert personnel."[138] Technological optimism assumes that the expertise and tools necessary to sustain nature will be created, and will further "effectuate certain outcomes regardless of time, space or usage patterns."[139] Thomas Hobbes observed that three things were needed for innovation: discontent, pretense of right (symbols), and hope of success. James Fleming[140] documents discourses dating from the nineteenth century grounded in the myth of technological mastery over the natural world, culminating in the ideas of geoengineering the planet. In this doctrine, "it is neither necessary nor responsible to make the detour through messy democratic debates, thereby wasting time in the face of a looming ecological catastrophe."[141] As such, this myth is not incompatible with the ecological horror stories of Rachel Carson or Bill McKibben. Rather, it carries the promise of the Industrial revolution into the future. It is into this looming ecological catastrophe, our means of detecting it, and our myths for response that chapter 2 continues.

2   Urgency Manifest

Sometimes, no matter how much and how carefully you prepare, the disaster is just too big.
—Zhang Qiang[1]

Introduction

The way in which the world is imagined determines at any point in time what men will do. It does not determine what they will achieve.
—Walter Lippmann[2]

Although the Battle of Solferino was uncommonly large, there was nothing inherently novel about the horrors of the European battlefield, technologies in use, nor the nature of customary relief efforts, when Jean-Henri Dunant happened upon the conflict in 1856. Nevertheless, today Dunant's presence there is understood as initiating the doctrine of humanitarian relief. How did his accidental and relatively marginal role in a customary humanitarian relief effort come to symbolize the very initiation and purpose of global humanitarian initiatives? And how does the myth[3] of his agency shape the role and purpose of professional humanitarian relief since? The answers to these questions matter for how agency in Anthropocene disasters might be cast. Consider Dunant's own account of the Battle of Solferino—*A Memory of Solferino* (1862)—and the way in which his agency is represented today.

Dunant was traveling to Northern Italy to seek an audience with Napoleon when several armies converged. Witnessing the violence, he took keen interest in the challenging logistics of tending to the dead and wounded and their families. During the battle and in its aftermath, Dunant describes a bustle of customary relief efforts.[4] He observes first-aid posts near the field of battle, wealthy benefactors offering goods and services, villagers paid to bury the dead, distribution of food and water supplies, medical practitioners from nearby villages and convents helping the wounded, and efforts to make contact with relatives of the slain. Documenting the customs associated with battle response, Dunant writes: "A black flag floating from a high place is the usual means of showing the location of first-aid posts or field ambulances, and it is tacitly agreed that no one shall fire in their direction."[5] Among the French army, he observes that their prisoners of war were served "the same food as the French officers, and their wounded were treated by the same doctors."[6] As the battle ended, wounded began to move from the field of battle, and Dunant says that "every church, convent, house, public square, court, street or pathway in [the surrounding] villages was turned into a temporary hospital."[7] He follows one cohort of injured soldiers making their way into the village of Castiglione. Once there, Dunant notes that the villagers "had plenty to do in taking care of the wounded officers within its doors." The scale of the battle and its casualties overwhelmed the village, and Dunant despaired at the unattended suffering of hundreds of soldiers that had arrived in one of Castiglione's churches. It was then that Dunant first began corralling volunteers. Every household was already busy helping wounded, yet he nevertheless "succeeded … in getting together a certain number of women who helped as best they could with the efforts made to aid the wounded."[8] Dunant continued recruiting volunteers among villagers who could be spared from assisting elsewhere and among visitors like himself. He purchased linens and other supplies to support his actions, and so began his efforts to form relief societies.

Dunant is an important symbol of the now-global Red Cross and Red Crescent movement. This movement, the foremost volunteer emergency preparedness and response organization in the world today, was formalized through the first Geneva Convention of 1864. Its doctrine is exemplified by the mission of the International Federation of Red Cross and Red Crescent Societies (IFRC), founded in 1919 "to inspire, encourage, facilitate and promote at all times all forms of humanitarian activities by National Societies, with a view to preventing and alleviating human suffering, and thereby contributing to the maintenance and promotion of human dignity and peace in the world."[9] The organization is founded on a doctrine of impartiality, neutrality, independence, voluntary service, and universality. Since

1864, new humanitarian organizations have emerged at all scales, providing assistance to millions of disaster victims across the world. In globalizing Dunant's efforts, however, the flood of international responders and resources can marginalize traditional logistics that have emerged in place over centuries of experience with similar events.[10]

Today, the IFRC doctrine is attributed to Dunant himself, yet its origin in the customary responses to European battles is seldom recognized. For instance, the agency of the people of Castiglione and neighboring towns is not apparent on the pages of the IFRC, which writes the following of Dunant's role at battle of Solferino: "Dunant organized local people to bind the soldiers' wounds and to feed and comfort them," as "some 40,000 men lay dead or dying on the battlefield and the wounded were lacking medical attention."[11] Similarly, Jean-Henri Dunant is described to have "swiftly mobilized the local people into action, setting up crude infirmaries in churches, monasteries and makeshift tents. All the wounded soldiers, regardless of which side they were fighting on, were given care. 'Tutti fratelli'—they are all our brothers, said the women who helped Dunant at Solferino. The germ had been sown."[12]

Casting Dunant as the originator of humanitarian relief efforts implies that, previous to Dunant's discovering the horrors of battle, there was a want of aspiration or capacity to respond. Of course, Dunant's own account of the battle does not presume to have invented, nor indeed directed, humanitarian responses. As myths evolve, complex and contextual factors often transform into symbolic heroes, victims, and villains. This evolution, inevitably, has resulted in material impacts today, in which local incapacity is assumed.

Three key observations can be drawn from Dunant's account. First, he witnessed a disaster that resulted when the battle exceeded local response capacity. Second, Dunant learned from, and was inspired by, the humanitarian efforts he observed on the battlefield and in Castiglione. Third, Dunant addressed governments, calling for humanitarian relief to become a responsibility to be planned for, funded, and managed over longer time scales and through new networks of coordination. The 150 years since Solferino has seen humanitarian aid increasingly taking on a formula that addresses only the third of these insights. International aid workers arrive at disaster sites with a prescribed mode of response, a standard of logistics, and a common set of metrics, unified by their doctrine of impartiality.[13]

In this standardization, traditional and customary experiences of hazards, whether and when hazards should be interpreted as disasters, and what networks should be deployed to administer response, have been treated as peripheral or indeed as hindrances to professional expertise in disaster risk reduction and response.[14]

This history raises the question of what is customary or traditional about the disasters of the Anthropocene. In forging a focus on the processes that produce the hazards of the Anthropocene—storm, heat, flood, fire, and drought, among others—the international humanitarian project has developed strategies based on the natural dimensions of disasters. There are several conditioning factors to be considered in this focus: (i) the importance of myths about the "natural" ranges of climatic variability; (ii) the creation of vulnerability through wealth, policy, or colonial practices; and (iii) the potential for hazards objectively outside the realm of any human experience.

As an example of the first factor, consider the ways in which European myths of forest fire as rare, destructive, and preventable have shaped New World approaches to fire disaster preparation and response.[15] A resulting policy of fire suppression since the colonization of North America has contributed to an accumulation of combustible materials in forests in close proximity to centers of human habitation.[16] United States wildfires over recent decades have caused millions of dollars in damages (figure 2.1). Discourse on fire management is exploring the recognition that fire-suppression policies have created the exposure of human communities and ecological systems to late-season, high-intensity wildfires, but disagreements on the nuances in the scientific epistemological community persist.[17] Indeed, a combination of expert doctrines and external political pressures,[18] both grounded in symbols of catastrophe, appear to influence the trajectories of individual fire events. In any case, peri-urban forests are desirable real estate. As a result, the rates of increase in damages and lives threatened have outpaced the increase in area burned over the last five decades (figure 2.1).

In an example of the second factor, doctrines concerning free agricultural markets contributed to the African famines of the late twentieth century. This doctrine drove proposals—indeed, coercion—by the World Bank and International Monetary Fund to sell emergency grain reserves and remove trade barriers.[19] Traditionally, these stores were protected in sealed

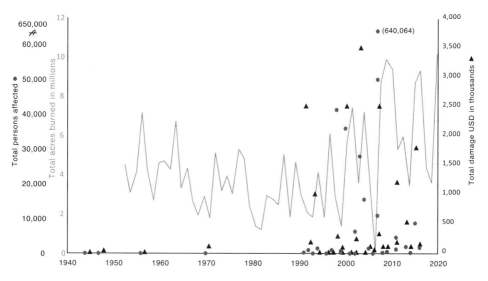

Figure 2.1
Wildfires in the United States, 1940–2016. Total persons affected, total damage in US$, and total burned acres.
Source: Data from EM-DAT and the National Interagency Fire Center.

containers as insurance against the inescapable droughts, floods, and pest outbreaks of the region, exemplifying the "science of the concrete."[20] Furthermore, intraregional transportation of grain was known by local farmers to lack the infrastructure and institutional capacity that would support productive regional markets.[21] But European traditions of food production characterized drought as unusual and short-lived, flood as manageable, and pests as amenable to technological solutions. This doctrine reinterpreted grain stores as obstacles to free regional trade by keeping prices unnaturally low. Meanwhile, the Sahelian drought deepened. Crops failed, and hunger followed; communities could no longer rely on grain reserves nor afford to buy grain on the open market. Internationally, the famine was seen unquestioningly as resulting from the natural hazard of drought.[22] For donors, foreign grain relief was an urgent, immediate, and unquestionably necessary response to an abnormal weather event affecting helpless people. And aid was indeed urgently needed. Yet this response was also blind to the contributing factors related to neither weather nor deficiencies in customary capacity to manage drought.[23]

The third factor presents the most precarious element of urgency manifest in the Anthropocene. The modern era is rife with reports of disasters that are the most intense, the most extreme, the greatest cost or largest death toll. These are the "unimaginable risks" with which the Anthropocene presents us: "As a consequence today we all face *ontological insecurity*[24] because we have neither experienced nor prepared for these new risks and our future is unclear."[25] Unimaginable risks are not unique in the Anthropocene—humans have always faced unprecedented challenges, from megafauna extinction to white sails on the horizon—but the hazards of global change are not always nor completely caused by proximate human activities. This question of causation, this attribution, becomes central to many of the symbols that surround the Anthropocene myth.

A case in point is the Australian Millennium Drought (1996–2010). This long-lasting dry in southeastern Australia set many records for both temperature extremes and rainfall deficits. Very warm ocean temperatures in surrounding seas at the time were ascribed to human-induced climate change.[26] It is possible that these ocean temperatures influenced continental rainfall patterns. That is, there is some scientific basis for attributing this specific drought to climate change. Indeed, the Bureau of Meteorology's head of climate analysis, Dr. David Jones, was quoted in national newspapers as saying, "It may be time to stop describing south-eastern Australia as gripped by drought and instead accept the extreme dry as permanent."[27] But a definitive attribution was beyond the capacity of climate science at the time, and communities had no basis for making this distinction. In the context of profound ontological insecurities, communities reverted instead to their dominant myths.[28]

What, then, are appropriate metrics for detecting and attributing disasters, and what are appropriate responses to urgency in the Anthropocene? The potential for disaster outside the realm of human experience creates a challenge that is unique in the phenomena associated, rigorously or tenuously, with climate and global change, and in the ways in which urgency itself is construed.

The Phenomenology of Urgency

Following our attention to the Anthropocene as a coupled problem of phenomenon and discourse, we here distinguish between scientific disciplines' attention to *phenomena* as observable or measurable material events in the world and philosophical disciplines' attention to *phenomenology* as a study of objects of direct experience—specifically, the subjective experience of urgency. The unique features of the manifestations of the global change problem—irreversible transformations, high-impact events with variable probabilities, and very long planning horizons—mean that confronting disaster and its potentials is, increasingly, a matter of urgency.[29] Yet the character of this urgency, how it is experienced, by whom, and with what power to act, is neither universal nor predictable.

The contribution of Edmund Husserl's study of phenomenology was to place the natural sciences into a social context by considering the historicity and directedness of scientific disciplines themselves. He saw in the sciences historical processes involving their own myths, as we illustrated in chapter 1 in the case of geology. Husserl supported the purposes and benefits of science but recognized that scientific insight is a product of both path-dependence and social context. His project was not a postmodern descent into relativism but a means of describing phenomena as they are positioned within the lived world. Perhaps for this reason, arriving at a unified definition of the methods and aims of phenomenological analysis is itself is challenging, and there may be as many phenomenologists as there are approaches to phenomenology.

Here, we draw attention to the work of Emmanuel Levinas, who wrote extensively on the face-to-face encounter with the suffering other. Levinas postulated that the historicity of cognition is always located within a person's intentional field of experience—or myth—situated as an object that filters and interprets all sensory input. Levinas considered that before any intentional field of experience can arise, the sensibility and affectivity in the face-to-face encounter remains at the foundation of human cognition.[30] Faced with what Hannah Arendt called "the banality of evil" of mid-century Europe,[31] Levinas came to reject the idea of any real understanding of the world outside of the immediate now of the face-to-face encounter in the material world.[32] It is for this reason that in the urgency of the phenomena we describe in this book, we do not seek to attribute unequivocally any particular event to any particular global change process, but rather to consider these events as critical symbols in the ongoing narration of global change as a source of security in the rapidly changing world.

Political urgency meets increasingly pressing narratives about catastrophic climate change, environmental destruction, and environmental injustices across the world. Although polarized in nearly every other respect, activists across the political spectrum can agree that the ongoing crises emerge from an incongruity among the key values and ideas that would move societies toward human dignity for all. There is a mounting perception that socialist, environmental, conservative, and libertarian protagonists want fundamentally different things and that the only game is an oppositional one. Edmund Husserl argued such crises arise when failing to grasp the complexity, diversity, and synergy of human experience and worldly phenomena.[33] Insisting on acontextual categories and schemes of interpretation to identify goals and solve problems, he reasoned, produces a blindness to the potential for common ground that may exist outside preferred myths and their symbols. For example, carbon-neutral futures can be achieved without needing to agree on whether, as an environmentalist might maintain, there is a moral imperative to mitigate climate change to save species, or, as a Tea Party member might contend, the United States' national security depends on achieving energy independence.

The following sections examine the phenomena and phenomenologies of urgency through descriptive case studies. We consider the urgency experienced and expressed by narrators of the event. When is the urgency of climate-related hazards generated by the events finding purchase in ongoing social discourse, and when do they empirically constitute catastrophes? How does this distinction affect our ability to make policy and develop systems of governance that are equal to the task?

Unimagined Extremes

A crisis is a terrible thing to waste.
—Paul Romer[34]

The lead-up to and aftermath of Super Typhoon Haiyan embody the challenges of matching capacity to prepare for extreme events with the actual scale of disasters; this presents a warning for a world under climate change. The Philippines had strengthened preparedness efforts during the years before the event, and state-of-the-art technologies were employed by many of the participants. For instance, the storm surge model of the Japan Meteorological Agency (JMA) for the first time released a storm surge forecast publicly in advance of the typhoon;[35] the World Health Organization used social media for the first time as part of its risk-communications strategy; and the international humanitarian community for the first time responded to a Level 3 activation for a sudden onset disaster, resulting in extraordinary resources. Nevertheless, Typhoon Haiyan far exceeded model projections and emergency-response capacity, and its impacts became a political lever for renewing national leadership. The unprecedented scale of both the typhoon and of the preparedness efforts, and the concomitant incapacity of the latter to match the former, may be indicative of Anthropocene extremes. The broader warning is against mistaking skill at detecting, predicting, and communicating an event for the capacity to respond.

Detecting a Disaster

At 4:40 a.m. on Friday, November 8, 2013, Typhoon Haiyan passed by the small city of Guiuan in the Eastern Philippines with the highest wind speeds ever recorded for a tropical cyclone making landfall. By 6:30 a.m., Haiyan hit the major city of Tacloban before passing over the Central Visayas, an area that had suffered a powerful 7.2 magnitude earthquake just a few weeks earlier. Haiyan's effects were felt as "tsunami-like" storm surges[36] and gales that crushed well-built schools and makeshift earthquake shelters "like a giant hand from the sky."[37] Locally known as Typhoon Yolanda,[38] Haiyan is estimated to have been the deadliest typhoon in Filipino history. Final reports recorded that the storm left 6,300 people dead, over one thousand people missing, and over twenty-eight thousand people injured.[39] The storm displaced more than sixteen million people and left another four million homeless. It caused an estimated US$9.6 billion in damage.

The Philippines finds itself in the path of between three and six typhoons per year. The country ranks twelfth of two hundred countries and territories in which people are most at risk from natural hazards, according to the United Nations International Strategy for Disaster Risk Reduction. And Typhoon Haiyan was the thirty-first tropical storm of the season in the western North Pacific. The highly favorable conditions for typhoon development meant that forecasts and warnings of storm formation and track were accurate and timely.[40] Landfall was predicted to occur around low tide. But Typhoon Haiyan was unusual in several ways. The warm sea surface temperatures and high ocean heat content, aided by a genesis location unusually close to the equator, resulted in increased sea levels and ample

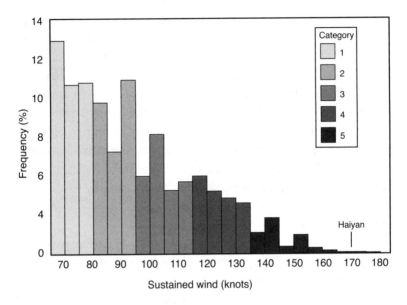

Figure 2.2
Historical distribution of maximum wind speeds in the Western North Pacific, 1951–2012. Typhoon Haiyan recorded landfall wind speeds faster than observed before or since.
Source: Figure developed based on data from Esteban et al., "Storm Surge Awareness" and Takagi et al., "Track Analysis." Takagi et al. reanalyzed the best track data from the Joint Typhoon Warning Center (JTWC).

thermodynamic forcing. Low vertical wind shear and upper-level diffluence provided additional support for what became an explosive cyclogenesis. These ideal conditions led to a rapidly moving typhoon, traveling at 28 to 43 kmph, which allowed Haiyan to maintain Category 5 strength even as it had multiple encounters with land. The Joint Typhoon Warning Center determined one-minute-sustained winds as Haiyan passed over Tacloban to be as high as 315 kmph (figure 2.2). The storm surge in Tacloban set an official record of 7.5 m high, and eyewitness reports place the water as high as 9.1 m. The rapid forward movement of the storm contributed to the unusual tsunami-like waves, sometimes called *meteotsunamis*.[41]

Typhoon as Symbol

As a physical phenomenon, Typhoon Haiyan violated the expectations of communities, weather forecasters, the government of the Philippines, and international aid agencies. Post hoc scientific analyses suggest that the full impact of the typhoon could have been anticipated based on an understanding of the physical system,[42] but the operational postanalysis from the Joint Typhoon Warning Center indicated that the explosive intensification and the rapid propagation of the storm could not have been predicted with currently available tools. Similarly, post hoc scientific analyses conclude that the warm sea surface temperatures, high ocean heat content, and increased sea level can be unequivocally attributed to anthropogenic climate change. Typhoon Haiyan possessed, in this context, a ferocity that might be anticipated with a high level of confidence.[43] However, these thermodynamic attributes are insufficient to draw a line of causation from climate change to this disaster in this place at this time, and debate continues in the scientific literature on this point.[44]

Nevertheless, Typhoon Haiyan was immediately invoked as a symbol distinct from other humanitarian crises ongoing at the time, including the Indian floods, the Syrian conflict, and violence in the Central African Republic. This invocation was despite the fact that climatic elements could be connected to these other crises, ambiguously or not, in various ways.[45] That said, the timing was fortuitous for symbolic construction, as the UN Framework Convention on Climate Change (UNFCCC) commenced its nineteenth session of the Conference of the Parties (COP19) in Warsaw on November 11, 2013. On that first day of talks, Philippine representative to COP19 Naderev (Yeb) Saño stated: "To anyone who continues to deny the reality that is climate change, I dare you to get off your ivory tower and away from the comfort of your armchair. ... What my country is going through as a result of *this extreme climate event* is madness" (emphasis added). UNFCCC head Christiana Figueres was quoted in *TIME* magazine, stating that the typhoon was part of the "sobering reality" of climate change.[46] On the same day, Max Fisher of the *Washington Post* emphasized the extraordinary nature of the event: "The single most important factor may be that, quite simply, this storm was just too big; with winds well beyond 200 miles per hour and sea levels surging across coastal communities, no country could absorb it unharmed."[47]

Within days, the symbol of the super typhoon as an unprecedented phenomenon and thus as an emblem of anthropogenic climate change was combined with the vulnerability of the affected population to invoke climate change as global injustice. The head of the UN Office for Disaster

Risk Reduction, Margareta Wahlstrom, noted on November 12: "It is clear that education, early warnings, urban planning and building codes are key issues for renewed consideration in a world where all bets are off in terms of disaster impacts."[48] "Typhoon Haiyan brought into sharp focus how climate change is intensifying the severity of extreme weather events, which hurts the poor the most," said World Bank President Jim Yong Kim on November 18, 2013.[49]

Thus, a single urgent phenomenon is brought to task in the service of multiple goals: a scholarly debate on attribution science, a call for international agreements for the reduction of greenhouse gas emissions, an invocation of the "slow violence" of inequitable risk distribution. Haiyan becomes not just a physical phenomenon, but a symbolic object that serves to "point backward to global crimes of environmental racism ... and forward as global portent."[50] But under a comprehensive analysis, this typhoon is unique, and the significance of Haiyan to the urgency of the Anthropocene depends on the details.

Disaster Response

The context matters: As noted earlier, the Philippines is in a high-risk area. It lies in the path of the world's most active zone of tropical cyclogenesis and is situated on the Ring of Fire, where 90 percent of the world's earthquakes occur. The Bohol earthquake in the Central Viyasas region of the Philippines occurred just three weeks before Typhoon Haiyan. The earthquake killed more than two hundred people, injured nearly one thousand, and displaced about 350,000 to temporary shelters. The low-lying Tacloban City, which bore the brunt of the typhoon's impacts, is situated at the head of a narrow, deep waterway that serves to channel and amplify storm surges. Tacloban City is located in one of the country's poorest regions, although it is a local hub for trade and education. The region surrounding the city is mountainous and difficult to traverse, making evacuation extremely difficult. Over the past fifty years, the Philippines has lost up to 80 percent of its protective coastal mangroves through aquaculture and human settlement and has lost protective upland forests to illegal logging and mining.[51] Throughout the nation, the population is concentrated in extensive low-lying coastal areas distributed among over seven thousand islands.

The World Health Organization's social media initiative meant that coverage was extensive leading up to, during, and after the typhoon. "The Emergency Relief Coordinator formally activated an Inter-Agency Standing Committee (IASC) Level 3 emergency response the following day (12 November), noting that the magnitude of this sudden-onset humanitarian crisis justified system-wide resource mobilization. A massive international response was launched, and more that 450 international, surge-capacity staff of various expertise were deployed within three weeks. The United Nations Humanitarian Coordination Team in the Philippines issued a humanitarian action plan on the same day as Level 3 activation."[52] Images published internationally, intended to mobilize humanitarian responses, emphasized the physical and sociocognitive remoteness of the affected population.

The United Nations coordinated an appeal, with the aim of raising over US$780 million. By July 2014, this appeal had raised over US$460 million. In addition to cash in the hundreds of millions,[53] the US government contributed around 13,400 military personnel, sixty-six aircraft, and twelve naval vessels in the six weeks immediately following the typhoon, aiding in the delivery of relief supplies and the evacuation of thousands of people.[54] Over fifty governments contributed aid, ranging from a single medical team to millions of dollars. Nongovernmental organizations also contributed, sometimes to an extent that dwarfed their own governmental responses (figure 2.3).

At first glance, we see an unprecedented phenomenon, exacerbated by climate changes caused by first-world profligacy, impacting a highly vulnerable population. But is this the whole picture?

As in the case of the Sahel drought, the information marshaled for humanitarian purposes (a laudable immediate goal) omits important elements when seeking to understand the deeper lessons. These include the fact that the Philippines is in the medium-development category by international human-development standards, with life expectancy, incomes, and education all increasing, at least until 2015. Internally, inequality is far below the average for East Asia. Governance, particularly with regard to environmental concerns, was improving at the time. In 2009, the Philippines implemented a coordinated strategy to mainstream climate-resilient development into local planning. As part of this program, the Disaster Management Assistance Fund administered by the Department of Finance

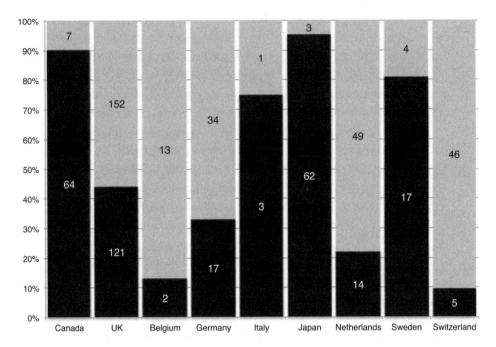

Figure 2.3
Proportion of funds raised for Typhoon Haiyan from government (dark gray) and nongovernment (light gray) sources for a selection of countries. The amounts raised in US$ millions as of July 3, 2014, are also shown.

offered loans to local government at low rates to assist in the building of resiliency to disaster. In 2011, the government of the Philippines allocated US$714 million for its disaster-response, recovery, and risk-reduction activities. This was nearly six times the humanitarian assistance provided by the international community that year.[55] This trend continued through 2012 and, importantly, 2013.

In directing responses following the typhoon, the government of the Philippines led the way, making the relief and recovery effort a collaborative domestic and international operation. The "government of the Philippines has similarly and consistently eclipsed international contributions and, in response to Typhoon Haiyan, also demonstrated the primary coordinating role a domestic government can play in disaster relief."[56] "Moreover, the good organizational networking by the Philippine government down to the village level facilitated humanitarian efforts by local and foreign agencies once aid started trickling in."[57] The local knowledge and experience of Filipino responders was critical for the collaborative emergency response.

To ensure accountability, the government of the Philippines asked the International Aid Transparency Initiative (IATI) to track donations. Because donors did not consistently adhere to IATI guidelines, the government of the Philippines subsequently created an online platform to record cash and in-kind donations from governmental organizations. This Foreign Aid Transparency Hub (FAiTH) was not perfect—it did not record private and nongovernmental donations—but demonstrated a strong commitment to aid transparency. Around six weeks after the typhoon's passage, FAiTH reported over US$239.4 million in nonfinancial assistance, which was comparable to the international responses to the Pakistan floods of 2010 and the Indian Ocean tsunami of 2004 (in annually adjusted US$).[58]

The story is not wholly positive, of course. "The lack of familiarity with the capacities of a middle-income country; differences between international and national planning time frames; and different views on the boundaries and linkages between emergency relief, early recovery and recovery all contributed to the complexities of transitioning from relief to recovery programming."[59] In addition to mismatches between local and international practitioners, an influx of ad hoc groups of volunteers was enabled by a temporary relaxation of visa and immigration regulations. This led to a certain amount of chaos, whereby inexperienced foreign volunteers themselves became a burden on the coordinated government response. In addition, providing health care services to affected populations was particularly difficult—largely because of lack of access to transportation and the ability to widely communicate health information. The damage to health care infrastructure was also a critical concern.[60] Importantly, in-kind donations of medicine presented particular problems as many were out-of-date or not appropriate to current needs: "Medicine management during the response was difficult and was compounded by receiving donations of short-dated, near-expiry and unnecessary items which created additional burden on the health system."[61]

Disaster as Symbol

When manifest as extreme phenomena that exceed the emergency response systems we have created, climate becomes a complex agent of urgency. The impacts of changes in the frequency and intensity of extreme weather phenomena will depend at least as much on the symbols that attend them as on the events themselves. This is because "narrative structure simultaneously constitutes the basis for knowing how the world can be changed and manipulated (epistemology), while shaping the individual and cultural cognition that engenders a sense of being-in-the-world (ontology)."[62] Narratives shape and are shaped by the myths that determine what is possible, what can be withstood, what is to be feared, and what cannot be imagined.

Iconic events that are related in a concrete way to the vulnerabilities of greatest concern—climate injustice, say, or environmental sustainability—serve as an important common focus for government, researchers, and community members, even as they embody different meanings. In this way, the extreme as an organizing principle is used to steer the narrative, as in the case of Haiyan, to stimulate the political will to invest in climate change mitigation and adaptation.[63] But even in this, outcomes can be unexpected.

Of particular interest is the way in which the postdisaster narrative has shaped democratic politics in the Philippines.[64] In a belated visit to Tacloban after the storm, President Benigno Aquino "refused to believe reports that the city of 220,000 people was 95 percent devastated"[65] and reprimanded community members for complaining about hardship and loss instead of being grateful for still being alive. During the recovery period, Aquino followed international practice in designating some destroyed sites in the region to be "no build zones" without consulting the local community. In stark contrast, Rodrigo Duterte, who was the mayor of Davao City when Haiyan struck, sent aid to Tacloban immediately. "'It's our turn to help him' said posters plastered around Tacloban" during Duterte's subsequent presidential bid.[66] To Haiyan survivors, Duterte could not be more different from Aquino: a political outsider, not an heir to a political dynasty; a man of the people, not of the elite. One of them. After he was elected president (in May 2016, with 38.5 percent of the popular vote), Duterte threatened to shoot the government official he had put in charge of Tacloban's recovery if that official failed to act quickly enough.

Duterte continued to use the narrative of Haiyan as an example of environmental injustice, further setting Filipinos against the outside world: "Haiyan is just a creation of climate change, which the industrial countries also created."[67] Duterte characterized the Philippines as a victim once again, this time of the energy-hungry Global North. The paradox, of course, is that even as Duterte restores human dignity to those devastated by earthquake and typhoon, he acts outside the rule of law to attack other vulnerable communities. The ways in which extreme phenomena have an impact on democracy raises many open questions. Indeed, "it is established, for instance, that democracies are not always pacific; they do not always protect the human dignity of their citizens; they do not invariably abolish poverty; they do not always eliminate illiteracy; they do not always prevent themselves from accepting dictators who transform themselves into despots."[68] Democratic governance is emerging as deeply problematic in the Anthropocene.

The New Normal

A wet year won't beat California's never-ending drought.
—Peter Gleick (January 22, 2017)[69]

We had to act as if we were having our own millennial drought that would last 10 years. It was definitely DEFCON 1.
—Felicia Marcus, California Water Resources Control Board (March 10, 2017)[70]

The symbols to which Typhoon Haiyan has been harnessed, from ordinary hazard to first-world hegemony, from clear evidence of climate change to a story of local resilience, demonstrate the complex role that discourse can play in the urgent Anthropocene. Slow-moving disasters take on something of a different character, whereby narratives of the atypical, exceptional, and abnormal vie with a sense of a "new normal" emerging. This tension has been nowhere more evident than during the recent drought conditions in California.

California Dreaming

In *The Grapes of Wrath*, John Steinbeck (1939) follows the fortunes of displaced Oklahoman farmers pushed westward by social and biophysical processes beyond their control or understanding. Decades of tilling the deep soils that had been kept in place by ancient prairie grass met with years of dry weather, and helpless farmers saw their crops blow away in the Dust Bowl. Unable to repay bank loans that had covered previous losses, the farmers were foreclosed upon, as distant investors seized the opportunity to take over small properties, consolidate, and industrialize production. Steinbeck situates the reader alongside the family watching a tractor tilling their homes and fences into the soil, and has the masked driver suggest to them: "Why don't you go on west to California? There's work there, and it never gets cold. Why, you can reach out anywhere and pick an orange. Why, there's always some kind of crop to work in. Why don't you go there?"[71] The book was published on the four-year anniversary of Black Sunday, the most severe and terrifying of the dust storms that named the Dust Bowl of the 1930s. The book, with its tragically specific family, resonated so strongly with the American public that "it almost seemed to cheapen the novel."[72] From Eleanor Roosevelt and Woodie Guthrie engaging their public platforms to *Grapes of Wrath* parties, Steinbeck's novel incited public urgency to respond with donations and offers of work. In the midst of the compassionate outpouring of aid, however, the response of Kern County appeared equally urgent. Offended at the insinuations made in the book against the empathy of county residents, the book was burned, and the Bakersfield town hall meeting of August 21, 1939, passed Motion 47 to ban the book from the library and schools (box 2.1).

Box 2.1
Motion 47 of the Board of Supervisors, Kern County, passed with a vote of four to one (from Wartzman, *Obscene in the Extreme*, 8)

WHEREAS, John Steinbeck's work of fiction, *The Grapes of Wrath*, has offended our citizenry by falsely implying that many of our fine people are a low, ignorant, profane and blasphemous type living in a vicious and filthy manner, and

WHEREAS, Steinbeck presents our public officials, law enforcement officers and civil administrators, businessmen, farmers and ordinary citizens as inhumane vigilantes, breathing class hatred and divested of sympathy or human decency or understanding toward a great, and to us unwelcome, economic problem brought about by an astounding influx of refugees, indigent farmers, who were dusted or tractored or foreclosed out of Oklahoma, Kansas, Nebraska, Arkansas, Missouri, Texas and others of our sister states, and

WHEREAS, Steinbeck chose to ignore the education, recreation, hospitalization, welfare and relief services, unexcelled by any other political subdivision in the United States, made available by Kern County to every resident in Kern County, and

> WHEREAS, *Grapes of Wrath* is filled with profanity, lewd, foul and obscene language unfit for use in American homes, therefore, be it
>
> RESOLVED, that we, the BOARD OF SUPERVISORS, in defense of our free enterprise and of people who have been unduly wronged, request that production of the motion picture film, *Grapes of Wrath*, adapted from the Steinbeck novel, not be completed by Twentieth Century-Fox Film Corporation and request that the use and possession and circulation of the novel, *Grapes of Wrath*, be banned from our library and schools.

Might the inhabitants of Castiglione have reacted similarly if they were confronted with a narrative that they had turned their backs on the wounded of Solferino? That Dunant alone rallied them into benevolent response? If the people of Castiglione did protest, it is not widely known.

Steinbeck also set the stage for how the Dust Bowl would be remembered in the American foundational or cosmological myth. Although descriptive of the catastrophic social, environmental, economic, and political conditions of farmers in the West during the Great Depression, Steinbeck's book does "not offer codified or institutional solutions." Rather, his narrative "leads us deeper into complexities those issues raise by historicizing beneficence, sympathy, compassion, and relatedness,"[73] concepts that continue to be critical to the American identity. The book's ending offers closure neither to the family nor to the industrial transformation of the agrarian societies of Oklahoma and California. This story continues today—in the displacement and exploitation of farm workers, on the path of agricultural development,[74] but also in the continuing absence of formal Native American relationships and rights to water. No treaties have been made with Californian tribes, such that the Winters Doctrine that assures water rights in other US states cannot be evaluated.[75]

Water continues to play a central role in the story of California. Rainfall deficits are common in the region, as are very wet years (figure 2.4). When rainfall is insufficient to support agricultural and human use, the mining of ground water has offered a steady supply. Indeed, in California, in the absence of local ordinances and until the Sustainable Groundwater Management Act of 2014, the default situation was that land ownership was conflated with groundwater ownership. Starting in the 1920s, electric bore wells made groundwater irrigation simple and lucrative, providing a stable and highly productive agricultural system. Extractions in some

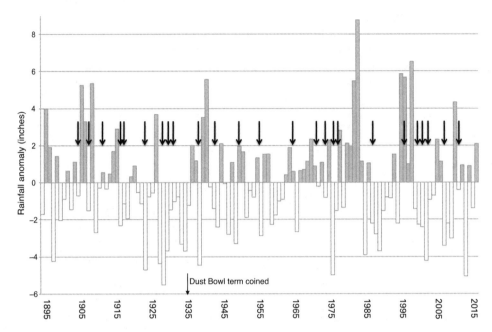

Figure 2.4

Rainfall anomalies (differences from the 1901–2000 average) for the western region of the United States, in inches. The thick black arrows indicate La Niña events of varying strengths. Typically, the pattern of Pacific Ocean temperatures and atmospheric circulation known as La Niña leads to drier than average conditions in the western United States. But La Niña cycles are not sufficient to explain drought conditions; they are part of the picture, but not the whole.

Data: National Oceanic and Atmospheric Administration (NOAA)'s National Centers for Environmental Information.

areas reached twice the rate of natural recharge (figure 2.5). As a result, the urgency that has attended other extended droughts, such as those in Australia and the Sahel, has been mitigated by a bridging solution the unsustainability of which has not been visible until recently.

The Metrics of Drought: Supply

Drought is not simply low rainfall; it can also be caused by extreme heat, unreliable rainfall, excessive extractive use, or land clearing. Because people use water in so many different ways, there is no universal definition of drought. The World Meteorological Organization collates a not-exhaustive list of fifty methodologies for detecting drought in the *Handbook on Drought*

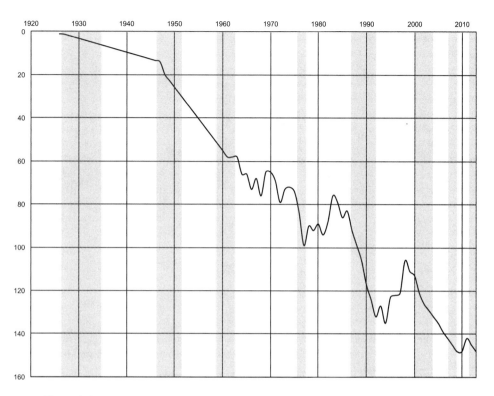

Figure 2.5
Cumulative groundwater depletion in cubic kilometers, 1920–2013. Gray shading indicates periods of officially designated drought.
Source: Based on Choy and McGhee, "Groundwater." Additional data used from the US Geological Survey.

Indicators and Indices. One of the most commonly used metrics in the United States and in the academic literature is the Palmer Drought Index,[76] developed by Wayne Palmer in the 1960s for the US Weather Bureau (see figure 2.6). This index, like many others, is a measure of water supply. Palmer created the index by applying recent precipitation and temperature to a simple "bucket" model to produce a standardized index of soil wetness, from -10 to 10. Palmer chose this "strictly meteorological" approach to avoid "many of the complicating biological factors and arbitrary definitions" and instead derive a "climatic analysis system in which drought severity is dependent on the duration and magnitude of the abnormal moisture deficiency."[77] Critically, Palmer considered drought a deviation from "normal" conditions, a climatological attribute that cannot always

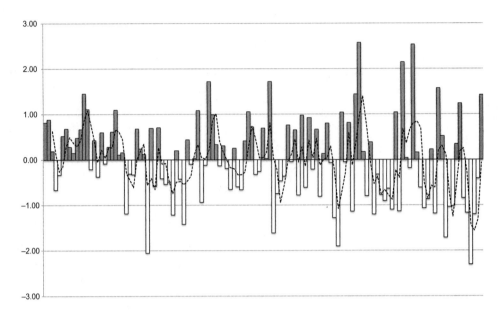

Figure 2.6
Palmer Drought Severity Index for California for September–August in 1895–2017, with a three-year moving average shown as a dashed line. The slight downward trend is not statistically significant.
Data: Accessed from NOAA National Climatic Data Center, 2017.

be defined usefully (see, e.g., figure 2.4). In regions of high rainfall variability around the world, human and ecological water usage is far from simply a climatological matter. It is a matter of context and perspective. Steinbeck was already aware of this: "But Adam, looking out over his dry dust-obscured land, felt the panic the Eastern man always does at first in California. In a Connecticut summer two weeks without rain is a dry spell and four a drought. If the countryside is not green it is dying. But in California it does not ordinarily rain at all between the end of May and the first of November. The Eastern man, though he has been told, feels the earth is sick in the rainless months."[78]

Because it is widely used, the Palmer Drought Severity Index (PDSI) and its variants permit intercomparisons of drought conditions across space and time—which in turn leads to the index being even more widely used. This tendency toward standardization assists in making the problem comprehensible to the state. From its earliest beginnings in Europe, the state's interests in natural resources led inescapably "to rationalizing and standardizing what was a social hieroglyph into a legible and administratively more convenient format."[79] However, operational weather and agricultural services typically adopt their own locally relevant definition of drought, which may include information regarding rainfall deficits and elevated temperatures but may also consider direct measurements of stream flows, water table depths, soil moisture, industrial allocations, crop types, and timing.

At present, the United States Drought Monitor (USDM) maps drought designations across the United States. This map draws on expert interpretation across five measures comprising the Palmer Drought Severity Index, together with a more sophisticated soil-moisture model, weekly stream flow measurements, additional precipitation measures, and a variety of other objective drought-indicator blends based on seasonal and interannual precipitation patterns and satellite-based measurements of vegetation health and soil moisture. In addition, some blends might consider groundwater levels, reservoir storage, and pasture/range conditions. Finally, to map drought severity, the USDM draws on reports from 350 experts across the country to make a qualitative judgment of drought severity. The organization asserts that it is "this combination of the best available data, local observations and experts' best judgment that makes the U.S. Drought Monitor more versatile than other drought indicators."[80]

The Metrics of Drought: Demand

The feedbacks between people and drought are not fully understood, and this renders drought management inefficient. Because we are now in a human-influenced era, Van Loon argues that "we need to rethink the concept of drought to include the human role in mitigating and enhancing drought."[81] As noted, meteorological measures of drought have been critiqued for not offering useful metrics to respond to and plan for drought. Furthermore, many of the measures that go into a drought designation have already had the hand of extractive water use and land-use change in their records.

Stream flow, the volume of surface water in a system, is an important example. Clearing watershed vegetation leads to decreases in canopy interception of rainfall, surface roughness, transpiration, and ground-litter storage of water. All these factors cause a change in the pattern of runoff into

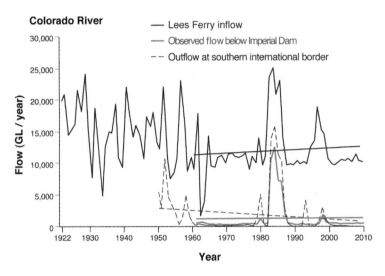

Figure 2.7
Observed inflows at Lees Ferry and outflows below the Imperial Dam and at the international border between the United States and Mexico, in gigalitres (Gl) per year. Trend lines for inflow, observed flow, and outflow are shown.
Source: From Grafton et al., "Global Insights," figure 2a, 318.

streams and rivers, resulting in faster stream flows and higher volumes over shorter time periods. Faster and higher volumes of stream flows diminishes the amount of water available for groundwater and aquifer recharge and can lead, somewhat perversely, to more frequent flash flood events. Furthermore, the extractive use of surface water often can far outweigh the deficits of freshwater due to evaporation or reduced rainfall.[82] For example, flows in the Colorado River were allocated in 1922 in perpetuity by volume rather than proportion of flow, with a complex set of regulations governing senior and junior rights and cross-boundary trade. The Colorado River is primarily a snow-fed river system that passes along the edge of California on its way to Mexico, supplying water to more than nineteen million people and adding $970 billion to the economy in Southern California.[83] By treaty, the United States is obliged to supply 1.845 km^3 of freshwater per year to Mexico, a volume that has not been met in all but a few years over the last several decades (figure 2.7). As a result, no freshwater has reached the sea during that time. Finally, in 2010, the US Bureau of Reclamation confirmed for the first time that water extractions were exceeding the supply.

The depletion of groundwater (figure 2.5) is another strong indicator that there is a discrepancy between water demand and supply in California. The cumulative depletion of groundwater in California has steadily increased to over 140 km^3 of freshwater in 2014, or four and a half times the capacity of the state's largest reservoir. Corporate and family farms have together contributed to the steepening downward curve of groundwater use. While on a trajectory of increasing predominance, factory farms account for around one-quarter of agricultural acres in California today.[84] The effects of their groundwater use are well understood. From salinization and land subsidence to impacts on ecosystems and townships, groundwater overuse has received considerable scrutiny. As surface reservoirs sank to record-low levels across California toward the peak of the drought in 2016, the visible face of California's thirst engendered unprecedented attention to the state's water supplies—but there are few drought indicators that target groundwater. In the World Meteorological Organization's inventory of drought indices, only the Standardized Water-Level Index (SWI)[85] uses well measurements to indicate how groundwater recharge is impacted by drought. There are ongoing deliberations that explore means of better understanding groundwater dynamics.[86]

But for the SWI, the metrics used to detect drought do not consider social and economic choices about water use relative to "normal" conditions.[87] That is, they do not invert the question and attempt to measure the point at which socioeconomic decisions draw the human-natural system into a state of moisture deficit—based, for instance, on the consumptive or evapotranspirational characteristics of a region. Of course, that has not been the intention of drought detection since Palmer's first research in the 1960s. Before considering whether the time might have come to include socioeconomic choices in drought detection to meet the water demands of the future, we will turn to the kinds of droughts that are rendered visible using today's metrics.

Detecting a Slow Emergency

The key challenge of detecting when a significant drought has commenced is that the drought is declared when the supply runs low, not when the demand is high. Governor Jerry Brown declared the drought in California on January 17, 2014, after one of the driest years in California history. A formal declaration can result in a positive feedback due to farmers' insurance and aid schemes, in which farmers increase production in good years and receive compensation in bad years, and in that way remove any incentives to adjust production to local conditions.[88] Farmers respond by planting crops in places that can receive compensation and are compensated based on the metrics. And those metrics are based upon a moisture balance that only measures unusual weather conditions, not maladaptive water use. Common to all these metrics is the insistence on measuring drought as an anomaly. By 2017, rain and snowpack were far above average. Northern California received its entire annual average precipitation in the month of January alone. Some officials declared that the "precipitation drought" was over, but they were cautious about suggesting that a "return to normal" should be considered. The question arose: What is the baseline for normal conditions?

Calculated based on more than a century of data, the California PDSI demonstrates large year-on-year variability, in part because of the strong relationship between California rainfall patterns and the El Niño/La Niña pattern of variation in the tropical Pacific (figures 2.4 and 2.6). The first two years of the most recent drought illustrate a considerable departure from the 119-year record. There is no objective basis on which to designate any part of this record as "normal." The North American Drought Atlas (NADA) offers a historical reconstruction based on hundreds of tree-ring chronologies of North American climate for the past two millennia. The year 2014 stands out in this data as a severe drought year, but the inferred rainfall was not outside the envelope of natural variability over that time.[89] Indeed, the "reconstruction reveals that the climate system is capable of natural precipitation deficits of even greater duration and severity than has so far been witnessed during the comparatively brief 2012–2014 drought episode."[90] In large part, then, the experienced and narrated severity of the most recent drought can be attributed to a combination of elevated temperatures and unsustainable water extraction practices. Certainly, the current expectations for water use in California renders even historically typical rainfall variation unusual or extreme.

California Awakening

As cogently expressed by Peter Gleick, asking "Is the drought over?" is the wrong question.[91] Seasonal forecasts of rainfall are rapidly improving, but predictability remains a few months in advance at best. More importantly, the factors that conditioned the impacts of the drought are only some-what related to rainfall deficits. Also largely moot is the question "Was the drought caused by climate change?" There is some evidence that the high temperatures and strongly coherent circulation structure (the "ridiculously resilient ridge" of popular parlance) that accompanied the rainfall deficits were more likely to have occurred under climate change.[92] Some authors go so far as to suggest that "diminished snowpack, streamflows, and reservoir levels have resulted in a convergence of reduced surface water supply with heightened demand that appears to be unique in modern California his-tory."[93] But a "new normal" this is not: in fact, water resources demand and regulation have been out of balance with supply for many decades, as con-tinued drawdowns of the aquifers during wet periods attest. How urgency is identified and addressed in Californian water management will arise from an enquiry into the multidimensional relationship between water and humans in the Californian context.

If we are to speak of drought as a disaster affecting humans, we need met-rics that measure drought as something human. This means using metrics in a way that looks not for anomalies in weather, but for chronic overuse due to impossible expectations of human-nature relations. Before the Dust Bowl, California already had a reputation for being a lush Eden. The state's name reveals the mythical status of California: Califa, a mythical island paradise described in *Las sergas de Esplandián* (*The Adventures of Esplandián*) by Garcia Ordonez de Montalvo (a Spanish romance written about 1510), was the source from which the state got its name. The so-called Mediter-ranean climate is only found in four other locations worldwide and is key to global food production. Californian oranges, grapes, avocados, almonds, and smaller crops, such as strawberries, blackberries, blueberries, and rasp-berries, are exported worldwide, hydrated with the Central Valley Aquifer. California has been seen as a productive agricultural region with intermit-tent droughts that are unusual, but the most recent drought of 2012–2016 has changed that perception—at least temporarily—and directed attention to a symbol of a "new normal." This characterizes a transformed condition that differs markedly from what came before. But the climate record shows that more severe rainfall deficits are relatively common in the region. As a symbol, the "new normal" may lie less in the climate record and more in the human perception of California as a periodically drought-stricken state with poor water governance.

Responding to a slow crisis such as drought depends on the ability to mobilize the symbol of drought in more positive ways. This symbol is fundamentally useful for the ability to see the situation as real, significant, and actionable. Emmanuel Levinas observes that the situation is always relational, always apparent in the meeting between the self and the other. How does this apply with these drought metrics? Can the drought be seen in other ways than by personally observing an empty reservoir, or watching crops or forests withering from lack of water? Here, the Australian Millennium Drought offers important lessons.[94] In the early years of this iconic Australian drought, sanctions were available but not invoked by government to enforce adoption of demand-reductions measures. Instead, water-demand management became a shared journey, as illustrated by the forty separate stakeholder briefings and twenty-one public forums attended by more than 1,300 people, resulting in 670 submissions to inform the process of creating the overarching document *Our Water, Our Future*, which then led to dozens of individual pieces of legislation. This process allowed the drought to be storied and known. Minister for Water John Thwaites noted at the time: "You can be fined, but no one has ever been fined. Community pressure does the job."[95] Community pressure is evidence of the consent of the governed, allowed for by the ethical engagement between the governed and the state.

In California, this shared journey was not taken, at least not with deliberation. Instead, during the early stages of the drought, Governor Jerry Brown asked Californians to voluntarily reduce potable water use to 20 percent below predrought levels. Commercial, industrial, and institutional sectors (two-thirds of the water usage) were not asked to reduce demand at all. Largely, voluntary reductions were not achieved until sanctions and incentives were introduced across the board. In effect, drought management in California suffers from a goal substitution in which the goal—living with inevitable drought—has been replaced with a means, that of improving water infrastructure, thus eliding improved human relationships with water.

Thus, effective policy and inclusive governance in the face of a slow-moving catastrophe present a particular challenge. That said, formulae that recognize that all crises are shared journeys, that knowledge is distributed, and that seeking the "normal" is unproductive have been successful—and they can be again.

Dangerous Climate Change, Here and Now[96]

If you think adventure is dangerous, try routine; it is lethal.
—Paulo Coelho[97]

The United Nations Framework Convention on Climate Change (1992) adopted an ultimate objective of limiting global average warming below 2°C, and the most recent Paris Agreement maintains this objective.[98] This specification has been understood as preventing "dangerous anthropogenic interference with the climate system."[99] What "dangerous" means in this specification depends on judgments of values, and as time passes since the identification of the danger, the question becomes less salient.[100] The Anthropocene now presents very different challenges to the world of global average targets; challenges that are beginning to emerge in extreme phenomena.

For example, there was a severe heat wave in Europe during the northern summer of 2003. France experienced seven consecutive days with daytime temperatures over 40°C. Temperature records were also broken in Brogdale, United Kingdom (38.5°C); Roth, Germany (40.4°C); Grono, Switzerland (41.5°C); and Amareleja, Portugal (47.3°C). Reservoirs and rivers used for public water supply and hydroelectric schemes either dried up or ran extremely low. Exemptions to allow the release of water above ecologically safe temperatures into rivers were granted to at least six nuclear reactors and several conventional power stations. Farm animals perished and crops withered. Railway lines buckled. The mass of European Alpine glaciers decreased by 10 percent and nearly 650,000 ha of forest burned. Europe as a whole experienced an estimated death toll of over thirty-five thousand people, and financial losses exceeded €13 billion.[101]

"The physical nature of a heat wave itself is not unambiguous: several definitions of the term heat wave exist within the international meteorological community."[102] Furthermore, the direct impacts of heat stress on the human body have been well characterized by the medical community: "A slight positive deviation from the desired body-core temperature triggers two thermoregulation mechanisms in the hypothalamus"[103]—these result in an increase in cardiac output and a loss of considerable amounts of water. These responses can be linked to epidemiological records to quantify the resulting mortality.[104] The mortality statistics can be further categorized by age, gender, socioeconomic status, and urban form. But the human nature of the disaster cannot be communicated by these factors. For example, consider the case of France.

As with all heat waves, the media narrative began with reports of inconvenience and images of children at play in water. These are the universal symbols of the summer heat wave. Before two weeks had passed, however, almost fifteen thousand people had died in France, and unclaimed bodies piled up in makeshift coffins for weeks afterward. Power and water supplies failed at a critical time. Absent from the disaster were President Jacques Chirac and his ministers. Even when government action was initiated, "instructions were given to limit dissemination of death numbers."[105] Blame was apportioned to health practitioners on vacation and inattentive families. "'We're all guilty,' declared the front-page headline of Tuesday's popular daily Le Parisien."[106] Once the extent of the catastrophe became more apparent, the public symbols changed dramatically. "Is it normal that last night there were 300 people who hadn't been buried because the family had not turned up to claim the body?" was the question posed by the state secretary for the elderly, Hubert Falco, as some victims were buried in unmarked graves.[107]

This was not the most recent heat wave to cause massive mortality in Europe. Indeed, close to 95 percent of human mortality from natural hazards in the developed world have been attributed to extreme temperatures.[108] Conceptually, the warming global temperatures associated with anthropogenic climate change have been understood as a shift in the mean of a normal (Gaussian) distribution, with no change in variability. However, the events of 2003 have come to symbolize a regime in which extreme temperatures, both hot and cold, have manifest more frequently and become more intense. The 2003 European heat wave constituted one of the first weather events that could be attributed to global climate change—or, in the careful words of attribution science, "we estimate it is very likely (confidence level >90%) that human influence has at least doubled the risk of a heat wave exceeding this threshold magnitude."[109] The variability of temperature—that is, the width of the normal distribution—has increased.[110] Put another way, in many places heat waves are increasing in frequency and intensity more rapidly than the average temperature is increasing, and so are cold snaps.[111]

It is apparent that extreme temperatures and other excursions of natural variability that are manifest now can or will be attributed to anthropogenic climate change. But while the obvious symbolic change that is occurring in the global change discourse is one of dangerous changes in the natural system, the most critical symbolic change that could occur is a narration of the social amplification of risk. Science recognizes the discursive limits and possibilities of scientific knowledge, while the public discourse often, and perhaps paradoxically, treats science as describing an essential perceived reality. This perceived reality has an important cultural component: this is most evident when technological risks are perceived as more hazardous, when people have little sense of control over their exposure to hazards, or where there is a social stigma attached to vulnerability.[112] Even so, in the realm of the unimaginable, the Anthropocene will provide ample opportunities to overcome the social attenuation of risk. "In a catastrophic age, trauma itself may provide the very link between cultures."[113]

Will Steffen and colleagues identified a "second stage" of the Anthropocene from 1945 as the *Great Acceleration*.[114] Many contributing factors were documented through increases in exposure of people and the things they value to losses, in addition to characterizing people as agents of catastrophic change. In this context, "risks do not register their effects in the abstract; they occur in particular regions and places, to particular peoples, and to specific ecosystems. Global environmental risks will not be the first insult or perturbation ... ; rather, they will be the latest in a series of pressures and stresses that will add to (and interact with) what has come before."[115] That is, the Anthropocene renders urgently actionable results from attending to particular relationships between phenomena and conditions in the lived world, not from universal metrics of emergency.

3   Urgent Policy

Of course, causes of climate-related disaster have always been social.
—Jesse Ribot[1]

Our understanding of the behavior of the climate system is so deeply rooted in the basic physicochemical properties of the water molecule that we can confidently conclude that global warming from anthropogenic emissions of long-lived greenhouse gases poses serious risks.
—Bjorn Stevens[2]

Introduction

More urgently than ever, we need ideas and theories that will allow us to conceive the new which is rolling over us in a new way, and allow us to live and act within it.
—Ulrich Beck[3]

In the warm weather of July 26, 1943, Los Angeles, California, was blanketed in smog so dense that some residents thought that they were under chemical weapons attack by the Japanese.[4] A synthetic rubber plant was blamed, and the plant was promptly shut down. But smog episodes continued; they got worse. It took nearly a decade for chemist Arie Haagen-Smit to determine that ozone, a gas harmful to humans, is formed when nitrogen oxides and volatile organic compounds react in the presence of sunlight. Nitrogen oxides are emitted from fuel-burning sources including electric utilities, industrial boilers, and vehicles. Sources of volatile organic compounds include paints, inks, solvents, and gasoline. The result, then, was what became known as *photochemical smog*. Other scientists (some funded by automobile companies) immediately disparaged Dr. Haagen-Smit's work, and it would take another decade before his work earned acceptance.

In 1968, Dr. Haagen-Smit became the first head of the statewide Air Resources Board. As more became known about the sources of photochemical smog, lawmakers in California and nationwide began to focus on regulating them—creating standards for the maximum amounts of pollutants in the air and deadlines for meeting these standards.

The federal Air Pollution Control Act of 1955 and the Clean Air Act of 1963 took many of their core concepts from California-based research. California was the only state that retained its freedom to regulate as state policymakers saw fit. As result, Californian standards continue to be able to further restrict United States federal standards. These regulatory developments occurred in the tumultuous years in which activism for civil rights and environmental protection came to define a generation. Books such as *Silent Spring, Never Cry Wolf, Desert Solitaire,* and *Our Synthetic Environment* made the UN Decade of Development (1960–1970) a particularly important time in environmental thought.[5] Rachel Carson's *Silent Spring* in particular went on to inspire worldwide environmental awareness of air and water pollution and to garner support for urgent changes in the modern approach to industrialization and development.[6]

President Nixon established the National Ambient Air Quality Standards as part of the Clean Air Act of April 1970, and he signed Reorganization Plan No. 3 to establish the Environmental Protection Agency (EPA) in July. The Senate confirmed William Ruckelshaus as the first administrator of the EPA in December. The act was in response to mounting calls for better regulation and established the EPA as an independent agency (but not as a Cabinet department). As a result, EPA experts could determine standards in a rules-based system. The standards methodology that is the core of the EPA policy approach is based on the idea that a regulation specifies a range or limit of either ambient concentrations or individual emissions, and then relevant industry engineers determine the means to meet the target in the most economically efficient manner. This methodology often is called *technology forcing*, and it has worked well for reducing sulfur emissions from coal-fired power plants, removing lead from gasoline, and reducing emissions of nitrogen oxides and particulates from power plants and vehicles. Some United States jurisdictions have explored technology forcing as a means to reduce carbon dioxide emissions to mitigate climate change. To date, however, it has proved insufficient for solving the smog problem in California.

The requirements of regulation rarely specify a zero limit. For that reason, a discourse has evolved around the idea of *sacrifice zones*—zones of pollution, disturbance, or destruction that allow other areas to remain free from contamination. The sacrifice zone has become a symbol of environmental injustice for communities and places where polluting industries are permitted in order to serve other ends, such as economic or national security. Stories of destruction and injustice provide effective narratives in the political process. But serving the common interest is a different commitment that rewards steering away from urgent post hoc protests and toward early civil engagement.

Air quality in Los Angeles remains among the worst in the nation, with, on average, seventy-seven days exceeding ozone pollution standards in the decade from 2005 to 2014. In 2016, ozone levels exceeded federal standards on ninety-one days. Clearly, there are many factors that contribute to the tenacity of the problem. The worst pollution burden is evident in census tracts with majority low-income Latino residents and areas that host landfills, refineries, railyards, and factories. In addition to these zones of environmental injustice, there are wider factors. Southern California's population has almost doubled, and vehicle miles traveled have more than doubled, since 1970. Although California has been quite successful in regulating car efficiency, traffic delays (estimated at 500 million hours per year in Los Angeles alone) mean that Californians are only averaging a fuel economy rating of twenty mpg per vehicle. California emissions regulations apply only to new vehicles, and small businesses in particular keep their trucks, which are a major capital investment, for as long as possible. Furthermore, cargo volume at California ports has increased dramatically in the last decade and is projected to triple by 2030.

It is apparent that Los Angeles's air-quality policy suffers from two key malfunctions. The first is goal substitution. This is a process whereby a limited set of policy levers—from new vehicle emissions guidelines to electricity market regulation—have been redefined as the policy goals, rather than means to achieve the goal of reducing pollution. The goal of pollution reduction has been redefined as regulating and managing EPA-defined "safe limits." When reducing pollution per se is not explicitly retained as the goal, alternative policies are not explored and other contributing domains, such as public transport or urban planning, remain hidden. Nevertheless, environmental policy operating under the standards-based approach has become the norm internationally. Today, most nations utilize an environmental impact assessment process with the authority to determine safe limits and compliance. Importantly, goal substitution limits the ability to recognize the social and political context of the pollution problem. Because of their inherent complexity, encompassing social and natural processes, environmental policies in particular can result in this substitution. With targets and timetables, safe limits, and compliance requirements, often the result is that necessary social processes—and the innovations that can arise therefrom—are sidelined.

A second important malfunction in the environmental policy process arises from the sometimes concealed influence of dominant myths. In the case of Los Angeles air pollution, a predominant myth is one of the individual car culture. This myth is particularly powerful in the city because the widespread adoption of cars coincided with the dramatic growth of Los Angeles in the 1920s. The doctrine of car ownership was supported by the Federal Road Act of 1916, the poor performance of streetcars, the lack of geographic limitations to urban spread, and the availability of local oil resources. Individual car transportation became symbolic of a progressive and modern culture. Alternative policy approaches, when they emerge, do so in ways that are founded upon myths that offer a sense of familiarity and rectitude, providing ontological security.[7]

Faced with unprecedented threat, people find ontological—existential and cosmological—security in myths that pinpoint who, what, where, and when we are in order to characterize problems, set goals, and identify solutions. This creates a narrowing of standpoint that can prevent the imagining of alternatives. A study by the University of California, Los Angeles found that in the decade leading to 2015, solo car use increased by 3.5 percent, carpool use decreased by 24 percent, and public transportation use decreased by 6 percent.[8] As a result, solutions that involve electric car ownership typically gain more traction than solutions that involve public transit. This tendency to revert to foundational myths for inspiration and direction to navigate crises is evident globally.[9] Expressions of ontological insecurity are often at play in responses to or reactions against extant proposals.

Although it has proved inhibiting in Los Angeles, the idea of safe limits has entered the vocabulary of global environmental policymaking.[10] The hypothesis holds that beyond certain thresholds, earth systems, being highly nonlinear, are likely to undergo a catastrophic shift. In the ensuing epoch, biogeophysical processes in the earth system "cannot continue to function in a stable, Holocene-like state." In this way, "planetary boundaries," like safe limits, can define an estimated maximum quantifiable value for key earth system processes, within which humanity "has the freedom to pursue long-term social and economic development."[11] Planetary boundaries and safe limits helpfully drive understanding and raise awareness by using quantifiable metrics to determine environmental decisions. But are they sufficient? Setting "safe" limits can produce goal displacement, substituting the goal of reducing pollution with meeting or staying within set limits, while undermining the political processes necessary to identify common interest outcomes.

Incongruously, the slow change in environmental policy may arise precisely from myriad urgencies that prevent the opportunity to achieve more fundamental policy change and instead depend on a perpetuated reliance on established patterns. Maarten Hajer's insight that the discourse that permitted discovering environmental crises is paradoxically limiting us from imagining solutions[12] still rings true. The considerably more bureaucratic process of arriving at "good enough" transformation requires opportunities for civic organization, with academia, industry, and government. Transformative ideas emerge from critical engagement not just with the symbols of global environmental change but also with the doctrines that underlie them. There is, still, a great global diversity in ways of understanding and shaping earth processes, with much redundancy that can be drawn upon to innovate, if given opportunities for situated engagements.[13]

Decoupling from the Wild

The cowman who cleans his range of wolves does not realize that he is taking over the wolf's job of trimming the herd to fit the range. He has not learned to think like a mountain.
—Aldo Leopold[14]

When Michael Shellenberger and Ted Nordhaus published *The Death of Environmentalism* in 2005, they intended to shake the foundations of the

United States conservation movement. Shellenberger, an environmental activist, and Nordhaus, a political strategist, had interviewed environmental leaders and examined the track record of US environmental organizations—and they concluded that the environmental movement had failed in its core mission. This was ascribed to several causes, including using "science to define the problem as 'environmental,'" "crafting technical policy proposals as solutions,"[15] and failing to recognize that US political processes were not amenable to predominantly European approaches.[16] As a result, Shellenberger and Nordhaus suggested that environmentalism had been rendered a special interest, rather than a common interest with a holistic vision for the future. The solution to this failure emerged in the "Ecomodernist Manifesto" of 2015,[17] which outlines a "good" Anthropocene that depends on a "radical decoupling of humans from nature,"[18] as exemplified by cities, which "both drive and symbolize the decoupling of humanity from nature."[19] In defining their solution, meanwhile, the ecomodernists invert the scale to focus not on the United States' environmental policy, but on the need for decoupling worldwide.[20]

It is important to note that the ecomodernist proposal exists as a conversation outside the canons of peer reviewed academic discourse. The movement has signatories from several distinguished academics, primarily in the United States, but is focused on a wider discourse. The manifesto speaks less of policy than it does of providence: the inevitability of the good Anthropocene and the ecomodernist future. That said, there is an orientation toward some key symbols—including nuclear energy, cities, and synthesized food production—that could be developed as pathways for policy.

In the following sections, we examine how the spaces offered by the United States Wilderness Myth of Henry David Thoreau, John Muir, Aldo Leopold, and Edward Abbey direct ecomodernist alternatives and the ongoing discourse on the strategy of decoupling humans from nature. We argue that shared symbols and partially incorporated formulae from a broad range of philosophical, political, policy, and scientific orientations create action spaces full of contradictions and incongruences that will need to be resolved for meaningful dialogue to take place. Careful disambiguation will be needed to ensure that narratives of decoupling, combined with urgency, do not perpetuate or substantiate territorial injustices. Finally, we offer a reflection on the role played by ontological insecurity in engendering the wilderness myth and its alternatives. Our aim is neither to celebrate nor to demonize ecomodernist efforts to transform myths of the Anthropocene, but to engage in democratic and pluralistic debate over visions for the future.

The American Wilderness Myth

To understand the ecomodernist revolt against environmentalism, one needs to appreciate the Wilderness Myth of the United States. Here, the figures of Henry David Thoreau (1817–1862), John Muir (1838–1914), Aldo Leopold (1887–1948), and Edward Abbey (1927–1989) loom large. These men mythologized wilderness into the heart of the United States foundational myth and continue to shape the imagination of environmentalists and activists across the world today. Their legacy in the form of national parks and wilderness areas has become the chief manner in which the United States encounters the more-than-human world: turning its gaze from the traces of human activity to distill a perspective of "pure nature." An early advocate of the restorative powers of nature, Thoreau, a scholar and abolitionist, sought refuge from the "lives of quiet desperation" around him. Thoreau's studies led him to transcendental philosophy and a rapturous exploration of close encounters with nature: "We need the tonic of wildness. ... At the same time that we are earnest to explore and learn all things, we require that all things be mysterious and unexplorable, that land and sea be indefinitely wild, unsurveyed and unfathomed by us because unfathomable. We can never have enough of nature."[21]

In this, Thoreau was in step with his time, as the age of Romanticism celebrated the remote and the wild. In the United States, the Hudson River School exemplified this; its members emphasized the untamed and dangerous power of wilderness, combined with a secular faith in nature's capacity to uplift and enlighten.[22] Throughout the nineteenth century, this symbol actively supplanted the classical pastoral landscape as a safe space of harmony, order, and control. *Walden* reads as much as a partial escapism from the confines of the author's contemporary society, with its reliance on slavery, as it does a practice of transcendental philosophy. To be fair, Thoreau's narrative of solitary life is shadowed by a contrapuntal story in which his clothes are washed and his groceries purchased for him, and visitors were encountered frequently at home and in town. Nevertheless, this lyrical work, as well as his earlier writings on civil engagement,[23] inspired social change-makers from John Muir to Gandhi[24] to Martin Luther King Jr.[25]

John Muir, a naturalist and prolific writer, was a teenager when Thoreau published *Walden*. Muir's memoirs of the American West, accompanied by photographs of Yosemite and Yellowstone, evoked in the young nation a profound sense of longing for and proprietorship over the natural domain of North America. Muir's vision of preservation of the natural world lay the foundation for a new myth of native ecosystems in the New World: enlightened transcendence in nature, in which human hunting, farming, and industry were absent. In Yellowstone and Yosemite, in national parks across the United States, this meant the removal of all human activity. The cattle owned by settlers acting on manifest destiny were as unwelcome as the towers of acorns stored by the Ahwahnechee.[26]

When Aldo Leopold, an early graduate of the Yale School of Forestry, first published *A Sand County Almanac*, he espoused a harmony with nature that was more sympathetic to conservation (with sustainable use) than preservation (with humans prohibited). In his role in the new Division of Forestry in the Department of Agriculture, Leopold founded the science of wildlands management, offering an alternative to the wilderness preservation ideals of Muir. Rather than seeing wilderness free of people, he argued, "Control comes from the coordination of science and use. ... Game can be restored by the *creative use* of the same tools which have heretofore destroyed it—axe, plow, cow, fire, and gun."[27] Leopold's thinking shifted over time, however. Ever the empiricist, Leopold found that the control he sought was elusive. By 1935, he was advocating for "an intelligent humility toward Man's place in nature."[28] That year, Leopold joined with others to form the Wilderness Society, a group dedicated to protecting and extending designated wilderness areas in a spirit of preservation. In that way, his later philosophy aligns most closely with that of the ecomodernists nearly a century later.

Edward Abbey (1927–1989) was one of many prominent activists who inherited the wilderness mantle. Abbey wrote *Desert Solitaire* during the Decade of Development[29] and drew on the revolutionary currents of his time to transect anarchist notions of fierce independence with conservation ideals and the need for solitude in the wild.[30] Although sharing with ecomodernists this ideal of freedom from the political spectrum and freedom in nature, Abbey departs markedly from their prescriptions. Instead, he would likely reject the implicit hierarchical interdependence that ecomodernist urbanization might demand and espouse the alternative of energy independence through closeness with nature.[31]

Of course, not all United States natural philosophers of the twentieth century subscribed to the views of these grandfathers of the Wilderness Myth. But the legacy of Thoreau, Muir, Leopold, and Abbey has come to shape successive generations of environmentalists and academic ecologists. As a result, the American Wilderness Myth demonstrated a remarkable tenacity throughout a twentieth century focused on control of and mastery over nature. New generations of Americans have found not only inspiration, but a cosmological doctrine of wilderness, vast and untamed. Not static in formulae or symbols, the rich American wilderness has served as a foundation for the power of progress and the wealth of the nation. This myth is important for understanding that Shellenberger and Nordhaus may have intended to upend environmentalism when *The Death of Environmentalism* was published in 2005, but they nevertheless continued building on the foundations of an American cosmology of a separate wilderness. Yet with undeniably strong evidence, United States environmentalists had to agree that a change in thought was required. "We will never be able to turn things around as long as we understand our failures as essentially tactical, and make proposals that are essentially technical … a more powerful movement depends on letting go of old identities, categories and assumptions."[32] Over the decade since, they have become part of a radical rethinking of what it means to have agency in the Anthropocene.

The Ecomodernist Refinement

The ecomodernist proposal directs our attention to two primary symbols: an untrammeled wilderness free from humans, and radically optimized human settlements. The proposal builds upon the Wilderness Myth to articulate the necessary ramifications for humans to survive and thrive: self-contained and habitable sacrifice zones. The direction of social, technological, political, and economic evolution under modernity is understood in this proposal as ultimately resulting in a *decoupling* of human well-being from the natural environment. Martin Lewis introduced the idea of decoupling more than two decades ago when he argued that the coupled cycles of resource use that drive human development and the cycles of environmental processes needed to revolve separately.[33] This, he argued, would happen through *substitution*, which relies on synthesized products to replace organic ones so that the environment can be spared. Another symbol is the *half-earth*, presented by E. O. Wilson as a world in which carefully selected regions amounting to half the planetary area are set aside for preservation.[34] But it is the new and growing sense of urgency that has lent these symbols new potency.

The ecomodernist proposal identifies two doctrines in the service of decoupling but provides less detail on the formulae that might support them.[35] The doctrine of *nature without humans* builds on the Wilderness Myth. This doctrine, with its formulae, is a well-traveled road through existing thought about preservation and ecosystems in a context evolving from command and control to adaptive management. The Wilderness Myth—a construct of the New World and of the United States in particular—is well supported by prescriptions such as national parks, environmental impact statements, and EPA regulations. But critically, the malfunction of the Wilderness Myth is ascribed in the ecomodernist proposal to the failure to develop workable prescriptions for the corollary *humans without nature* doctrine. Ecomodernist formulae lack prescriptive detail, relating in general to the inevitability of intensification in the realms of settlement, energy, food, and water. Settlement formulae are focused on cities. The United Nations reported that in 2016, four billion people lived in urban areas—over 50 percent of the world's population, occupying less than 3 percent of the world's land area (excluding Antarctica).[36]

The justification, then, for ever-larger cities is a combination of resource-use efficiency and small footprint. The concentration of populations would be further encouraged by (unspecified) engineering technological innovations and "by convincing our fellow citizens that [wild] places, and the creatures that occupy them, are worth protecting." The energy formulae are centered upon small-footprint, energy-dense, zero-carbon solutions: "Nuclear fission today represents the only present-day zero-carbon technology with the demonstrated ability to meet most, if not all, of the energy demands of a modern economy. ... In the long run, next-generation solar, advanced nuclear fission, and nuclear fusion represent the most plausible pathways toward the joint goals of climate stabilization and radical decoupling of humans from nature."[37] Agricultural production and water management formulae are predicated on the argument that Indigenous and traditional (extensive) farming systems and livelihoods are incapable of supporting the population of the future. Indeed, "whether it's a local indigenous community or a foreign corporation that benefits, it is the continued dependence of humans on natural environments that is the problem for the conservation of nature."[38] Production of food and fiber is envisioned instead as a combination of agricultural intensification and factory synthesis. Water—both freshwater supply and waste treatment—is considered to be an issue of plentiful energy supply: "Energy allows humans to … desalinate sea water to spare rivers and aquifers."[39]

Of course, these policy prescriptions can be contested

• on technical grounds, particularly with regard to assumptions about near future technological advances (batteries, fusion, nuclear waste) and legacy infrastructure;

• on pragmatic grounds, such as the fact that the same UN cities report highlights that 56 percent of cities are already at high risk of exposure to at least one type of natural disaster that is projected to increase in frequency and intensity in coming decades;

• on political grounds, since the assumption is made that "the strength of any given political proposal turns more on its vision for the future and the values it carries within it than on its technical policy specifications;"[40]

• on moral grounds, as Indigenous peoples and small-scale farmers are urged to abandon their ancestral connections to the earth based on selective use of evidence on causes of Pleistocene extinctions;[41] and

• on ecological grounds, because the actions of small-scale farmers and Indigenous peoples can maintain ecosystem diversity and function by sustaining habitats and crops' genetic materials, while lowering the risk of catastrophic wildfires.[42]

What directs the ecomodernist proposition, then, is the standpoint that decoupling is inevitable and, indeed, already underway. As such, there is an expectation that human innovation under the right vision and values constitutes mere facilitation. This might explain why the ecomodernist myth seems to elide detailed policy prescriptions, despite some clear opportunities for synergies with ongoing global deliberations.

The ecomodernist proposal might be read as an alternative to the large-scale planning and monitoring of the United Nations policy of decoupling, or perhaps as an assumption that the ecomodernists' effort is part of the providence of a decoupled future. The process of decoupling might be understood as a kind of reflexive modernity—one that is, or at least should be, happening outside the large-scale policy planning that drove the change from feudalism into the first modernity of industrial society.

This is presented as a third way, of policy through technology and persuasion through liberal democracy. Yet in seeking to avoid any talk of politics, these proposals are not devoid of political implication. The symbol of decoupling might beneficially be disambiguated to ensure the goals do not surreptitiously justify the means. Specifically, the boundaries between the decoupled worlds of humans and nature will need to be governed and will require some degree of sacrifice: in the inevitable need to locate polluting industries somewhere, there will be connected human settlements and natural systems exposed to industrial hazards.

Environmental justice activists have shown that expert-driven decisions over the placement of polluting industries disproportionately affect already marginalized portions of society. Furthermore, authoritarian dispossession of biodiverse landscapes has a long history, from African colonialism to the creation of western US national parks systems.[43] Finally, sacrifice zones can be created by a hands-off approach to nature. For example, the replacing of Indigenous fire-management practices with fire suppression has been found to increase the risk of catastrophic fires while also lowering biodiversity. At present, all these sacrifice issues are typically managed through regulation.

These necessary corollaries of decoupling as a silver bullet for the problems of the Anthropocene have been taken to task by Bruno Latour in his laboratory studies. He convincingly shows that progress does not remove humans from nature, but instead proliferates human entanglement *in* nature. From research on antibiotic resistance to water management,[44] the idea of proliferation sheds light on a blind spot in the apparent providence of decoupling: we are not removing ourselves from nature through technology and cities, but ever deepening our dependence on understanding the finer linkages of our entanglement. To move forward, Latour asks, "If we can no longer separate the work of proliferation from the work of purification, what are we going to become?"[45] Answers call for understanding the behavior of the more-than-human and how coupled human-natural systems change. The aim is to develop symbols that can better navigate our entanglement in earth processes.

Partial Incorporation

Although complete decoupling of human and natural environments at planetary scales is a radical proposal, the symbol of decoupling is shared with the United Nations, as noted above. Its origins in environmental policy lies in the "life cycle" perspective put forward by the Oslo Symposium on Sustainable Consumption and Production in 1994. A decade later, the proposal to decouple life cycles of human development and of environmental processes was put forward, first by the ten-year framework of programs in 2002 and then the Marrakech Process in 2003. Decoupling then appears prominently under the Sustainable Development Goals of 2015. For example, Goal 8 includes an aspiration "to decouple economic growth from environmental degradation" by 2030, "in accordance with the 10-year framework of programmes on Sustainable Consumption and Production." The ecomodernist proposal identifies two types of decoupling that relate to this lifecycle thinking.[46] These are *relative decoupling*, in which the "cycle of human consumption is decoupled from the natural systems that produce raw materials," and *absolute decoupling*, in which "the growth rate of the environmental parameter is zero or negative."[47] The Sustainable Development Goals similarly maintain that it is only through decoupling that continuing economic growth—in the context of finite material, energy, and ecosystem resources—can be sustained. In this way, decoupling has become a central symbol of the good Anthropocene. At the same time, the ramifications of settlements as sacrifice zones and the denial of land tenure is not incorporated into international prescriptions.

The Ecomodernist Manifesto does not mention the Sustainable Development Goals nor the Sustainable Consumption and Production framework, leaving shared meaning hypothetical for the purposes of this discussion. The seeming inevitability of progress toward decoupling may be emerging from a faith in the continued success of United Nations policy. The Sustainable Consumption and Production framework measures decoupling through one of six core metrics.[48] To measure decoupling, the Sustainable Development Goals draw on fifteen core indicators that were developed by the Organisation for Economic Co-operation and Development (OECD) in 2002 to monitor sustainable development. Here we come full circle to the efforts to curb air pollution in the United States using safe limits. But the ecomodernist proposal characterizes setting boundaries and safe limits as "Malthusian echoes," "a poor basis for policy," and "misleading."[49] In this view, if boundaries were to be set, they would be variable in space and time, tensile depending on human innovations, and as such have very little usefulness. Such critique of the planetary boundaries concept may be warranted. Nevertheless, the lack of a clear policy framework, the rejection of international governance regimes, and the potential for territorial dispossession makes the ecomodernist proposal an unsatisfying response to urgency in the Anthropocene. In particular, the strain between suggesting (a) an incapacity of local and Indigenous peoples to take care of nature and (b) legacies of dispossession under the guise of preservation is troubling. The critique offered by Kareiva and colleagues,[50] while apparently otherwise supportive of the ecomodernist project, warns of such risks. By operationalizing decoupling, humans by definition live in a sacrifice zone.

When Shellenberger and Nordhaus recognize the futility of "seeing the environment as a separate 'thing,'" over which humans are "superior," they double down on the Wilderness Myth. When reflecting Latourian notions of propositions[51] by saying that environmentalists tend "to see language in general as representative rather than constitutive of reality,"[52] they remain attached to their own constitutive reality in devising a vision for the future. Perhaps for this reason, the Wilderness Myth is never grappled with in ecomodernism. Rather, it remains implicit in that if you accept the Wilderness Myth, nature without humans, then you accept humans without nature. Rather than reject or even problematize wilderness as a construct, the wilderness ideal is expanded to allow *wilderness* to mean any area in which humans do not extract resources. Rather than a return to pre-European environmental conditions, the ideal is shifted to a modern version of pre-human earth. Rather than reject human separation from nature, the ideal is shifted toward a future in which we do a "better job" to operationalize separation than did Thoreau, Muir, Leopold, or Abbey, than the National Parks Service, than the Environmental Protection Agency. In this way, the ecomodernist myth both accepts that humans have never been decoupled from nature and proposes that we now, finally, decouple.

Transformed Futures

Sustainable Development Goals that keep human societies within a "safe operating space" are indeed now urgently needed ... but even a strong, sustained program of policy adjustments may be insufficient to counter harmful trends. ... What is now needed is nothing short of major transformation—not only in our policies and technologies, but in our modes of innovation themselves.

—Melissa Leach[53]

The Bright Arrow of Human Development

On June 26, 1945, the forty-six nations that had signed the Declaration by United Nations in 1942 to fight the Rome-Berlin-Tokyo axis met in San Francisco to sign the Charter of the United Nations. Their signatures established the United Nations and its General Assembly, the Security Council, the Economic and Social Council, the Trusteeship Council, the International Court of Justice, and the UN Secretariat. Theirs was a fresh attempt at bringing nations together for peace, after the 1919 League of Nations had failed in its mission to prevent a new global war. It is this post-war yearning for sustained peace that continues to drive forward negotiations in this imperfect global forum. To reach the goal of sustained peace, the charter seeks to target root causes of social strife and national aggression. The Universal Declaration of Human Rights followed in 1948. Over many years of efforts to extend agricultural technologies, education, health care, and industry, the United Nations came to develop mandates for a host of human development needs.

The language of sustainable development and environmental concern that now dominates the United Nations discourse is a more recent addition to the portfolio. The Brundtland Report of 1987, *Our Common Future*, incited the United Nations Conference on Environment and Development that took place in 1992 in Rio de Janeiro. The Millennium Development Goals (2000) articulated ambitious efforts to improve key human development indicators. Determination buttressed by the partial success of these goals, the United Nations celebrated seventy years since its establishment by agreeing to officially begin implementation of the 2030 Agenda for Sustainable Development on January 1, 2016.

The seventeen Sustainable Development Goals (table 3.1) might be the most Anthropocentric symbol of any policy prescription to date.[54] The declaration announces "a comprehensive, far-reaching and people-centred set of universal and transformative Goals and targets ... an Agenda of unprecedented scope and significance" that "is accepted by all countries and is applicable to all."[55] "If we realize our ambitions across the full extent of the Agenda, the lives of all will be profoundly improved and our world will be transformed for the better."[56] The scope is global and immediate, visionary and practical. Implementation includes developing two indicators for each of the seventeen goals, with continuous appraisal and mobilization of funding to perform the necessary tasks, each of which has been designed to

Table 3.1
The United Nations Sustainable Development Goals

No Poverty	Zero Hunger	Good health and well-being	Quality Education	Gender equality	Clean water and sanitation
Affordable and clean energy	Decent work and economic growth	Industry, innovation, and infrastructure	Reduced inequalities	Sustainable cities and communities	Responsible consumption and production
Climate action	Life below water	Life on land	Peace, justice, and strong institutions	Partnerships for the goals	

be achievable within current economic means. The goals are designed for synergy with other existing and emerging efforts, such as the Addis Ababa Action Agenda and the Paris Agreement. They are an impressive feat of transborder deliberation in the service of the common good.

This summary reads as a bright arrow out of the shadows of war and into a better future, a narration of the Anthropocene from the middle of the twentieth century. As such, the United Nations has been on a trajectory of discovery in which it has, through target-and-timetable approaches, permitted progressively broader and more ambitious aspirations to come into focus. Without due attention to the creation myth of the UN, however, the human rights and environmental protections that have joined the agenda might seem to have been undetectable until quantification and its associated discourse could say something about them. In particular, with World War II as year zero for the United Nations myth, the centuries of colonial history from which many nations are still reeling in terms of health, employment, education, political empowerment, and religious rights remain poorly acknowledged. The Permanent Forum on Indigenous Issues has not yet substantively influenced the myth, either as a means of understanding the context in which development assistance became necessary or as a means by which to innovate alternative pathways to sustainability.

As such, the Sustainable Development Goals risk succumbing to *cockpitism*, "the illusion that top-down steering by governments and intergovernmental organizations alone can address global problems"[57]—as though there could be no other framework for global human dignity. That said, the

UN is proving malleable to the discourses of its constituents, if slowly and nonlinearly, finding "norms and their content and boundaries as dynamic" in the development of policy.[58] Many voices are still not heard, and many remain at the fringes. The discourse continues to present a technical approach to a global biopolitics of human development. But further evolution is possible. The Sustainable Development Goals "might be genuinely global and hence destabilise long-standing divisions between 'developed' and 'developing' societies ... and might challenge existing growth paths of resource-intensive development."[59]

Symbols of Sustainable Development

As we have argued throughout this book, symbols matter. Experience from the Millennium Development Goals shows that ambitious targets and timetables for human well-being can be met effectively with voluntary international efforts. Nevertheless, we acknowledge the limits of the Millennium Development Goals. The discourse was narrow, focused on symbols of capacity deficit in subjects "summoned by the goals, that is, young women, slum-dwellers, the hungry, and so on."[60] Still more critical have been commentaries observing that "perhaps we should prefer humility and reversibility over hubristic mega-schemes for revisioning global development."[61]

The Sustainable Development Goals seek to meet these criticisms head on with Goal 17: Partnerships for the Goals. But the goals retain a normative function.[62] Each goal represents a symbol, but together they are preceded by their overarching symbols: people, planet, prosperity, peace, and partnership. In this, the Sustainable Development Goals seek to present a doctrine we can all get behind, "eradicating poverty in all its forms and dimensions, combating inequality within and among countries, preserving the planet, creating sustained, inclusive and sustainable economic growth and fostering social inclusion."[63] These symbols are vague enough to permit negotiation over their normative implications. Nevertheless, they prescribe a particular vision of the future based on market mechanisms and regulatory limits. In aligning national policy according to the attainment of SDG targets, these mechanisms and limits in turn become substituted for goals in themselves. Consider each symbol in turn:

People: "We are determined to end poverty and hunger, in all their forms and dimensions, and to ensure that all human beings can fulfill their potential in dignity and equality and in a healthy environment."[64] If the SDGs have a stated primary goal for achieving sustainable development, it is for people to have financial, food, water, and (to an extent) cultural security. Given, for example, devastating statistics that one in eight persons live in extreme poverty and around 800 million people suffer from hunger, change is urgently needed. People are at the center of the SDGs, and their presence there is detected and determined in terms of numerical indicators of what a person is: years in school, salary level, life expectancy, time spent in unpaid work, amount of resources consumed, and so forth. The purpose of the goals is to hold nations accountable to targets based on these metrics.

Following the extended definition of poverty, all seventeen goals are about eradicating poverty some form, including access to education, freedom to pursue political and spiritual life, and the ability to live in a healthy environment. Hence, the symbol of "people" is in different ways implicitly at the locus of all five core symbols, but it has disappeared in the statistics of infrastructure and biodiversity. For instance, Goal 14 to protect marine resources cites pollution, overfishing, environmental degradation, and climate change as key challenges. These all require people to act at multiple levels. The solutions they mention concern protection through conservation, as well as maintaining harvested species "within biologically sustainable limits" based on maximum sustainable yield. Granted, there is very limited space for nuance in the SDGs, but bringing the symbol of people into this goal would permit saying something about the loss of diversification through local fisheries as industrial and foreign competition assert themselves. It would also permit commenting on unsustainable practices and the role of conflict.[65] If hunger is to be combatted, a focus on people would permit concepts of food aid to expand beyond surplus exotic hybrid varieties people cannot plant or do not know how to cook (see chapter 2). Noha Shawki writes that the deliberations that built the Sustainable Development Goals did include terms such as "tenure security, and community, informal, and customary land rights" but that these did not make it into the final document, except as "equal access to land" in Goal 2.[66] Leach argues, "If SDGs around reducing global hunger are to be met, addressing such place-specific agricultural sustainability challenges must be taken seriously." To this end, the goal, future efforts might include language about effective and robust democratic institutions and transparent and inclusive decision processes, so as to provide legitimacy to SDG targets.

Planet: "We are determined to protect the planet from degradation, including through sustainable consumption and production, sustainably managing its natural resources and taking urgent action on climate change, so that it can support the needs of the present and future generations."[67] That is, the planet is presented cosmologically: "We reaffirm that planet Earth and its ecosystems are our common home."[68] More specifically, it is the planet as the *world-for-us* that symbolizes the foundational myth of the Sustainable Development Goals. This is achieved by presenting the planet as a phenomenon measured by indicators that may be observed only at present, according to the limited quantifiable baselines available to us. Such presentation avoids symbols that invoke the *world-in-itself*, with concomitant myths about the creation of the earth, with nature and humans in coexistence.

Human history older than the 1865 International Telecommunication Union is not mentioned in the historical overview offered by the United Nations, and human events earlier than 1974 are not referenced in the SDG reports for 2016 and 2017. In contrast, deeper planetary evolutionary history features as a touchstone for addressing sustainability in the SDGs. The 2016 SDG report uses the earth's deep history to provide perspective into the level of species extinctions and global sea ice levels.[69] In this way, the SDGs narrate our home as existing at the intersection of geological history on the one hand and the immediacy of the past few decades and the coming years on the other. As such, a metaphor for our home might appear more as a modern house built on Gondwanan lands than an ancestral home among companion species. As a result, the action space facilitated by the SDGs appears out of sync with the timelines experienced by and meaningful to people. This apparent trick of time is achieved by presenting the planet as measured by indicators, which dictates the historicity of our planetary home according to the baselines natural scientists have made available to us. The Sustainable Development Goals thus invoke the American Wilderness Myth, storying humans as visitors to nature at best and invaders of nature at worst. As such, policy prescriptions invoking decoupling are provided support from this symbol.

Prosperity: "We are determined to ensure that all human beings can enjoy prosperous and fulfilling lives and that economic, social and technological progress occurs in harmony with nature."[70] Prosperity is the most surreptitious symbol of the five. Commentators have raised concerns that the Sustainable Development Goals, like the Millennium Development Goals before them, constitute a means of normalizing market liberalization.[71] Indeed, while the "agenda is a plan of action for people, planet and prosperity,"[72] the goals themselves place prosperity squarely in the context of economic performance. For example, reporting on Goal 8 observes that "sustained and inclusive economic growth is a prerequisite for global prosperity,"[73] and metrics are limited to labor productivity, unemployment, percentage of persons with bank accounts, and gross domestic product. This quantifiable narrative is what Weber calls the "market episteme,"[74] in which social and environmental processes are identified within a market logic. That economic growth is a key concern is also clear in the references made by the Sustainable Development Goals to other synergistic agreements. Commitments to World Trade Organization agreements are affirmed (Goal 10, 14, 17), while other relevant agreements, such as the Food and Agriculture Organization's "Voluntary Guidelines on the Responsible Governance of Tenure"[75] and the United Nations' "Declaration on the Rights of Indigenous Peoples," are not. There is also concern that "current GHG emission trajectories are simply not compatible with the SDGs."[76] Indeed, economic growth and industry (Goals 8 and 9) are disconnected from emissions (Goal 13), with no attempt at synergy. Because "no scenario exists by which the SDGs of 2030 could be met in a world transformed by climate change,"[77] this approach contains the seeds of its own failure.

Peace: "We are determined to foster peaceful, just and inclusive societies which are free from fear and violence. There can be no sustainable development without peace and no peace without sustainable development."[78] Peace is, of course, the foundation symbol of the United Nations. It continues to be an achievement of the unprecedented level of international deliberation that constitutes the United Nations. There are signs, however, that stability is mistaken for peace. For example, the Elders[79] have raised concerns that UN Security Council members pass vetoes on interventions in war-torn regions without offering alternative pathways to securing human dignity. Territorial conflicts across the world perpetuate within and across boundaries drawn by colonial governments, as ethnic groups renegotiate relationships. The impacts of climate change inflame these tensions in many cases.[80] Although the renegotiation of territorial sovereignty is a complex challenge beyond the scope of the United Nations mandate,[81] there is an opportunity to address the ongoing role colonizing institutions have, for instance, in perpetuating the socioeconomic and environmental inequities that bring about the need for sustainable development policies. Goal 16 is based on "respect for human rights, the rule of law and transparent, effective and accountable institutions,"[82] but the metrics focus on safety and security of the individual as the locus of liberation and agency. Quantification of participation in democratic institutions, though apparently needed is, perhaps, not possible.

Partnership: "We are determined to mobilize the means required to implement this Agenda through a revitalized Global Partnership for Sustainable Development, based on a spirit of strengthened global solidarity, focused in particular on the needs of the poorest and most vulnerable and with the participation of all countries, all stakeholders and all people."[83] In the United Nations, partnership has been focused on the relationships between national leaders. In this tradition, the Sustainable Development Goals continue to focus on the role of nations and the global community in fostering sustainability. Partnerships mentioned by Goal 17 include those related to finance, trade, and technologies for collaboration, as well as the capacity building needed to support the statistical management of nations. The symbol of partnership, therefore, appears to be the capacity to report on metrics for each of the other sixteen goals. There is little mention of vertical partnerships. Leach and colleagues see a parallelism in the development of national-level policies and grassroots-level partnerships that intersect poorly,[84] and the Sustainable Development Goals are no exception. As long as "capacity deficits"[85] are understood as something developing nations have, and developed nations can fill, these deliberative arenas will be difficult to arrange.

Transformation

The Office of Decolonization in the United Nations suggests that dependent territories were reduced from around one-third of countries at the end of World War II to only a handful today (figure 3.1). At present, there are seventeen UN-recognized non-self-governing territories, but not all nations removed from the non-self-governing list since 1946 gained independence as such. In addition, the ongoing efforts by Indigenous peoples to reclaim their self-determination are absent from this description. The Unrepresented

Figure 3.1
The world in 1946, showing independent countries (dark gray, the founding members of the United Nations and the defeated Axis powers) and non-self-governing territories (light gray). The map outlines are for 2017.

Nations and Peoples Organization has almost fifty members, and there are many nonparticipating peoples, including Australian Indigenous nations, the Dene Nation, Ka Lahui Hawaii, the Maasai people, and others. As such, the characterization by the Office of Decolonization represents an oversimplification of the history both prior to and since World War II.

As long as the United Nations retains a geological context for the post–World War II period, the baseline for transformation is rooted in a symbol of capacity deficit. Where culture is mentioned in the Sustainable Development Goals, it is in connection with economic growth through tourism; where knowledge is mentioned, it is attained in formal schooling. The most vulnerable often lack the resources to engage with and influence the political economy through which their lives are shaped, but that does not mean they lack capacity.[86] Rather, this means there is a need for capacity building among actors within the international regime to better recognize these knowledges and skills. A different doctrine might see the world's peoples less as blank slates ready for capacity building, and more as loci of capacity to be drawn upon. Furthermore, it is apparent that "environmental sustainability is inconsistently covered in the framework of SDG goals that have emerged from political negotiations so far."[87] With quantifiable metrics steering the work of transformation, the aspirational futures may be elusive.

In the urgency to tackle the major challenges of our time—human dignity, environmental sustainability, and disaster risk reduction—the United Nations has responded within its existing formulae. The negotiations over the Sustainable Development Goals have displayed an impressive effort at integrating a broad and complex set of concerns. This has stimulated an ongoing renegotiation over the meaning and core elements of development. Although urgency to act within this regime can appear painfully slow, its true urgency is to deliberate over shared meanings, goals, and prescriptions. Given the continued efforts to achieve peaceful international cooperation, the United Nations myth is a target-and-timetable agenda; it seeks to set targets, measure metrics of progress, and then set new targets, in the service of transformational change. The modality is to "create conditions for," rather than to prescribe, a particular future. It is, perhaps, premature to be planning for the next set of goals. But in the interests of furthering human dignity and environmental sustainability, a perspective that tackles the topic of land tenure would support transformation. Further, we would propose that the next set of goals embody more explicit attention to the many innovations that have, do, and will continue to come from the myriad myths of peoples globally. Future goals could focus on capacity building within the United Nations to foster coexistence within a broader historical context. Writing the history of exploration, trade, exploitation, and cultural transformation into these next goals can have transformative potential by offering alternative formulae for the five key symbols of the Sustainable Development Goals.

We Have Always Been Humanitarian

As climate-related disasters have increased, they have become a rallying point in the negotiations—a tangible, immediate reason to push for more ambitious climate action.

—Lisa Schipper and colleagues[88]

From Hazard to Disaster

Since Henri Dunant inspired the global humanitarian movement, efforts have been made to monitor, assess, and improve how this domain assists persons affected by disaster. The International Federation of Red Cross and Red Crescent Societies focused on supporting the capacity of local communities to respond to humanitarian disasters. Attention to the root causes of war became woven into the United Nations founding mission to reduce the risk of armed conflicts through the Charter of the United Nations. This core mission of the United Nations was soon augmented by increasing attention to natural disasters.[89] It would take another half century to follow the philosophy of the UN on armed conflict: to attend not only to capacity to respond after the event but to also focus on preparing for the risk of disasters.

The United Nations Office for Disaster Risk Reduction was established in 1999 after a series of catastrophic natural disasters placed the threat of violence from earth processes on the UN policy agenda. Landmark events that sparked global disaster reduction efforts included the 1962 Buyin-Zara earthquake that struck Iran and killed more than twelve thousand people; the 1970 Bhola cyclone that is estimated to have killed almost half a million people in what is now Bangladesh; and the severe El Niño cycle of 1997–1998 that caused compound disasters across the world—from famine to landslide, cholera outbreak to wildfire.

The first response was the creation of the United Nations Disaster Relief Office (1972), with an aim to "prevent, control and predict" natural disasters, according to the command-and-control doctrine of the era. Mounting evidence on the complex drivers of disasters initiated the International Decade for Natural Disaster Reduction (1989–1999). Lessons learned led to several publications: the 1989 "International Framework for Action"; the 1994 "Yokohama Strategy for a Safer World: Guidelines for Natural Disaster Prevention, Preparedness and Mitigation" and its "Plan of Action"; the 1999 "International Strategy for Disaster Reduction"; and the most recent "Hyogo Framework for Action: Building the Resilience of Nations and Communities to Disasters" (2005). With each iteration, international research has helped to reframe earlier policies.

Throughout these decades, the focus has been on disaster response: the ability to respond to disasters as they occur to reduce the severity of their impacts. This focus had been critiqued since at least the 1970s[90] on two grounds: (1) the need to recognize the social dimensions that contribute to disasters and (2) the need to consider preparation, readiness, and exposure in advance of extreme events. These critiques, importantly, made the distinction between a *disaster* and an *extreme event*, or *hazard*. The requirement of these critiques, in addition to disaster response, is to reduce the likelihood of disasters, even when the likelihood of many hazards and extremes themselves cannot be restricted. If populations are well prepared, their exposures limited, and their vulnerabilities addressed, extreme events result less frequently in a disaster that exceeds the capacity for people and their governments to respond. In this way, ongoing research worked to redirect policy toward the arena of disaster risk reduction that the Sendai Framework for Disaster Risk Reduction (SFDRR; adopted in 2015) prescribes.

The Sendai Framework rests on seven broad targets, each with goals for 2020 and 2030, and an ultimate outcome: "The substantial reduction of disaster risk and losses in lives, livelihoods and health and in the economic, physical, social, cultural and environmental assets of persons, businesses, communities and countries."[91] In aiming for this outcome, the framework explicitly seeks to align and synergize with other frameworks—in particular, the Sustainable Development Goals, for building resilience to extreme events; and the Paris Agreement,[92] for mitigating the drivers that influence the severity and intensity of extreme events. These three international institutions together address the three core concerns of our time: human dignity, environmental sustainability, and disaster risk reduction. There is reason to expect that the intersections of these concerns will be difficult to address.[93] By their nature, the implementation of these institutions will be inconsistent in their requirements and goals for, for example, energy generation or water quality. The Sendai Framework doctrine is that "vulnerability is the main cause of disasters and disaster risk yet climate change affects mainly hazards,"[94] yet the framework "has not made reducing underlying drivers of disaster risk one of its priority areas."[95] Furthermore, the Sendai Framework downplays "the political root causes of disaster vulnerability, even while SFDRR appropriately highlights vulnerability and root causes, as per the definition of disaster risk reduction."[96] Although not as limited in doctrine as the Sustainable Development Goals, the opportunity to prioritize multifaceted strategies—those that, for instance, reduce exposure to hazards and greenhouse gas emissions at the same time—is lost. Thus, urgent and inextricably linked humanitarian and environmental issues are being compartmentalized into discrete international institutions, rendering invisible the interactions between them and limiting the capacity to integrate them.[97]

In this context, the partial integration of symbols across the three arenas indicates a lack of shared understanding of the concepts in question. For instance, Sustainable Development Goal 2.4 on food security lists the need to "strengthen capacity for adaptation to climate change, extreme weather, drought, flooding and other disasters." Climate change, extreme weather, drought, and flooding are not disasters per se. Rather, they are earth system processes that in some contexts become hazards, with potential to cause a disaster. An achievable goal from the disaster risk reduction standpoint is adaptation actions that reduce the vulnerability and exposure of populations in the face of such hazards.[98] Similarly, Sustainable Development Goal 11 on human settlements speaks of the need to decrease economic losses from "disasters, including water-related disasters, with a focus on protecting the poor and people in vulnerable situations." The imprecise language demonstrates a lack of understanding of and engagement with disaster risk reduction as a practice.

More useful goals would seek to reduce exposure to water-related hazards, or address poverty and other factors contributing to vulnerability. These apparently fine distinctions are significant: protection of people in vulnerable positions is not the same as reducing their vulnerability. The allocation of attention and resources is limited. There is need for careful disambiguation to ensure that, between disaster events, the reduction of vulnerability takes priority over protection while vulnerable. Appropriate integration of symbols across arenas is critical to this task. In the following, we examine three key symbols in the emerging disaster risk reduction discourse: resilience, risk, and culture.

The Sendai Framework and the preceding Hyogo Framework both focus on *resilience*—the ability to recover after a disturbance to resume a former state.[99] Although resilience has a carefully defined academic discourse concerning the dynamics of social-ecological systems, the Sendai Framework is focused specifically on hazard: "The ability of a system, community or society exposed to hazards to resist, absorb, accommodate to and recover from the effects of a hazard in a timely and efficient manner, including through the preservation and restoration of its essential basic structures and functions."[100]

This is distinct from the Sustainable Development Goals, in which the goal of transforming societies explicitly erodes the resilience of the ingrained ways of life that have produced injustices and environmental crises. To some extent, however, these are compatible prescriptions, in that they work on different scales. Resilience in the Sendai Framework focuses on the ability to rebound after a specific hazardous event and to "build back better" in the process. As such, the resilience concept is here based not on the space and time scale of a society, but on the space and time scale of the hazard.[101] But there is much potential lost by the Sendai Framework's attention to resilience only at the hazard scale. Disaster risk reduction so defined obscures the resilience of people as individuals or the kind of resilience a population may exhibit. Furthermore, the Sendai Framework appears unprepared for the unimaginable risks at large spatial scales and long temporal scales that could eventuate from uncontrolled global climate change. These unimaginable risks suggest that "the geological circumstances of the Anthropocene require a different biopolitics, one that understands that securing the biohuman is now the danger, and ... one that conventional understandings of risk management cannot adequately encompass."[102]

The idea of risk is at the core of the Sendai Framework, and has a very specific definition in the academic literature on disasters. This has significance for the myth shaping today's global policies on Anthropocene disasters. In the same way that "natural disasters" have been transformed by insights on the socio-economic drivers of disasters, "acts of God" were transformed by the "probability calculus" developed in 1657. Both Ulrich Beck and Michel Foucault invoke *Don Quixote* (1616) as prefiguring this transformation, moving from prescriptions in a world in which God's design and purpose is to be interpreted from similitude[103] toward ideas of *contingency*, a newly discovered ability to speak of both possible and actual hazard or extreme events. That transformation manifested in a new doctrine, the idea that the universe unfolds according to a range of quantifiably probable outcomes. The Decade for Disaster Risk Reduction has refined this doctrine, defining a quantified risk probability constituted from the exposure (a population, structure, place, or other phenomenon capable of experiencing harm) and the vulnerability to that exposure (its likelihood of experiencing harm).[104] This construction allows two policy levers—reduction of exposure and reduction of vulnerability—that using only the probability of a hazard would not provide. Nevertheless, this refined doctrine coexists with a series of risk domains that offer alternative prescriptions (table 3.2).

The study of risk perception has enabled the legacies of hazard probability approaches to become acquainted with alternative symbols.[105] For example, the Southern Paiute use the symbol of the angry rock to exemplify the unimaginable risk represented by the transport of radioactive materials through ancestral territories. Unimaginable risks upend our most basic feelings of security in the world.[106] The Southern Paiute are concerned that the angry rock blocks the path to the afterlife; this appears metaphorical to the doctrine of risk, and hence not a critical target for policy formulation. For the Southern Paiute, the inability to treat the risk of their family members not reaching the afterlife due to the presence of nuclear waste presents as an unnatural disaster[107] that violates the core of their cosmological myth. For the Anthropocene risk manager, an unnatural disaster occurs through the inability to treat risks in the context of unpredictable, complex, and dynamic social processes.[108]

In failing to grapple with its own symbols, the international doctrine to reduce the risk of disaster is hampered by institutional designs that reproduce disasters. In its commitment to respond rapidly and with immediate effect, the humanitarian movement has become caught up in its own "permanent state of emergency."[109] The formulae developed from the intertwining of military capacity for rapid intervention with humanitarian ideals of eliminating human suffering too often sow the seeds for the next disaster. For example, the annual cycle of humanitarian response through the United Nations, Red Cross, and Red Crescent predictably revolves through visits to prioritized disaster areas, interspersed with donor-funding campaigns to meet the ever-increasing demand for resources and the writing of reports about the year that was and the year ahead. In the constant state of emergency in which humanitarian organizations operate, humanitarian organizations and their supporters face multiple institutional constraints that prevent attention to the structural issues that reproduce vulnerability.

The "missing dimension" of cultures in creating and mitigating risk remains an open question, and only recently has "practical [disaster risk reduction] ... gained more from an approach that sees hazards, vulnerability and resilience as social constructions."[110] *Culture*, like *resilience* and *risk*, has a very specific meaning in the Sendai Framework, articulated as

Table 3.2

Frameworks for risk measurement

Risk measure		Definition	Application example
Fatalities	Individual	The probability that an average unprotected person, permanently present at a certain location, is killed due to an accident resulting from a hazardous activity.	Hazardous installations, transportation routes
	Societal	The relationship between frequency and number of people suffering from a specified of harm in a given population from the realization of specified hazards.	Nuclear industry, airports
Economic damage	Monetary valuation	Probability of loss in currency units.	Settlements
		Valued in proportion to a person and population potential economic production. Utility-based approach models the behavior of consumers and producers.	Estimating economic damage to give the system higher value
Environmental damage	Probabilities and energy valuation	Probability of exceedance of the time needed by the ecosystem to recover from the damage. Energy loss caused by injured and dead humans and animals expressed in units of energy (e.g., joules).	Offshore drilling
Integrated measures		Various types of consequences in one expression or framework.	Transportation of dangerous goods
Potential damage		Potential consequences of a hazard, irrespective of probability.	Dams

a commitment to ensuring "the use of traditional, indigenous and local knowledge and practices, as appropriate, to complement scientific knowledge in disaster risk assessment and the development and implementation of policies, strategies, plans and programmes of specific sectors, with a cross-sectoral approach, which should be tailored to localities and to the context."[111] But the challenges of working with cultural institutions is highlighted in several places, particularly in cases in which doctrines negate the existence of, or the need to address, hazards. Although there is no lack of agreement placed on the importance of cultures in disaster risk reduction, there is a lack of effective policy frameworks that permit doing so.

The *World Disasters Report: Focus on Culture and Risk* of 2014 from the International Federation of Red Cross and Red Crescent Societies takes on this "challenging theme."[112] This report notes that "climate change can be a window of opportunity in which [disaster risk reduction] organizations can check and change their own outlook, beliefs and behaviours, and learn from the very visible cultural responses and blocks to dealing with global warming that are apparent in high-income countries and some religions."[113] The report also recognizes the limited capacity of national and global organizations to reach every location and thus the inevitable need for some internationally and nationally imposed policies. They refer to the "sandwich approach,"[114] which draws on the opportunities and capacities of national and local scales to work in synergy. A particular benefit of this approach is the recognition of the close link between colonial thought and vulnerability studies. For example, European travelers to the West Indies in the nineteenth century considered the tropics inherently dangerous— making tropicality itself a symbol of hazard.[115] As the *World Disasters Report* concludes, "Only recently have people begun to rediscover and adapt traditional construction practices to make safer homes in the future, with some [disaster risk reduction] organizations playing a significant part in promoting the change. But the impact of disaster too often involves a loss of confidence in traditional values and structures, including local building cultures."[116]

Living with Hazards

A transformative line of inquiry into risks in the Anthropocene is to question what it might mean to coexist with hazards. This is not a new idea; its tenets are represented in the core insights of the International Decade for

Disaster Reduction. For example, David Alexander's work on the "disaster cycle" presents disasters not so much as preventable but as recurrent and predictable. Earlier, Gilbert White, a Quaker and geographer, opened the space for this discourse in his doctoral dissertation, "Human Adjustment to Floods," defended in 1945 at the University of Chicago. It was through his work on flooding that White came to understand, like Aldo Leopold, that control of nature is not a tractable goal. However, he understood that this lack of control presents an opportunity for the reconciliation of the integrity of nature with human dignity, which he considered to be the core concern of geography: "What shall it profit a profession if it fabricate a nifty discipline about the world while that world and the human spirit are degraded?"[117]

To coexist with hazards takes on a new dimension within the framing of the Anthropocene and its unimaginable futures. The need to reduce exposure and vulnerability to hazards sits squarely within the concerns of human development and global change.[118] Indeed, risk-management and risk-assessment approaches have a long history in climate change–adaptation research[119] and are starting to be considered for some aspects of emissions mitigation.[120] These approaches provide motivation for bridging the gaps at the international level between the Sustainable Development Goals, the Sendai Framework, and the Framework Convention on Climate Change, among others.[121] A focus on the intersections between policy arenas requires a more contextual approach. In coexisting with hazards, the emphasis is placed inside the realm of life lived, rather than in the siloed approaches of transnational agencies.

This is not to suggest, of course, that a goal of reducing the frequency and intensity of extreme events through addressing the drivers of those hazards—greenhouse gas emissions, for example—should be abandoned. Far from it. Rather, it is a recognition that this goal can be coupled productively with opportunities for reducing exposure and vulnerability, for seeking substantive decolonization through situated engagement, and for making the balancing of interests more explicit. Moreover, the coexistence of multiple doctrines allows for "uncertainty as to fact and disagreement over values."[122] The work of John Rawls and others in the articulation of deliberative democracy and, indeed antithetically, the analysis of Chantal Mouffe and others of agonistic pluralism suggest that coexistence of multiple doctrines is both necessary and effective in seeking just outcomes.[123]

A policy of redundancy that "permits several, and competing, strategies to be followed both simultaneously and separately" reduces the risk of single-point failures while also making space for "surplus meaning."[124] The benefits of redundancy imply the need of a multiplicity of myths—how we treat them not as formulae—policies and prescriptions—but as hypotheses, methodologies, epistemological rapproachements toward the world-for-us under rapid, dynamic change. As observed in chapter 1, what we narrate as the Anthropocene is a small part of every-when.

In this way, the urgencies of global change, the risk of disasters, the exigencies of poverty and hunger have the potential to provide a stimulus for doctrines that aspire to more than compromise between irreconcilable differences. Ideally, these formulae are embedded, without resolution with an international rubric, in local and traditional contexts. Innovations can be shared from one context to another without passing through the international generalization, with their conditioning factors and unique contributions intact. Multiple, changing, and ubiquitous human myths can embolden proposals for experimental and exceptional policy alternatives. In the next chapter, we address modes of governance that might usher in such a transformation.

4   Urgent Governance

There is nothing a government hates more than to be well-informed: for it makes the process of arriving at decisions much more complicated and difficult.
—John Maynard Keynes[1]

Introduction

The great problem concerning ends is to discriminate between those which are "good" in a near-by and partial view, and those which are enduringly and inclusively good.
—John Dewey[2]

On July 14, 2012, the Ocean Pearl set out from Massett, on the northern coast of Haida Gwaii,[3] around 50 km west of British Columbia, Canada. The Ocean Pearl, a 35 m commercial fishing vessel, had been chartered by the Haida Salmon Restoration Corporation (HSRC), a Vancouver-based company set up jointly by the Haida Gwaii of Old Masset and United States businessman Russ George. The voyage aimed to leave Canadian waters and deposit about 120 metric tons of iron oxide and iron sulfate into the ocean. This was accomplished largely by hand, over six days, as the crew opened bags, mixed the contents into a slurry with sea water, and pumped the slurry over the side. As an essential plant nutrient, the intention was for the iron to induce a phytoplankton bloom that would both sequester CO_2 through photosynthesis and feed salmon.

The Haida Gwaii of Old Masset had invested CA$2.5 million in this project, secured by the Northern Savings Credit Union, and representing nearly a third of the annual federal transfer payments the Haida Gwaii receive. Although subsistence hunting and fishing remain an important component of island life, the region has seen an economic downturn in recent decades due to declines in the forestry and fishing industries. The opportunity to increase the salmon run through iron fertilization of the phytoplankton on which salmon rely was an important one. The opportunity to make millions from certification as a carbon credit standards organization was even more attractive for the ailing community. The Old Masset reserve's economic development manager, John Disney, who had married a local and had been living on the reserve for over two decades, introduced the project. The plan Disney presented was to set up a company owned jointly by the Old Masset reserve and a company called Panktos Science, owned by Russ George. The Haida Gwaii would contribute all the cash, and George would contribute expertise and proprietary technology. The president of the Haida nation at the time, Guujaaw (Gary) Edenshaw, said that the village expected the project to be of great environmental and cultural benefit. "The village people voted to support what they were told was a 'salmon enhancement project' and would not have agreed if they had been told of any potential negative effects or that it was in breach of an international convention," Guujaaw said.[4]

By the time the project took place, Canada had withdrawn from the Kyoto Protocol and hence could not trade internationally in carbon credits. Although there is some evidence to suggest that the government agency had prior knowledge of the plan, charges for environmental violations from Environment Canada soon followed.[5] In the months following, George was removed as a company director of HSRC and the case was tangled in suits and countersuits in the British Columbia court system. The Parties to the Convention on the Prevention of Marine Pollution by Dumping of Wastes and Other Matter[6] met in late 2012 and expressed "grave concern" regarding this activity. The Conference of the Parties to the Convention on Biological Diversity also met in late 2012 and reaffirmed its precautionary approach to geoengineering,[7] but also noted that customary international law constitutes an incomplete basis for global regulation.[8]

Russ George maintains a strong defense of his advocacy for this project and others like it: "Yesterday's CO_2 is in effect already a lethal dose which will equilibrate into the ocean water as carbonic acid, acidifying the ocean, and stopping most of ocean life from having access to the calcium and silicon it needs to survive."[9] There is a sense in which George acted on a correct understanding: to limit warming and other impacts of climate change at any level whatsoever, the net emissions of greenhouse gases must eventually reach zero. Some way to remove already emitted greenhouse gases from the atmosphere and ocean appears to be necessary to achieve this goal.[10] Further, NASA imagery does seem to indicate a response in the region where the dumping was thought to have occurred: Dr. James Acker found that the *chlorophyll a* concentration was, for a short time, at least two to four milligrams per cubic meter higher than the decadal average.[11] And reported salmon catches in the region to have grown by 40 percent in the twelve to twenty months following the experiment.

There have been thirteen known, sanctioned experiments in iron fertilization of the open ocean between 1990 and 2017. These trials, unlike the uncontrolled experiment in the HSRC case, have sought to test whether encouraging phytoplankton growth through iron fertilization can increase the amount of carbon dioxide that ocean organisms absorb, with the ultimate fate of being deposited on the ocean floor. Quantifying the carbon dioxide that is sequestered during such experiments has proved difficult, however, and scientists have raised concerns about potential adverse effects, such as eutrophication.[12] Particularly because of the lack of baseline measurements, it is ultimately not possible to ascribe cause and effect in the case of the Haida Gwaii and Russ George. For the Old Masset village, therefore, the carbon credit income promised to the reserve never eventuated. Beyond these specifics, however, there are issues of governance to consider.

In October 2017, the second international Climate Engineering Conference was held in Berlin. The series of conferences was motivated by the developing interdisciplinary conversation incited by Paul Crutzen's famous 2006 essay on climate system intervention.[13] This essay opened the discussion of climate change responses from adaptation of impacts and mitigation of emissions to identifying technologies that could ameliorate changes in the system.[14] The least controversial of two classes of intervention is carbon dioxide management (CDM): processes that allow reabsorption of carbon dioxide from the atmosphere or ocean. The 2015 report from the National Academy of Sciences considered CDM a straightforward mitigation that should be judged by its economic cost alone. Solar radiation management (SRM), on the other hand, is an indirect method, the full biophysical ramifications of which are not well understood, in part because the scientific uncertainties and feedbacks appear to be greater. As such, the National

Academy of Sciences report concluded that SRM approaches should be judged "last resort" options in the event of future climate emergencies.

Clive Hamilton has observed that "a fleet of planes daily delivering sulfate particles into the upper atmosphere would be a grim monument to the ultimate failure of unbridled techno-industrialism and our unwillingness to change the way we live."[15] This vividly illustrates the way in which short-term concerns regarding the economic cost of mitigation and the increasing urgency to respond to climate change have the potential to create a path dependency to SRM-based emergency responses. In this context, perhaps a more useful distinction among classes of geoengineering may be to differentiate between treatments that can be administered unilaterally and treatments that can only be administered cooperatively. These classes can include both CDM and SRM approaches. For example, adding iron compounds to the ocean removes carbon dioxide from the atmosphere and is therefore a CDM technique, but one that can be administered locally for large-scale, if not global, effects. On the other hand, painting rooftops white reflects more sunlight and is therefore an SRM technique, but it would require multilateral action to achieve a climate impact.

Furthermore, geoengineering raises issues of distributive justice: risk and benefit distributions arising from many geoengineering treatments can be highly uncertain. For example, ocean fertilization is potentially effective for enhanced photosynthetic uptake but may cause eutrophication that impacts the harvest of marine resources remote from the treatment region. Delivering sulfate aerosols to the stratosphere to reduce the amount of solar radiation reaching the earth's surface are likely to have unanticipated impacts on food productivity and water supply. Delaying any geoengineering treatment until some regions of the world have already experienced catastrophic climate change impacts bolsters support for geoengineering solutions more broadly but would be deeply unjust.[16] Moreover, the anticipated support may not eventuate: the experience and attribution of climate catastrophes are not necessarily connected, as discussed in chapter 2. Indeed, if geoengineering treatments are applied in response to emergency conditions, policy makers already will have failed to achieve distributive justice.

Perhaps most critical, however, is the inadequacy of our international institutions to address the challenges presented by almost any form of geoengineering. Clearly, "it is difficult to predict how the debate on climate engineering will influence—or be influenced by—future developments in technology, the climate system, or the international order."[17] But as John Dryzek has noted, "Once this technology has been chosen, there is no going back." That is, if geoengineering approaches are selected as a technology of choice in addressing anthropogenic climate change, this requires—for most of the available technologies—a regime of continuous and ongoing application. As a result, the institutions that govern these applications must be "global, paramount and permanent."[18] This is, emphatically, not a feature of the international institutions that we have been able to craft thus far.

Given the urgency of unabated climate change and the threat of unilateral response, however, there are concerted international efforts to put a regulatory framework into place. For example, the Solar Radiation Management Governance Initiative,[19] the Bipartisan Policy Center's Task Force on Climate Remediation Research,[20] and the Climate Geoengineering Governance project[21] are key groups coordinating and synthesizing research; meanwhile, existing formulae such as those on nuclear nonproliferation and the Montreal Protocol offer potential templates. As the world prepares for scenarios in which international agreements on mitigation prove insufficient, "the global community must develop an understanding of the social, environmental, cultural, political and ethical issues involved ... to determine whether any climate engineering approach is appropriate as an effort to address climate change, we must first enter into critical global discussions."[22]

A Question of Sovereignty

The strongest man is never strong enough to be always master, unless he transforms his power into right and obedience into duty.
—Jean-Jacques Rousseau[23]

The multifaceted nature of the geoengineering domain illustrates the ways in which scales interact in the Anthropocene, ways rarely seen in human history. Causes and effects, and the modes of governance used to address them, have the potential to impact life and livelihood, justice and equity, knowing and being, across the planet. Climate change is a domain in which the problematic framing of scale has been particularly impactful.

As observed by Sheila Jasanoff, two distinct dimensions of climate change shape our ability to conceive of the problems and their solutions. As a phenomenon climate change is irreducibly global, adhering to universal laws of physics and chemistry. As a policy problem, climate change is bound by national and international laws, treaties, and norms in a way that "detaches global fact from local value, projecting a new, totalising image of the world as it is, without regard for the layered investments that societies have made in the worlds as they wish them to be."[24] This scale disconnect was recognized as early as 1990 on the multilateral international journey of the climate change regime.[25] The problem has received much attention,[26] but the fact remains that a broad international consensus on climate change mitigation is the gold standard by which governing the Anthropocene is judged. This section provides a brief history of the international climate change regime, its failures, and its successes, and probes the potential for different types of multilateral engagement.

UN Framework Convention on Climate Change

Although the chemistry and physics underpinning the energy balance of the climate system have been known for more than a century, science placed global change on the policy agenda beginning early in the 1970s. One of the most important early developments was the World Conference on the Changing Atmosphere: Implications for Global Security, held in Toronto in 1988, attended by more than three hundred scientists and policymakers from forty-six countries. The resulting Toronto Conference Statement noted: "The Conference called upon governments to work with urgency towards an Action Plan for the Protection of the Atmosphere. This should include an international framework convention, while encouraging other standard-setting agreements along the way, as well as national legislation to provide for protection of the global atmosphere. The Conference also called upon governments to establish a World Atmosphere Fund financed in part by a levy on the fossil fuel consumption of industrialized countries to mobilize a substantial part of the resources needed for these measures."[27] The Conference enumerated eight specific actions to be taken, which included, most significantly, to "reduce CO_2 emissions by approximately 20% of 1988 levels by the year 2005 as an initial global goal. Clearly, the industrialized nations have a responsibility to lead the way."[28]

The Conference aimed for a global convention to be ready for negotiation and adoption by 1992, and noted that, because the full effects of climate change could not be foreseen, it was in the common interest of all peoples to "join in prompt action."[29] The Conference took place concurrently with a severe heat wave. As climate scientist Stephen Schneider quipped, "In 1988, nature did more for the notoriety of global warming in 15 weeks than any of us ... were able to do in the previous fifteen years."[30] By 1992, the United Nations Framework Convention on Climate Change (UNFCCC) (box 4.1) was duly established as one of three conventions, along with the Convention on Biological Diversity and the Convention to Combat Desertification, adopted at the Rio Earth Summit in 1992. Nevertheless, the UNFCCC was not the comprehensive international plan to protect the atmosphere that was envisaged by the drafters of the Toronto Conference Statement. It was not the legally binding "law of the air" many had hoped for. Indeed, the preamble to the Convention included specific reference to the fact that nation-states have "the sovereign right to exploit their own resources pursuant to their own environmental and developmental policies." As a result, there was no specific target or timetable adopted for the reduction of greenhouse gas emissions, but only an overarching goal to "prevent dangerous anthropogenic interference with the climate system" (Article 2).

What has followed is almost three decades of false starts, failed negotiations, and moments of progress (table 4.1). This is, in part, an example of

---

Box 4.1

Parties to the UNFCCC convention

The Annex I Parties are Australia, Austria, Belarus, Belgium, Bulgaria, Canada, Croatia, Cyprus, the Czech Republic, Denmark, Estonia, European Economic Community, Finland, France, Germany, Greece, Hungary, Iceland, Ireland, Italy, Japan, Latvia, Liechtenstein, Lithuania, Luxembourg, Malta, Monaco, the Netherlands, New Zealand, Norway, Poland, Portugal, Romania, Russian Federation, the Slovak Republic, Slovenia, Spain, Sweden, Switzerland, Turkey, Ukraine, United Kingdom, and United States. These are broadly divided into two groupings: Annex I EIT that are "Economies in Transition" and Annex II that are the remaining members of Annex I, aside from Cyprus, Malta, and Turkey. All other countries are Annex B, or not parties to the convention (Andorra, Palestine, and South Sudan.)

Table 4.1
A brief overview of the primary decisions in the UN Framework Convention on Climate Change (UNFCCC) regime, also known as the Rio Convention, between 1992 and 2016

Decision	Name	Year	Expectations	Primary outcomes	Key details
	Rio Convention	1992	Very high. The Rio Earth Summit launched three new conventions.	Into force: 1994 Commitments included the establishment of the Secretariat, the Conference of the Parties (COP), the Annex I and Annex II country lists (see figure 4.1), and national inventories. Also included were aspirational goals for emissions reductions (to 1990 levels), adaptation, technology transfer, research, and financing.	Article 4, paragraph 10, which agrees to "take into consideration in the implementation of the commitments of the Convention the situation of Parties … with economies that are vulnerable to the adverse effects of the implementation of measures to respond to climate change." At COP1 (Berlin, 1995) it was agreed that the commitments of the convention were inadequate.
1/CP.3	Kyoto Protocol	1997	Medium. Negotiations were tense and complex.	Into force: 2005 Intended to implement the objectives of the UNFCCC. Commitments included quantified but differentiated emissions targets of six greenhouse gases to be achieved in the period 2008–2012 by the countries specified under Annex B (see figure 4.1). The Clean Development Mechanism (between Annex I and non-Annex I countries) and the Joint Implementation (among Annex I countries) were also developed.	Article 18, in which the COP agrees to "approve appropriate and effective procedures and mechanisms to determine and to address cases of non-compliance with the provisions of this Protocol, including through the development of an indicative list of consequences, taking into account the cause, type, degree and frequency of non-compliance."

Table 4.1 (continued)

Decision	Name	Year	Expectations	Primary outcomes	Key details
1/CP.7 2/CP.7 9/CP.7	Marrakesh Accords	2001	Low. The United States delegation declined to participate in the negotiations.	In Decision 2, which was the main thrust of the accords, the COP adopted a detailed new framework for capacity-building in non-Annex-I countries. The negotiators could not reach agreement, and therefore deferred several elements of Article 3 of the Kyoto Protocol, including provisions to make compliance with agreed targets legally binding and procedures whereby non-Annex-I countries might make future commitments.	The Marrakesh Accords were prefaced with a Ministerial Declaration (Decision 1) that noted, in item (3), that "the problems of poverty, land degradation, access to water and food and human health remain at the centre of global attention." The focus in this meeting was squarely on development.
1/CP.13	Bali Action Plan	2007	High, in the context of the unequivocal findings of the fourth IPCC assessment.	The decision in this case is focused on process: to institute an Ad Hoc Working Group to meet frequently "in order to reach an agreed outcome and adopt a decision at its fifteenth session..." that will include "including quantified emission limitation and reduction objectives, by all developed country Parties," as well as adaptation, technology transfer, and financial support.	The preamble uses the term *urgent* or *urgency* four times in regard to both mitigation and adaptation, including: "Recognizing that deep cuts in global emissions will be required to achieve the ultimate objectiveof the Convention and emphasizing the urgencyto address climate change." Then, "the process shall begin without delay."

Table 4.1 (continued)

Decision	Name	Year	Expectations	Primary outcomes	Key details
1/CP.16	Cancun Agreements	2010	Very low, following the failure to secure a binding agreement at Copenhagen in 2009.	Few solid commitments were made at this meeting, although there was an affirmation of the need to realize the Bali Action Plan and to strengthen programs for adaptation to unavoidable impacts of climate change. Indeed, the actions of adaptation were the strongest elements of this decision, apart from Article 4.A, paragraph 102, which established a Green Climate Fund, with the World Bank as interim trustee.	This meeting was primarily about mending fences after the disappointment of Copenhagen by explicitly recognizing the claims made by all parties. That said, the preamble recognizes that "climate change represents an urgent and potentially irreversible threat to human societies and the planet, and thus requires to be urgently addressed by all Parties" and raises the prospect of a 1.5°C target.
1/CP.17	Durban Platform	2011	High, as the first Kyoto commitment period was due to end.	The primary outcome of the decision was to extend the work of the Ad Hoc Working Group that was instituted in the Bali Action Plan. Notably, the work ahead was to include a legally binding instrument to replace the Kyoto Protocol from 2020. The target date for this protocol was "no later than 2015."	After two weeks of negotiations, a decision was reached on the last day after sixty hours of continuous negotiations. The preamble uses almost identical language to the Cancun Agreements regarding the "urgent and potentially irreversible" nature of climate change, and it reaffirms the aspirational 1.5°C target.
1/CMP.8	Doha Amendment	2012	Low	Not yet in force. This process is part of the Kyoto Protocol negotiations, rather than the COP, and includes commitments for some of the Annex I parties to take on commitments in a second commitment period from 2013–2020 (see figure 4.1).	The United States, the Russian Federation, and Canada, among others, remain at arm's length from the Kyoto commitments and actively worked against agreements concerning financing for less developed countries.
1/CP.21	Paris Agreement	2015	Very high.	Into force: 2016 The focus is on "nationally determined contributions" (discussed in more detail elsewhere in this chapter)..	The preamble included a reference to the "urgent threat of climate change" and maintained the aspirational 1.5°C target.

the dilemma of path dependence in the global climate change regime. Even without considering the technological lock-in costs that may pertain in society more broadly, the knowledge systems and institutions that support the regime resist change because the participants have developed material stakes in the stability of the regime. Simply by organizing ourselves—as scientists, as policy makers, as citizens seeking to understand and address climate change—we increase the costs of changing course.[31] Indeed, as an institution, the UNFCCC and its components have acted to modify the social environment in such a way as to attenuate the impact of alternative approaches.[32]

The Paris Agreement

On October 5, 2016, less than a year after the agreement was negotiated, the threshold for the Paris Agreement to enter force was reached. This threshold required at least fifty-five Parties to the Convention accounting for at least 55 percent of global greenhouse gas emissions to deposit their instruments of ratification with the depositary (Article 21). This contrasts with the Kyoto Protocol, which entered into force more than seven years after the negotiation, using the same criterion (figure 4.1) (Article 25).

The Paris Agreement explicitly signals a sense of urgency to reduce greenhouse gas emissions and adapt to already realized impacts. In terms of the individual targets and timetables for most Annex I countries, the Paris Agreement uses a different formula from the Kyoto Protocol, which expressed a commitment to meet a specified percentage of a base year or period, in addition to the overall commitments described in Article 3, paragraphs 1 and 2:

1. The Parties included in Annex I shall, individually or jointly, ensure that their aggregate anthropogenic carbon dioxide equivalent emissions of the greenhouse gases listed in Annex A do not exceed their assigned amounts, calculated pursuant to their quantified emission limitation and reduction commitments inscribed in Annex B and in accordance with the provisions of this Article, with a view to reducing their overall emissions of such gases by at least 5 per cent below 1990 levels in the commitment period 2008 to 2012.
2. Each Party included in Annex I shall, by 2005, have made demonstrable progress in achieving its commitments under this Protocol.[33]

The ratification of the Kyoto Protocol by each individual party took some time because these commitments were binding. With regard to the policies and measures mooted in the Protocol, even compliant countries

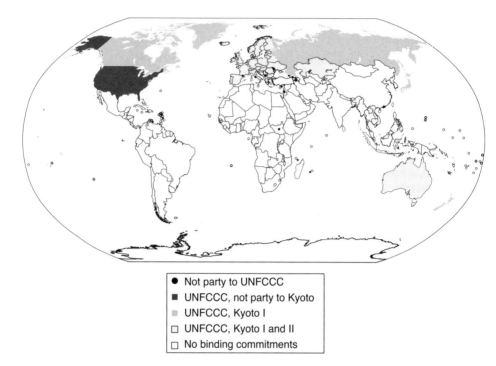

● Not party to UNFCCC
■ UNFCCC, not party to Kyoto
▨ UNFCCC, Kyoto I
□ UNFCCC, Kyoto I and II
□ No binding commitments

Figure 4.1
Parties to the UNFCCC Convention and the Kyoto Protocol. Dark gray countries are parties to the UNFCCC but not the Kyoto Protocol. Mid-gray and light gray countries are Annex B countries with binding targets in the first period of the Kyoto Protocol; light gray countries also have binding commitments in the second period. White countries are both non-Annex-I and non-Annex-B countries—that is, these countries have agreed to no binding commitments. Black countries are not parties to the UN-FCCC. Antarctica is shown for completeness but is covered by the Antarctic Treaty.

were unwilling to consider any strategy that might intrude upon their sovereign rights and responsibilities.[34] Instead, parties sought opportunities to generate political will though other existing formulae, such as via the Clean Development Mechanism or approaches for Joint Implementation. Similarly, the Protocol implemented the limitation of emissions from aviation and marine bunker fuels[35] as a hard requirement, in large part because there were international institutions[36] that could be responsible for implementation. In fact, Annex I countries demonstrated a net decrease in total emissions from fossil fuel burning over the commitment period. A large part of this decrease was attributable to the Global Financial Crisis, which led to a substantial global signal in greenhouse gas emissions and in atmospheric carbon dioxide concentrations starting in 2008.

In contrast, the Paris Agreement, with 195 signatories, is much more flexible, leaving commitments to be determined nationally and at a later date. In this way, the agreement certainly appears to adhere to the law that the least ambitious party will determine the outcome.[37] It has been characterized as a "triumph of diplomacy" by Chatham House, combining "a hard legal shell and a soft enforcement mechanism."[38] Part of this hard legal shell is Article 13, the establishment of a transparency framework, and Article 15, a mechanism to "facilitate implementation of and promote compliance" with the Agreement. Soft enforcement is also contained within these articles, in the form of expert review that is facilitative and nonpunitive, with no available sanctions. Indeed, beyond the overarching aims of Article 2—to avoid an increase in global average temperature below 2°C in comparison to preindustrial levels,[39] to adapt to unavoidable anthropogenic climate change, and to appropriately finance the effort—there are no targets and timetables in the Paris Agreement. This highly flexible and nonspecific set of commitments allowed most of the Parties to the original UNFCCC to ratify quickly. In this way, the Paris Agreement largely avoids the problem of "free riders" that was such a concern for the Kyoto Protocol.

The question arises: Why does this agreement not include more enforcement, even at the cost of free riders? A more credible agreement would have included, for example, a dispute settlement body such as that provided for in the World Trade Organization[40] or the United Nations Convention on the Law of the Sea (in Part XV). One reason this has not proved possible is the problem of who benefits when a country does not observe its commitments under the Paris Agreement. In a domestic quarrel, or indeed in a disagreement settled by the Dispute Settlement Body of the World Trade Organization, the breaching party is required to transfer a remedy—generally compensation—to the injured party.[41] But in the case of climate change, a breach of a single country's commitment to reduce emissions injures everyone, including the breaching country itself. If the only sanction is a loss of international reputation, then the breaching country experiences an additional loss, but none of the parties experience a benefit. Hence, the only available sanction for the international climate change regime is one that results in a net loss to all parties. Such conditions seem to align with Garrett Hardin's *tragedy of the commons*, wherein a polluting individual benefits while incurring a fraction of the costs.[42] But this metaphor has limits in the case of climate change, which represents instead a tragedy of open access.[43]

Despite this admittedly profound limitation, the Paris Agreement remains the only international, multilateral path available. From this standpoint, it includes many useful features. Most important is probably the *ratchet effect* of Article 4, paragraph 3: "Each Party's successive nationally determined contribution will represent a progression beyond the Party's then current nationally determined contribution and reflect its highest possible ambition, reflecting its common but differentiated responsibilities and respective capabilities, in the light of different national circumstances." There are many possible ways to comply with this provision that do not include substantive reductions in national greenhouse gas emissions, but nonetheless it is the first agreement to recognize that addressing climate change will be an ongoing process rather than a single task.

The Parties to the UNFCCC were encouraged to submit their post-2020 emissions-reduction commitments, called Intended Nationally Determined Contributions (INDCs), in advance of the twenty-first Conference of the Parties in Paris. This information had to include the baseline year or level, as well as the intended target and timetable. As of July 2017, 146 of the 152 parties that ratified the Paris Agreement had submitted these first INDCs. Most parties supplied a range of targets and in some cases made achieving those targets subject to access to resources not yet obtained, which made quantification of their impact on global greenhouse gas concentrations challenging for scientists. Furthermore, some countries submitted INDCs with emissions targets above their no-policy or current commitment baselines. Building on the monitoring and projection work of the UN Environment Program and several climate-modeling groups, Joeri Rogelj and his colleagues compared a range of climate scenarios implied by the INDCs.[44] They show that the corresponding atmospheric concentrations of greenhouse gases and climatic responses result in a median global average warming by 2100 of between 2.2°C and 3.5°C. This range incorporates the ambiguous relationships between emissions and concentrations, the unpredictabilities inherent in the climate system, and uncertainties that arise from elements that are missing from the INDC system altogether. These missing elements include bunker fuels, land-use and land-cover change, and emissions pathways of countries that are not parties to these agreements. Nevertheless, it is apparent that the Paris Agreement can be characterized as the science of the achievable.

Limits to International Governance

Environmental problems are wicked in precisely this way: not scientifically or technically complex so much as deeply engaged with the structure and limitations of social institutions. For example, the scientific concept of planetary boundaries articulates the many dimensions of global change.[45] These boundaries include but are not limited to climate change, and they encompass problems as broad as biodiversity loss, stratospheric ozone, ocean acidification, and freshwater availability. These are processes that span the entire earth system and involve many interacting phenomena. But as policy goals, the scientific challenge is relatively clear: emit less carbon dioxide, clear less forest, stop using chlorofluorocarbons, and so forth. The quantifiable tipping point implied by the boundary is open for debate, but the trajectory toward it is not. However, the policy measures themselves are a political question, and the wickedness arises: "Issue areas are more disparate, conflict lines are overlapping, and causation diffuses."[46]

In the face of the call for urgent action in international governance, national borders "lose precision in the frame of [its] dynamic and unstable character."[47] Of the planetary boundaries identified, only stratospheric ozone has a credible international institution to govern our approach toward the boundary, that of the Montreal Protocol. Is it possible, then, to do better institutionally than the UNFCCC on climate change or on any of the other pressing issues that threaten the capacity for humankind to survive and thrive?

Broadly, three paths might be considered: a multilateral international institution like the World Trade Organization; a series of bilateral and so-called minilateral binding agreements or clubs, like the Strategic Arms Reduction Treaty,[48] or a diverse, polycentric or networked approach encompassing many actors at the subnational level.[49] In this subsection, we will consider proposals for each, but we do not consider these to be mutually exclusive.[50] Rather, these proposals call for opening a space to consider approaches beyond the path dependencies that presently monopolize the time and attention of national and international leaders.

As an example of the first path, the Earth System Governance Project[51] puts forward a multilateral approach. The proposal is to create an international institution to address the novel challenges of the Anthropocene by repurposing existing political and institutional models. The framework does not suggest a minor shift in direction from the current regime, but rather a transformation to systems of global coordination to regulate national approaches to emissions-mitigation measures. Consider, for instance, the call to action made in advance of the UN Conference on Sustainable Development in Rio in 2012: "Incrementalism—the hallmark of the last decades—will not suffice to bring about societal change at the level and speed needed to mitigate and adapt to earth system transformation brought about by human action."[52]

A centerpiece of this approach could be, for example, to transform the UN Environment Programme into an organization that functions in a manner more analogous to the World Trade Organization.[53] In this way, binding agreements on matters ranging from financing to justice to transparency would become the norm, with appropriate adjudication and sanction measures. One of the more complex proposals in this globally public multilateral design has been the possibility of qualified majority voting—an approach that is highly contentious in the consensus-based model of the UNFCCC, particularly due to the ways in which votes can or should be weighted. Given the implications for global justice in any solution involving weighted voting, a middle path between weak consensus and binding votes may be an opt-in agreement that allows free riders, on the understanding that *any* progress toward emissions reduction is good progress.

Typically, advocates for the broadest possible participation over the binding nature of commitments believe that "parties will come to internalize the multilateral regime's norms and values through mere participation therein, even if the practical effects are nominal at first."[54] Global multilateralism does enjoy some additional advantages over other approaches. The institutions engendered by these processes enjoy considerable stability in the face of the costs of renegotiation (which can be a double-edged sword). These agreements can ensure that all parties benefit proportionally from the regime; for example, the United Nations Convention on the Law of the Sea includes countries with no coastal borders, thus allowing them to ensure continued access. Furthermore, any individual party possesses limited scope to veto a broadly acceptable agreement. Finally, it is almost certainly more efficient to negotiate a single multilateral agreement than many bilateral or minilateral ones.

The multilateralist claim emphasizes the importance of reputational incentives for compliance in multilateral agreements, but as we argued in the case of the Paris Agreement, the challenge in climate change mitigation is that any infringement benefits individual nations but leads to a net loss for all parties. For this reason, an alternative proposal has been to suggest that dispute resolution and enforcement of binding commitments may operate more effectively in a more limited participation setting. As an example of this second pathway, multilateral forums are often characterized in reality by a series of minilateral and bilateral negotiations,[55] though there has been little empirical work done on minilateral approaches in the climate change arena. As an example, consider the fifteenth Conference of the Parties (COP15) in Copenhagen in 2009. This meeting had strong participation by heads of state and very high expectations for an agreement following the Bali Action Plan (table 4.1). On December 7, a draft agreement known as the *Danish Text* was leaked to the media and conference participants.[56] This document, thought to have been generated by negotiators from the United Kingdom, the United States, and Denmark (the "circle of commitment"), stressed the urgency of the climate change problem and proposed abandoning the Kyoto Protocol.

Although the existence of such a draft was not secret as such, it included provisions that were immediately problematic to developing countries, organized as the G77. For example, consider Article III, paragraph 9: "The developing country Parties, except the least developed countries which may contribute at their own discretion, commit to nationally appropriate mitigation actions, including actions supported and enabled by technology, financing and capacity-building." And consider Article VI, paragraph 26: "In order to promote transparency and accountability the developing country Parties will report on the implementation of their individual mitigation actions and emission outcomes achieved in relation to their estimates in Attachment B. The supported mitigation actions and the related reductions are subject to robust MRV.[57] MRV of supported actions must verify that financing as well as action is delivering in full towards commitments." The leaked document led to a deadlock in Copenhagen—particularly vehement between the United States and the G77—which broke on the final day with a brief proposal, later dubbed the Copenhagen Accord, developed on the last evening between the United States and the BASIC group (formed of Brazil, South Africa, India, and China). Because of the lack of transparency in this process, the Copenhagen Accord was "noted" by the plenary rather than adopted.

COP15 is an empirical example of minilateral negotiations being both effective and ineffective. The ultimately ineffective efforts of the circle of commitment and the United States with the BASIC group reflected the power imbalance between the proposers and the rest of the parties. In addition, these groups were operating from a fundamentally different myth concerning the operation of international negotiations. The circle of commitment expressed the myth of a common future, symbolized by the biophysical and financial challenges. Furthermore, these parties placed a strong premium on consensus among all signatories, with no free riders. The BASIC group was underpinned by a myth of growing power and importance, signified by participating in minilateral processes. On the other hand, the G77 group remains committed deeply to processes that do not replicate colonial practices in any form. This case nevertheless demonstrates the effectiveness of minilateral arrangements, or *regime complexes*, identified by Keohane and Victor in 2011.[58] For example, it was at this meeting that the Small Island Developing States coalition emerged as a significant participant in negotiations. This coalition of fifty-seven countries was formally recognized in 1992 and has continued to have fruitful dialogs on questions of biodiversity, climate change, and adaptation financing. This group also proposed a draft that would legally bind some developing countries, including China, India, and Saudi Arabia, to mitigate their emissions (the Tuvalu Protocol). This proposal presented a way forward that included a broader raft of enforceable commitments, while paying due attention to postcolonial perspectives that are typically missing from the Conference of the Parties.

As an example of the third pathway, there is a rich literature providing theoretical and empirical analysis of decentralized, networked, bottom-up, polycentric, and adaptive governance approaches in the Anthropocene.[59] In many ways, this literature has been a response to the lack of progress in the international environmental regime, which has been observed to be "a diplomatic effort to identify a problem type that can earn agreement,"[60] rather than a pathway to addressing climate change. These proposed approaches respond to the power imbalances, the net costs to participants, and the inadequacy of the institutions that have been discussed in this section. For emissions control, perhaps the most significant expression of institutional diversity has been in the cap-and-trade arena. By 2005, six different systems had emerged, leading Victor, House, and Joy to cite this as an emulatable experimental approach to institutional designs.[61] Ideally, a universal trading system would be a more attractive alternative to prevent free riding on the efforts of others. But Victor observed that "this fragmented 'bottom-up' approach to carbon trading is not simply a stiff smile to be painted on the wreckage of grander visions for global trading. Rather, it is pragmatic and effective."[62] In addition, these diverse efforts recognize that benefits derived from the reduction of greenhouse gas emissions accrue at multiple scales,[63] and indeed different countries will ultimately make different assessments about risk, urgency, and opportunity associated with the impacts of these emissions.[64]

Decentralized approaches have the advantage of flexibility across policy domains: rules and measures can be adapted to the institutions, parties, and values at stake. These approaches also have the advantage of adaptability over time, which allows for learning from experience, and limits the negative impacts of path dependence in more entrenched situations. Ultimately, the orientation is toward more comprehensiveness, integrating additional considerations previously discounted or ignored but nevertheless relevant for designing institutions in the Anthropocene.

National Environmental Governance

Never hope to realize Plato's Republic. Let it be sufficient that you have in some slight degree ameliorated mankind, and do not think that amelioration is a matter of small importance.
—Marcus Aurelius (121–180 AD)[65]

Sovereign power is neither necessary nor sufficient to secure common interests, even if public procedures are employed. But effective sovereign power is a key element in responding to the challenges presented by the Anthropocene. For that reason, this section considers ways in which some forms of national governance are invoked for addressing global change in "an increasingly complex world of interrelated problems."[66] These forms of governance can be thought of as the political myth for a nation—and, often, the creation myth of the nation-state. Typically, the political myth of a nation is articulated through its constitution, if it has one. A nation may adapt to changing conditions without straining the interpretation of the political doctrine or the formal basis of power itself, if the constitution is resilient rather than rigid. That is, under the right conditions, constitutional change is possible without challenging the foundational doctrines of the nation.

One way to measure the resilience of a constitutional order is to consider the frequency of both replacements of and amendments to that constitution as modifications of the old order. For all countries since 1789, the average number of years between constitutional events in Western Europe and North America is 8.27 years.[67] This is higher than average,[68] indicated a reasonable level of resiliency, but not by a large margin. In these more supple systems, extra constitutional laws can develop, and these can encroach on the constitutional order without challenging the foundational doctrine. The same doctrine, then, can produce a variety of formulae: in this way, prescriptive norms of conduct, rules, statutes, and ordinances can be amended over time, new laws introduced, and old ones (occasionally) terminated. This flexibility creates space for proposals regarding alternative modes of decision making in a particular domain or, even more broadly, by consensus, deliberation, appraisal, contestation, and so forth.

But challenges to the political doctrine arise in the Anthropocene when proposed solutions challenge the foundational myth. In 1989, Charles Rubin was raising concerns about the ways in which environmental problems and their solutions were being theorized to be a threat to science, democracy, and indeed humankind.[69] The clearest evidence of this "environmental authoritarianism" is the way in which anthropogenic climate change is symbolized as a special interest. By narrowing the goal to reinstating "nature without humans," many advocates for robust national governance of natural resources and energy have set the terms of reference to exclude human interests. As such, this Wilderness Myth "has no guidance, beyond the caution that alternatives may not work, to judge the normative superiority of the existing ecosystem."[70] This has profound implications for the institutions required to govern the Anthropocene. The exclusion of even the possibility of trade-offs results in a rejection of the doctrines associated with climate change mitigation and adaptation in much of the current discourse across the political spectrum. This is not unexpected, according to insights of Lasswell, Lerner, and Pool: "The probability of the rejection of a political myth is increased if the adherents experience deprivations rather than indulgence; if attention is directed toward a new myth whose adherents are indulged; and if early adherence to the new myth is followed by relative indulgence."[71]

This is particularly the case in the United States, but the reputation (and sometimes actuality) of misanthropy and ecocentrism in the Wilderness Myth also has spread globally.[72] Examples include the case of the Arizona Cattle Growers Association, who brought suit against the United States Fish and Wildlife Service for its decision to set aside land to protect the Mexican spotted owl; the case of the return of the UNESCO-recognized Amboseli National Park in Kenya to local control by the Olkejuado County Council and the Maasai tribe; and the protests of farmers and Sami alike that they carry the costs of loss-reduction schemes for the protection of predators in Norway.[73] And in Australia, Rose contrasts Country that continues to be cared for by its Aboriginal families—quiet country—with Country from which its families have been expelled—wild country.[74] The concept of irreplaceability of individuals of a species has, in particular, led to claims that human interests such as economic development or native title are not legitimate. Of course, the counterclaim is made that any ecodoctrine does in fact require a recognition of some human interests, specifically access to a healthy biosphere to enable clean air, food, and water.[75] Alternatively, decoupling proposals such as that of the Ecomodernist Manifesto or those implicit in the Sustainable Development Goals requires decisions to be made around appropriate territories of sacrifice. These complex questions of competing interests must be addressed by national governments. In the following subsections, we review how different forms of national governance have addressed such questions.

Totalitarianism

The question of whether active concentration of authority and control should be employed to prevent unsustainable behavior cannot be avoided in the current state of urgency. The authoritarian response to the Anthropocene has been posed as a descriptive model and proposed as a prescriptive model.[76] Prescriptions that "humanity will have to trade its liberty to live as it wishes in favor of a system where survival is paramount"[77] came to prominence at around the same time as international multilateral negotiations started invoking urgency, although these propositions had been part of the environmental discourse for some decades in the form of "communist chic." Decoupling proposals imply a certain amount of authority and control in the ability to relocate communities from low-density to high-density settlements, and to relocate sites of production to designated sacrifice zones. As a result, it is relevant to consider the effectiveness of existing command-and-control approaches in efforts to govern the challenges of the Anthropocene.

Experience in China provides a useful example, particularly in the context of increasing centralized control by Xi Jinping and his allies in the Communist Party apparatus. China's environmental performance has come to prominence particularly since the upset polls around the world in the 2015–2017[78] period have contributed to a sense of deep insecurity in democratic nations. Furthermore, China has embraced a prominent position in the global environmental regime, from its key role as part of the BASIC group in Copenhagen in 2009 to announcing a "war on pollution" as part of the Communist Party Congress in 2014 to canceling "some 100 coal-related power plants across 13 provinces and metropolises."[79] Indeed, headlines such as "Only China Can Save the Planet" have become more common, and with them the sense that China can move more decisively than other actors in, for example, reducing greenhouse gas emissions or improving water and air quality.[80] There is a growing understanding, in China as elsewhere, that political responses to global change will determine possible futures.

The use of unambiguous environmental symbols in China has been evident for over a decade. China's eleventh five-year planning period (which ended in 2010) elevated quantitative environmental objectives in the regions, with a focus on emissions reductions and pollution control. Enforcement occurred through a process of "cadre evaluation"[81] rather than environmental regulation. This set the stage for a robust practice of gaming the system to ensure high evaluations for bureaucrats in distant regional centers. For example, there is evidence that local authorities shut down and reopened polluting manufactories multiple times to achieve targets.

The Chinese regime, at all levels, has a history of coopting environmental policy to attain other strategic objectives—a partial incorporation of symbols to serve a different doctrine. For example, the US$80 billion plus South-to-North Water Diversion Project has proved to be of limited benefit economically and considerable detriment environmentally and socially. Nevertheless, the symbols actively deployed by the Chinese government focused as much on environmental benefits as the need for water in northern urban centers. "After years of hard work, local governments in Jiangsu and Shandong, two provinces with the worst water pollution along trunk canals of the eastern route, have made obvious progress in curbing pollutions, Zhang Jiyao [a key minister] said. To date, constructions of all the 426 pollution control projects planned for the route has broken ground in the two provinces with 399 of them or over 94 percent of the total completed."[82] And from another source: "Recently, the Hubei Provincial Environmental Protection Committee informed the 2016 annual survey of ecological province construction results, Shiyan once again in the province's 17 cities ranked first."[83] In reality, local agencies and nongovernmental organizations have played a marginal role, as the central government used a combination of persuasive and coercive strategies to achieve the primary aims of food security and water allocation.[84]

Carbon dioxide–trading markets is another domain in which Chinese symbols of environmental governance have been employed, particularly since the Paris Agreement. China has introduced several regional cap-and-trade markets as a way of building capacity for a national market[85] and of engaging productively with international finance.[86] Given the preeminent contribution of China to global greenhouse gas emissions, this is an important initiative.[87] The nature of Chinese governance, however, leads to profound distortions in the market through central government intervention and poor regulatory infrastructure. In addition, there appear to be insufficient incentives, persuasive or coercive, to generate the regional demand that successful pilots require.[88] Because the markets operate in parallel, the standards of compliance are mixed. However, the planned launch of a national market in 2019 has the potential to benefit from the distributed learning that could be harvested. There are additional symbols at work, of course. A successful national emissions-trading scheme would provide for the prospect of accessing offsets in developing countries, as well as a new opportunity for gaining power in global markets and having a strong role in shaping the global climate regime without making binding commitments to emissions reductions.

The inverse of these arguments regarding authoritarian models is that the Anthropocene itself will engender a totalitarian turn. That is, the biophysical impacts of global change will directly affect the viability of democratic institutions. Some authors have suggested that even if environmental outcomes are poor in authoritarian regimes, a combination of economic and environmental stresses are more likely to entrench the authoritarian model in China.[89] The argument is that "authoritarianism is likely to persist because of the implacable material limits on economic development,"[90] that the overexploitation of natural resources will lead inevitably to an economic downturn. It certainly appears that the rapid economic growth of China followed by the Global Financial Crisis of 2008 and China's (albeit modest) slowdown since then have perhaps allowed China to bypass the "democratic moment" of Acharya[91] and strengthened the consolidation of power centralized under the leadership of Hu Jintao (2002–2012) and Xi Jinping (2012–). Even when effective agency in civil society enjoyed its moment in the sun, citizens did not use the opportunity to argue for environmental outcomes.[92] Finally, Chinese governance has in recent decades been particularly successful in coupling centralized authority and economic development. That said, the connection between economic performance and exploitation of resources in China is looking less and less inevitable in the twenty-first century.

Democracy

Democratic models of government do not "deny the power advantage enjoyed by those in charge of government, nor do they optimistically presume that democracies are free of the tendency for power holders to expand their control."[93] The task of democracies is to develop a model whereby bureaucratic and political power is balanced appropriately and explicitly with popular sovereignty. There are as many varieties of democratic governance as there are democratic governments. That said, there have been efforts to group and analyze these governments according to a variety of criteria, many of which were pioneered by Arend Lijphart. Although there is no standardized way of using these criteria, several relatively well-agreed-upon dimensions exist. One of those dimensions is the spectrum from consensual to adversarial democratic processes. The variation along this dimension has been advanced as a potential predictor for environmental performance.[94] There have, of course, been many critiques of the relevance of or even the possibility of comparing democratic attributes in generalizable ways.[95] Nevertheless, some kind of general distinction is useful for the purposes of better understanding the reasons for outcomes that serve environmental goals and those that do not.

Consensual democracies typically exhibit centralized power but with thick executive functionality; a vibrant multiparty political system; a proportional electoral system; and a relatively high degree of constitutional flexibility. Examples include countries such as Austria, Finland, and Germany. Consensual democracies tend to be highly correlated with neocorporatist approaches,[96] in which governments cooperate effectively with nongovernmental partners—interest groups, labor unions, private industry, and so forth—to negotiate shared solutions to national problems. Lehmbruch and Schmitter have argued that this last attribute of corporatism should be labeled *concertation*, but for the purposes of this discussion, these fine distinctions are not necessary.[97] Consensus-based democracies are also associated with *consociational* approaches, which are characterized by various types of democratic power sharing.

Adversarial or majoritarian democratic systems tend toward a thin and rather dominant executive; an inherent advantage accorded to the majority in a two-party political system; plurality or majority electoral systems; and more rigid constitutionality. Examples include Canada, the United Kingdom, and the United States. Adversarial democracies have the propensity to conflate success and virtue, in which "vulgar pragmatism does not ground values in existence, but takes as valuable whatever is existent. … Competitive success is taken to be at once the sign and the very substance of worth."[98] Or as Hegel might observe, whatever is, is right. Conventional wisdom suggests that adversarial systems, which are particularly prominent in the English-speaking democracies, are less likely to maintain strong environmental regulatory performance and participate in the global climate change regime: "While there is little agreement on the components of environmental performance indicators," Dryzek and Stevenson say, "there is a convergent validity across the findings of studies using different sorts of indicators."[99] This is possible to demonstrate on a case-by-case basis, but it is difficult to find universally applicable conclusions, as we show ahead.

Quantitative indices that measure these criteria are one useful tool in this process. For example, the Hicks-Kenworthy index quantifies *corporation* as the degree of cooperation among groups such as labor unions, industries, state, interest groups, and competing firms, among others. The Hall and

Gingerich index quantifies the ways in which nonmarket means are used in arenas such as labor organization and corporate governance. Majoritarian and consensus indices based on the work of Lijphart consider measures of plurality and centralization.[100] Lijphart and Crepaz famously analyzed eighteen industrialized democracies, based on the work of twelve neocorporatist scholars, to derive an expert index that measured the degree of corporatism between the late 1950s and the late 1970s.[101] More recently, Arsenault has applied a number of different indices to the "Lijphart eighteen," using data drawn from the 1960–2006 period.[102]

Similarly, quantitative measures of environmental performance are not standardized. However, Yale's Environmental Performance Index (EPI) has provided a useful and consistent set of twenty measures of various aspects of environmental performance—that is, outcomes rather than policies—over the last fifteen years.[103] The measures embody multiple issue categories, including energy, air quality, water quality and access, biodiversity, and agriculture, which are further combined into factors. For example, the Carbon and Energy factor is made up of two measures: Change of Trend in Carbon Intensity and Trend in Carbon Intensity per kWh. The twenty measures together are combined into two subindices (Ecosystem Vitality and Environmental Health), which are finally combined into a single index, the EPI score. This allows countries to be ranked, and the consistency of the approach allows change to be tracked from one year to the next.

An obvious difficulty with this kind of quantitative comparison is that the time scales are rather different. Further, the parameterized values depend on subjective value judgments. The measures of democratic style are estimated over many decades, the data to create them takes some time to assemble, and their determination may be politically influenced. Recent changes in the political landscape, which have been significant, cannot be captured by these measures. In addition, though the EPI score and its components are valid for the year 2016, and the eighteen countries selected are characterized by high-quality data, there are inevitable judgments that need to be made to turn a complex context into one, or a few, numbers. That said, there is consistency among the measures that suggests some reliability to the relative rankings at least.

Table 4.2 brings these two data sets together as correlations between quantitative measures. Significant correlations (indicated in this table by an asterisk) are not evident between any index of the degree of consensual

Table 4.2

Pearson correlation coefficient between various measures of environmental performance and various measures of democratic style during the preceding decades

Correlation between indices	2016 EPI score	Ecosystem vitality	Environmental health	Energy and climate factors	Emissions (per capita, 2013)*
Hicks-Kenworthy	-0.06	0.33†	-0.31†	-0.17	-0.37†
Hall and Gingerich	-0.11	0.54†	-0.51†	-0.12	-0.43†
Lijphart-Arsenault Cooperation	-0.10	0.43	-0.42	0.09	-0.35
Lijphart-Crepaz Cooperation	-0.06	0.44	-0.39	0.13	-0.26
Lijphart-Crepaz Corporatism	-0.03	0.61†	-0.48†	0.09	-0.47†

Source: Data obtained from the European Commission Emissions Database for Global Atmospheric Research.

*The final column shows emissions of carbon dioxide per capita in tons for the year 2013.

†Indicates a significant value.

democratic process and the overall EPI score for 2016. This is explained by the anticorrelation of the two primary subindices that make up the EPI score. Consensual democracies tend to perform better in measures of Ecosystem Vitality, whereas adversarial democracies tend to perform better in measures of Environmental Health. Furthermore, high levels of consensuality, cooperation, and flexibility do not predict a downward trend in carbon intensity of national energy systems and appear to be anticorrelated with emissions per capita. Similarly, a straightforward link between adversarial democratic processes and poor environmental outcomes is not generalizable. Attributes as varied as climate and geography on the one hand and class structure and party political mobilization on the other come into play in each case.[104] Detailed case studies have suggested that political and institutional factors are at least as important as population, relative wealth, or climate.[105] For example, countries that preempt a robust critique of environmental issues through consensus building tend to exhibit more modest environmental performance than others that either encourage it or, by exclusion, provoke it. Even those that employ corporatist approaches may exclude some interests and not others, leading to different outcomes with a similar model. Adversarial systems have not performed well in recent years in regard to the quality of public discourse, but the trends made explicit seem to be associated less with the political landscape and more with the relationship between economic growth and progress on decarbonization.[106] As a result, a normative commitment to democracy provides no guidance in advocating a preference for consensual or adversarial democracy in the Anthropocene. Quantitative measures in particular provide no empirical basis for this choice.

It is generally accepted that the vigor of discourse is what makes the adversarial democracy function well in regard to some measures of environmental performance. However, recent developments—in the United States and the United Kingdom, for example—may be of an entirely different stripe. Symbols of identification (nationality, ethnicity, homeland) have replaced symbols of demand (political position, ideology, and party). These symbols have fragmented across so many communities that they are displacing the more foundational political symbols, such as the Magna Carta (in the United Kingdom) and the Declaration of Independence (in the United States). Some have argued that this shift is enabled through responses to, and anticipation of, crises in the Anthropocene.[107]

Emergency Forms of Governance

Sovereign is he who decides on the exception.

—Carl Schmitt[108]

A sense of global emergency has prompted a sense of ontological insecurity that threatens to overtake emerging discourses of global stewardship. "If geoscientists across the disciplines are right," Noel Castree writes, "we are entering terra incognita by inadvertently ending the relatively benign conditions of the Holocene epoch."[109] In a present undergoing rapid change with accelerating exposure to extreme events and unknown effects on future states, the narrative of apocalyptic change presents an ecological horror story.[110] As we have discussed, the recognition of events as extreme and the attribution of these extremes to human activities carry with them a proposal that emergency forms of governance are necessary, invoking structures of power that promote efficiency over justice.[111] Even constitutional democracies can increase constitutional power and diminish constitutional restriction under certain conditions.[112] There is a very real sense evolving in which the principle of sovereignty is, ultimately, not a political but an antipolitical concept.[113] Drawing on the works of Hannah Arendt, Clinton L. Rossiter,[114] and Carl Schmitt,[115] Giorgio Agamben characterizes the sovereignty principle as resting in the power to suspend all political activity.[116] This "state of exception is not defined as a fullness of powers, a pleromatic state of law, as in the dictatorial model, but as a kenomatic state, an emptiness and standstill of the law."[117] This state reduces the political to "bare-life,"[118] "when 'who' someone is, is ignored."[119] But Agamben's analysis elides discussion of human-environment relations, taking territory as muted—the backdrop by which governance takes place.

Expanding on this line of thought, we have suggested that the emerging Anthropocene geopolitics constitute an unprecedented space of governance, lending itself to precipitating emergency authority. For example, De Larrinaga and Doucet argue that the human security discourse conceptualizes "a form of life rendered amenable to biopolitical technologies and rationalities while simultaneously defining the conditions of exceptionality that assist in sovereign power's ability to authorize international interventions meant to secure human life."[120] Agamben observes that the state of exception is "always something different from anarchy and chaos, in a juridical sense, an order still exists in it, even if it is not a juridical order."[121]

The Anthropocene state of exception, these scholars point out, is also different from the totalitarian notion of "complete state control of absolutely everything within a given territory."[122] To better understand how the state of exception relates to ecological politics, Smith therefore calls for "a critical analysis of the sovereign powers that states lay claim to over non-human nature."[123] There is a need to examine what states of emergency might mean for the emerging Anthropocene narrative. Yet these Anthropocene states of exception already have a designation in the environmental literature: they are sacrifice zones. As Rossiter writes, "No sacrifice is too great for our democracy, least of all the temporary sacrifice of democracy itself."[124]

The UNFCCC preamble asserts that nation-states have sovereignty to exploit resources according to their environmental and developmental policies. Countries that would comply with the Paris Agreement have yet resisted strategies that might erode their rights and responsibilities as sovereign states.[125] This sovereignty carries within it, however, the capacity to suspend rules of law *in extremis*. Dalby observes that the commitment to "promoting and securing the life of the biohuman means, indeed, that liberal rule must be prepared to wage war not so much for the human, but on the human."[126] In this vein, Smith argues, "if humanity is to avoid being reduced to bare-life and the living planet is not to become a bare rock then we should not confuse politics with process, or the creative constitutive political power of the earth's inhabitants with the constitutional power of the state to suspend such politics."[127] A specific space in which such structures of power are being invoked in the context of Anthropocene urgency is in the governance of migration.[128]

How might Anthropocene governance attend to the needs of refugees? If global anthropogenic temperature change exceeds 2°C, as seems likely, and if global land use change continues unfettered, then "those who suffer most from the situation will, ironically, be those most likely to find themselves reduced to bare-life."[129] Agamben sees "the camp as the nomos[130] of the modern."[131] By asking what a camp is and examining its political structure, Agamben leads "us to regard the camp not as a historical fact and an anomaly belonging to the past (even if still verifiable) but in some way as the hidden matrix and nomos of the political space in which we are still living."[132] The refugee camp is a place in which the state of exception materializes and subsequently creates a space consisting of a threshold of indistinction between bare-life and the juridical rule. As such, the risks presented by the camps of World War II, "merely the [places] in which the most absolute *conditio inhumana* that has ever existed on earth [were] realized,"[133] are present with us in the refugee and migrant camps of today. From the US Naval Station Guantanamo Bay detention camp to Australia's Christmas Island Immigration Reception and Processing Centre, there are ample specimens to illustrate Agamben's argument. The question becomes how these practices and sites we call *camps*, these sacrifice zones, are rendered within and through democratic governance in the Anthropocene.[134]

Scott Morgensen calls attention to the omission by Agamben of the internment camps that form part of the United States jurisdictional apparatus. Relocating Indigenous peoples, a process that dates formally to the 1837 Treaty of New Echota but was practiced from the earliest settlements, involved, for example, the internment of 1,700 Dakota people, of whom "over 300 died of starvation and disease."[135] The governance of reservations into which Indigenous nations were funneled certainly "would seem relevant to a history of the camp within Western modernity." The politics of settler colonialism is with us "right here, right now," Morgensen warns. Certainly, many Indigenous nations have been under "failed state" governance[136] since colonization devastated their preexisting social structures.[137] In the following section, we explore the limits of nation-state myths and doctrines in their coexistences with those of their Indigenous nations, and examine some implications of coexistence as a necessary inconsistency in law for governance in the Anthropocene.

Fragile Geographies of Coexistence

All land in Australia is held in consequence of an assumption so large, grand and remote from actuality that it had best be called royal, which is exactly what it was.
—W. E. H. Stanner[138]

Coexistence as a symbol for good environmental governance presents an alternative to increasingly polarized and authoritarian perspectives in the urgent domains of the Anthropocene. However, a tension exists between coexistence as an ideal and coexistence as a matter of fact in many contexts. For example, the idea of coexistence in Australian common law is one of necessary inconsistency in which private property intersects with

Indigenous Native Titles. But if understood as something more than a limited legal doctrine, coexistence is a state sui generis that needs to be recognized in its uneasy juxtaposition.[139] In this and other arenas, negotiating sustainable outcomes in the context of human dignity requires a means of governing the fragile geographies of coexistence,[140] in which simply adapting formulae under the same doctrine becomes untenable. Governing for sustainability requires recognition of myriad coexisting myths of Indigenous-settler[141] relations and beyond, as well as searching for doctrines that can better support the fragile geographies they engage. It is difficult to engage in this paradoxical space while remaining in generalities. Hence, we explore the difficult question of Anthropocene coexistence from the focused perspective of Australian Indigenous self-determination.

Native Title and Coexistence

When the ruling on the case of *Mabo v. Queensland* was issued on June 3, 1992, the High Court of Australia extinguished the Proclamation of Terra Nullius made by Governor Burke in 1835. Terra nullius was founded upon the Doctrine of Discovery, which was developed based on three Papal Bulls of the fifteenth century: the Bull Dum Diversas of 1452, authorizing the subjugation of non-Catholics; the Bull Romanus Pontifex of 1454, authorizing the dominion of Catholic nations over discovered non-Christian lands; and the Bull Inter Caetera of 1493, which granted dominion in perpetuity over all lands "found and to be found" in order to instruct inhabitants in the Catholic faith.[142] The doctrine was domesticated in British common law to include the principles that discovery carried with it rights against other Christian nations and that lands with no colonial presence could be legally occupied as terra nullius.[143] Thus, the doctrine held that Australia had been uninhabited when Captain Cook claimed possession in 1770, and hence all the continent belonged to no one before establishment of the British colony in 1788. For nearly two centuries, until 1967, Australian Indigenous peoples were denied citizenship of any form in the British Commonwealth. The ruling in favor of the plaintiff, Eddie Mabo and the Meriam people of the Torres Strait, finding that their tenure of their ancestral lands predated European colonization, overturned these centuries of legal doctrine.

The landmark *Mabo v. Queensland* ruling was soon followed by the Native Title Act of 1993, which "removes the common law defeasibility of native title." This hasty enactment was intended to resolve native title in advance of an anticipated landslide of claims prompted by the *Mabo* decision.[144] Three years later, the Wik peoples and the Thayorre people sought to test whether native title over their ancestral lands on the Cape York Peninsula could supersede the pastoral leases granted by the Crown under the 1910 and 1962 Lands Acts.[145] The High Court of Australia found that native title could *coexist* in law with pastoral leases. That is, where the Crown had issued leases for forestry, pasture, or private property under the presumption of terra nullius, the recognition of native title could not confer a right of *exclusive* possession. In effect, Crown leases would extinguish native title and instate a space of "necessary inconsistency." Clarifying, Justice Toohey in the court hearing said: "That is not to say that the legislature gave conscious recognition to native title. … It is simply that there is nothing in the statute or grant that should be taken as a total exclusion of the indigenous [*sic*] people from the land."[146] In rapid succession, the doctrine of terra nullius had been extinguished, native title recognized, and native title again extinguished under a new interpretation of coexistence.[147]

Research on settler-Indigenous affairs highlights that so long as national laws are set to govern relations with Indigenous peoples, the table cannot be set for a just, inclusive, and respectful negotiation of coexistence.[148] In the pastoral leases case, the Wik and Thayorre peoples had wished to test the inconsistency in fact of the leases, on the grounds that there were two legal regimes that had achieved "concurrent enjoyment of rights."[149] The court rejected this argument. Justice Kirby insisted instead that "the law was concerned with 'title' in respect of land and the existence or otherwise of legal rights in respect of the land, not the manner of their existence."[150] In this way, the court affirmed the understanding that the law itself is not positioned to rule on the manner of its own existence.

While the fragile doctrine of native title[151] is the first effort of the Australian government to find a means of representing Indigenous preeminence in law, the reality is, of course, that coexistence between Indigenous and British law has been ongoing since settlement. This coexistence continues today under forms of Indigenous recognition that are "regressive, dispossessory, the antithesis of justice and the mutually respectful coexistence that is urgently being demanded."[152]

Similarly, Indigenous peoples internationally are emerging as subject to legal frameworks such as the international labor standards and international human rights law. The significant shortcoming of these frameworks is their inability to articulate and protect the rights of Indigenous peoples to self-determination.[153] A milestone in international Indigenous governance, therefore, was marked by the United Nations Declaration on the Rights of Indigenous Peoples (UNDRIP), which was adopted on September 13, 2007, by 144 nations, with four nations voting against (Australia, Canada, New Zealand, and the United States). The declaration is significant because it recognizes that Indigenous peoples are more than individual subjects within national jurisdictions, and it enshrines in international law the principles of self-government and native jurisdiction.[154] Indeed, the "expression of sub-state group rights alongside individual rights is the UNDRIP's novel contribution to the body of international human rights norms."[155] As a new and developing ground in international law that could potentially reframe the doctrines of sovereign nations, this is, perhaps necessarily, a slow process. Significantly, the declaration is not legally binding, but rather "a standard of achievement to be pursued in a spirit of partnership and mutual respect" that represents "a further important step forward for the recognition, promotion, and protection of the rights and freedoms of indigenous peoples."[156] In the process of developing actionable formulae for this novel legal domain, the language of coexistence included by the Working Group on Indigenous Populations[157] was edited out of the final declaration. Paragraph 13 of the draft declaration preamble read, "Recognizing that indigenous peoples have the right freely to determine their relationships with States in a spirit of *coexistence*, mutual benefit and full respect."[158] This paragraph does not appear in the final declaration. Instead, the declaration expressed symbols of partnership, including "constructive arrangements with States" and "harmonious and cooperative relations."[159]

The declaration stands as testament to the burgeoning scholarly and civic work that examines the nature of Indigenous governance and its existence within, alongside, and across nations established through colonization. The academic literature contains many possible perspectives to begin to understand the tensions of coexistence. For instance, the proposition by Rawls of "overlapping consensus" between "conflicting and even incommensurable religious, philosophic, and moral doctrines"[160] provides one working symbol. Porter and Barry suggest that Mouffe's proposition of "agonistic pluralism" would permit the recognition of the "ambivalent character of human sociability and the fact that reciprocity and hostility cannot be dissociated."[161] For the doctrine of coexistence to become more than "a narrow, legally constrained space in which fragile Indigenous enti-tlements are circumscribed by the power of the state ... as a discourse of citizenship without the possibility of a diverse and pluralistic outcome,"[162] we can reflect upon the ways in which Indigenous myth provides "essential lessons about how to proceed."[163] Consider, for example, governance in the Murray-Darling River Basin in Australia.

Coexistence Constrained

The Murray-Darling Basin is home to almost fifty Indigenous nations that have inhabited this productive region continuously for over thirty thousand years. These nations each maintain relationships with discrete sections of the river system, which comprises 14 percent of the Australian continent, including its three longest rivers. For the Yorta Yorta, this profoundly place-based relationship is one of embodied connection with Country around the confluence of the Murray and Goulburn Rivers. Yorta Yorta man Lee Joachim says, "We identify the Barmah Lakes and the Moira Lakes as part of us—they are our kidneys. The narrows—what others call the [Barmah] choke—is like our central nervous system, and we are part of that ... the correct flooding period is controlled through those narrows and all aspects of flooding in the Barmah-Millewa Forest."[164] The relationship between the Yorta Yorta people and their Country is one of purpose, meaning, and duty rather than ownership. Importantly, this obligation extends beyond those entities native to their traditional lands: the well-being of any people on Country must be supported. This includes people from neighboring clans, European settlers, and any other visitors. Further, this obligation extends to *everywhen*;[165] there is no time dimension in the Western sense to this obligation.

While continuing relations with Country and with neighboring nations within the basin, the Yorta Yorta people are familiar with negotiating their sovereignty with non-Indigenous partners. Between 1860 and 1994, they submitted more than eighteen separate claims for land and compensa-tion,[166] which culminated in a 1998 decision by Federal Court Justice Olney: "The tide of history has indeed washed away any real acknowledgment of their traditional laws and any real observance of their traditional customs. The foundation of the claim to native title in relation to the land previously occupied by those ancestors having disappeared, the native-title rights and interests previously enjoyed are not capable of revival. This conclusion effectively resolves the application for a determination of native title."[167] Yorta Yorta appeals to the High Court argued that the Federal Court understood Indigeneity as something "frozen in the past,"[168] but their appeals were denied.[169] The standards by which Indigeneity was measured under common law could not accommodate Yorta Yorta cosmological myth.

For the Australian government, the stakes were high: the agricultural gross domestic product of the basin is valued at over AUS$6.7 billion, while accounting for more than 80 percent of consumptive water use nationally.[170] Apart from the Indigenous nations, over two million other Australians live and work in the basin. The urgency of governance challenges has reached a critical level in the Murray-Darling Basin through loss of biodiversity and productivity due to droughts and other extremes. The basin is also home to thirty-five species of endangered birds and sixteen species of endangered mammals. Twenty unique mammalian species that existed only in the Murray-Darling Basin are already extinct. Flow through the Murray, Darling, and Murrumbidgee Rivers is also one of the world's most highly variable surface water complexes. This variability is integral to the health of internationally important wetland ecosystems.[171] "Claims for 'business as usual' in the agriculture sector, and particularly with regard to irrigation, can no longer be supported as appropriate, or even valid."[172]

For the Yorta Yorta equally, the degradation of this river system, with which they have millennial knowledge of careful coexistence, is a critical issue. Since the *Mabo* decision, state and territory governments across the basin continued to allocate consumptive water entitlements with no regard for Indigenous preeminence.[173] The native title framework functioned to limit Indigenous water rights throughout the Murray-Darling Basin.[174] Writing about rights to water in the Murray-Darling Basin, Morgan, Strelein, and Weir urge that "native title should not be the only benchmark for the engagement of Indigenous Nations"[175] and propose that comanagement may be a viable path for Indigenous people, local government, the state, and federal government to work together.[176] In 2004, Premier Steve Bracks of the State of Victoria signed a cooperative-management agreement covering public lands, lakes, and rivers.[177] The agreement was intended to develop "mutual recognition and trust between the Yorta Yorta People and the State."[178] The comanagement agreement with the Yorta Yorta Nation Aboriginal Corporation was established five months after the high court upheld the lower court decision that native title did not apply to Yorta Yorta country. There is little doubt that the Victorian government pursued the comanagement route to alleviate the impacts of the native title defeat.[179]

Meanwhile, a severe drought afflicted southern and eastern Australia from 1997 to 2009. It was into the troubled context of this Millennium Drought that two distinct formulae for water governance emerged: cultural flows and environmental flows. The former is descriptive of water flows that are made for the purpose of cultural activities, which include both farms and Indigenous cultural practices.[180] The latter is descriptive of water flows to support ecological outcomes, and is synergistic with, but not equal to, cultural flows.[181] Environmental flows have been a fraught formula for ecosystems, because the label is often used for emergency measures, such as treating blue-green algae, for flows that can be unseasonal, or flows that constitute thermal pollution because of low temperature.[182] Through comanagement, the proposition of cultural flows would draw on Yorta Yorta *Caring for Country*[183] to ensure water flowed through the right places at the right time and with the right conditions, while also providing a means for Indigenous nations to "speak through" the prevailing governance arrangements[184] and support spiritual, social, and economic practices by Indigenous peoples.[185]

Diagnosing the uneasy coexistence between Indigenous and non-indigenous populations and the Murray-Darling river systems, Jessica Weir observes that engineering approaches—weirs, dams, meters, and allocations—had severely restricted capacity to maintain adequate flows through the Millennium Drought.[186] Drawing on the work of Bruno Latour, Weir shows that the effort to distill water into an isolated and separately manageable phenomenon instead proliferated its entanglement in the complex social and biogeophysical systems of the basin. Rather than relying on the river flood to flush out salinity, to ensure birds, turtles, and fish can hatch, feed, and travel, and that plants can flower and produce foods, water managers now need to take heed of everything from the microscopic to the basin-wide in their calculations.

Throughout the Millennium Drought, these technological water-management systems failed as farmers were faced with year after year of record-low rainfall, causing depression, substance abuse, and suicides,[187] as crops and farms were lost. To avoid any repetition of the impacts of the Millennium Drought, the Murray-Darling Basin Plan was signed into law in 2012 after a decade of painful negotiations. The plan included infrastructure improvements and water allocations that would ensure "environmental flows." The plan aggravated many farmers. In 2010, farmers were photographed burning the management plan in protest against measures that they said "would cause a permanent, man-made drought."[188]

In this space, the proposition of cultural flows—embodying the understanding that Indigenous water ontologies are "actually (as well as metaphorically) valid"[189] and that agriculture is also a form of cultural water use— have appropriately resisted functional parameterization. As a result, cultural water is a nexus of multiple views relating to distributive justice and restitution, as well as the role of technical experts and the prospects for integrating cultural flows as a formula into the comanagement regime.

As these conditions indicate, this space is not one of harmonious coexistence either among people, or between people and the water that sustains them. It is this fact that Chantal Mouffe[190] asks us not to shy away from or seek to simplify by way of deliberative, consensus-oriented politics in decision making: "Reciprocity and hostility cannot be dissociated," she argues.[191] To which Porter and Barry add, "A relational contact zone must reject outright any formula or prescription as completely anathema to its philosophical and ethical orientations. What can be developed are some analytical, ethical, and philosophical orientations for developing conceptual positions practices, and interventions that are counter-hegemonic, agonistic, and decolonizing."[192]

Acknowledging Coexistence

It is the work of nonindigenous persons to recognize coexistence, for the Indigenous peoples of the Murray-Darling have recognized it since contact. Furthermore, they have developed governance structures for coexistence on this river system over the tens of thousands of years that they negotiated relations with the cosmologies of neighboring nations. As a result, "Indigenous formulations are non-intrusive and build frameworks of respectful coexistence by acknowledging the integrity and autonomy of the various constituent elements of the relationship."[193] To move forward, then, nonindigenous people need to foster policies and prescriptions, processes and engagements, that recognize substantively "presence, coexistence and belonging."[194] This suggests that simplifying water management in the Murray-Darling Basin by way of deliberative, consensus-oriented politics is perhaps impossible, perhaps even undesirable beyond the shorter time scale.[195] Rather, conflict in decision processes must be tolerated, lest we mistake participation, sign-off, or consensus for agreement. Our aim in speaking of coexistence, then, is certainly not to propose a one-size-fits-all doctrine for urgent environmental governance in Indigenous-settler spaces. As Richie Howitt has stated, "there is no sense here of negotiated belonging; there is no sense of … settling of tensions."[196] Indigenous-settler spaces are resistant to the myths of nation-states and fragile against the rhetoric of law. Relational approaches that take seriously the need to engage Indigenous people in responding to global environmental crises cannot rely on existing formulae if committed to the common interest.[197] Hence, rather than seeking to "translate" Indigenous myths or prescribe Indigenous policy participation, we may begin to accommodate the coexistence of paradoxical spaces of governance. "Indigenous sovereignty is not," Howitt reminds us, "to be found like a pearl glistening in the archival documentation of whitefellas' generally warped understanding of pre-contact societies."[198] To recognize coexistence with Indigenous forms of governance we must first develop the conceptual tools, and this can only happen in situated engagements[199] with the radically place-based ontologies of Indigenous nations.

The preexisting and ongoing relations that govern Indigenous peoples and their ancestral lands and waters are only just beginning to gain presence in national and international legal frameworks. Although Indigenous governance remains dependent upon rights granted to Indigenous peoples by the sovereign legal regimes imposed on them, advances in Indigenous legal recognition do not lead inevitably to self-determination. Decolonization remains a difficult topic that, while increasingly well-defined in scholarly literature, finds numerous hindrances to actualizing. Indeed, the understanding of colonialism spans from, on the one hand, Linda Tuhiwai Smith citing activist Bobby Sykes as saying, "What? Postcolonialism? Have they left?"[200] to, on the other, the United Nations rubric indicating that only seventeen countries remain under colonial rule.[201] Indeed, the nearly ubiquitous "decolonized" territories since World War II[202] serve as an illustration of the erasure of Indigenous nations across the world. Against this apparent emancipation, Indigenous peoples are fighting for recognition of their coexistence within sovereign nations and to have their unique perspectives on the world-for-us contributing to governance in the Anthropocene.

The Included Middle

If our encounters situate us on a ground sufficiently shared to become meaningful and sufficiently differentiated to become provocative, what may erupt?
—Deborah Bird Rose[203]

As we have described, the same doctrine can produce a variety of formulae. In resilient governance systems, the foundational doctrine is not challenged, even when formulae encroach on the constitutional order. We have, in different ways, illustrated how sovereign states ensure this resilience as they negotiate international legal frameworks and relate to their Indigenous populations. Nevertheless, international and Indigenous regimes alike, by their nature, infringe on sovereignty even without the additional insult of legally binding agreements.[204] The doctrine of preeminent sovereignty "requires elections that hold elected leaders accountable to publics and other arrangements that hold non-elected leaders accountable to elected ones."[205] This doctrine is especially active in adversarial democracies at the present time (Australia, Canada, Ireland, New Zealand, the United Kingdom, and the United States). The prevailing symbol is that "international law has been hijacked by essentially undemocratic modes of supranational lawmaking."[206] In this myth, the amalgam of government negotiators, scientists, nongovernmental organizations, advocacy groups, and media engaged in international negotiation and discourse do not stand in for robust democratic process. The doctrine of the United Nations, on the other hand, acts in a process that "in fact prepares the ground for the operation of a form of sovereign power that claims the globe as its field of operation."[207] This has the potential to eradicate the conflict necessary in "the real politics (the public actions and expressions based on individual judgments—and the responsibilities that are coeval with this)."[208] In this space, the resistance to, for example, developing binding agreements for emissions reductions draws into sharp relief the ability of states to suspend constitutional order to act on states of exception. In response, "green sovereignty" argues that national sovereignty itself represents a hazard to ecological sustainability. As a result, Anthropocene geopolitics, in a state of urgency, risk becoming an arena in which the argument between preeminent sovereignty and green sovereignty will allow the state of exception to become "a global biopolitical norm."[209]

Seeking alternatives to the potential for exceptional governance, several theorists have staked out a middle ground, such as the polycentric governance of Elinor Ostrom,[210] the regime complex of Robert Keohane and David Victor,[211] and the deliberative democracy of John Dryzek.[212] In the context of urgency, however, as Dryzek observes, "haste to institutional prescription is also problematic, threatening to short-circuit the kind of learning process necessary in the novel and complex conditions accompanying the challenge of the Anthropocene."[213] An alternative to increasingly polarized perspectives, both between and within modes of democracy, is presented by the logic of the "included middle."[214] Bădescu and Nicolescu observed that "the logic of the included middle is a true logic, formalizable and formalized, multivalent."[215] Manfred Max-Neef emphasized that this construction, in which allowable states can be denoted as A, $not\text{-}A$, and T, is not a metaphor any more than Indigenous cosmologies are narrative equivalents of geological history.[216] In the Anthropocene, we can turn this logic to the need to learn through, rather than resolve, conflict, inconsistency, and uncertainty. The false haven of consensus, the mirage of the win-win, ceases to demand attention.

This much is clear, as the world-for-us is coming to be treated as a fungible commodity, the relationships between human societies and their place-based knowledge have been severed, and systems of global governance turn to bare-life metrics for human and more-than-human alike. Recognizing the unprecedented challenges and unimaginable risks of a world in transformation, in chapter 5 we will draw together insights to explore what coexistence might mean for Anthropocene urgency.

5   Coexistence

These times called the Anthropocene are times of multi-species, including human, agency: of great mass death and extinction; of on-rushing disasters, whose unpredictable specificities are foolishly taken as un-knowability itself; of refusing to know and to cultivate the capacity of response-ability; of refusing to be present in and to onrushing catastrophe in time; of unprecedented looking away.
—Donna Haraway[1]

Introduction

To some extent we are all blind and no doubt will remain so.
—H. D. Lasswell[2]

We have described many types of challenges that the Anthropocene proposition presents—from super typhoons to extreme heat, from multilateral agreements to unilateral ocean fertilization, from colonial legacy to water infrastructure. These are among the many examples that in recent years have provided us with opportunities to observe, respond to, and plan for unfamiliar events. We can, perhaps, imagine injustice, catastrophe, disaster—but not in the particular form presented by the Anthropocene. We know of our tendency to mistake skill at measuring disasters for ability to devise a response equal to the challenge. We are aware of our propensity to ignore the perplexing, the distressing, the threatening in the midst of other events competing for our attention—and the implications of doing so. The apocalyptic ending of the world so often implicated in the Anthropocene myth has happened again and again, but each time in a different guise, at a different pace, with different symbols and different myths. This new epoch does not lend itself to existing knowledge traditions to universally project, prepare, and respond to what is to come, be they within the frames of traditional knowledges, scientific modernism, or existing institutions.

The question that arises, then, is not whether we will need to transform social institutions for knowledge production, policymaking, and governance, but how to do so. We need new myths to imagine these alternatives. That is, our challenge is to populate the unimaginable changes to come with imaginative concepts, relationships, policies, technologies, and ways of governing.[3] Conversely, to imagine that we know the solutions based on the same concepts that created the problems is denial at best, hubris at worst.[4] The ability to detect variously defined anthropogenic layers in sedimentary strata, to map forest fires, predict cyclones, or project the future likelihood of drought does not directly correspond to the ability to determine appropriate goals and alternative pathways to reach them. To insist that because Enlightenment traditions are able to recognize problems, they are also most appropriate for finding solutions, is to react to the impulsive sense of urgency rather than to act on the outcomes that are sought. The realities of the last century speak to the precedence of ongoing global crises—though their precedence lies in the destruction of the oppressed, not in the nature of *this* destruction. Under unprecedented intensities of Anthropocene hazards, can we simultaneously admit the precedence of injustice? To do what is important, as well as what is urgent? Can the fact of coexistence in the more-than-human Anthropocene be recognized and be permitted to shape agency? If not, what is the alternative?

To offer a way forward, we first make the normative assumption that, where possible, people act in the common interest, by which we mean dignity for all. This may be interpreted as a provocation. From this standpoint, we examine the means of achieving dignity offered by some new myths and some old myths, including ecomodernism, neoliberalism, environmental justice, and Indigenous knowledge systems. Our purpose is to present these as alternatives that offer partial insights, to critique tendencies toward universality of any of them, and to argue for the innovation that arises from coexistence of the many ontological frames that are being explored. Coexistence itself is not a proposition, but an inextricably material condition. The challenge is how we navigate this coexistence. To persist according to the empty map of supposed decolonization,[5] to assume that ideological doctrines can be reconciled, to posit pristine wilderness without sacrifice is to deny and seek to erase coexistence. In this way, we postulate that governing the Anthropocene effectively will require "a space shot through by a multiplicity of disputes, critiques, [and] disagreements,[6] to ensure complexity is never sacrificed to argument. It *is* the argument.

All Seek Dignity

There is the story of the drunkard searching under a street lamp for his house key, which he had dropped some distance away. Asked why he didn't look where he had dropped it, he replied, "It's lighter here!"
—Abraham Kaplan[7]

Our common ground—shared across cultures, sectors, and knowledge traditions—is the demand for human dignity. This is recognized in the Universal Declaration of Human Rights, the "foundation of freedom, justice and peace in the world," under Article 1: "All human beings are born free and equal in dignity and rights. They are endowed with reason and conscience and should act towards one another in a spirit of brotherhood."[8] It is further crystallized by Article 30: "Nothing in this Declaration may be interpreted as implying for any State, group or person any right to engage in any activity or to perform any act aimed at the destruction of any of the rights and freedoms set forth herein."

Disdain for human dignity underlies conflicts from the personal to the geopolitical, while the aspiration for dignity forms the bedrock for successful interaction. But too often, the goal of dignity is displaced by a means for achieving it. For instance, the Universal Declaration of Human Rights has centered on the rights of the individual, unintentionally denying the rights to self-determination of subnational and international groups.[9] As we examine a selection of old and new myths for meeting the challenge of the Anthropocene, we recognize intent in each to achieve dignity, but we consider that each is one path among many, and each is dynamic and adaptable. We make this clear at the outset to this concluding chapter because it matters what stories we tell stories with,[10] what ideas we develop ideas from. With the pressing urgency of responding to climate-related hazards, we do not have the luxury of insisting that we all get in line behind one heroic and all-encompassing narrative of transformation. We wish to step into a deliberative, contested, political space in which each can recognize a common wish for dignity, in which we, as societies faced with unprecedented Anthropogenic risks, can intersect, interweave, debate, disagree, negotiate, reimagine, and find new myths to better navigate the fact of our coexistence.

In a polarized debate, the actors become archetypal heroes, victims, and villains, while the more complex protagonist loses ground, and it becomes easier to ascribe to opponents an antagonistic role. Particularly as the stakes become higher, the risks increase, and the urgency mounts, simpler stories are sought. Here we call for plurality and inclusion, for debating the content of policies rather than the identity politics of caricaturized others. All the following examples are means of exploring doctrine, formulae, and symbols of Anthropocene urgencies: not all of these are *right*; none of them is *just right*.

Ecomodernism and the Good Anthropocene

We affirm one long-standing environmental ideal, that humanity must shrink its impacts on the environment to make more room for nature, while we reject another, that human societies must harmonize with nature to avoid economic and ecological collapse.

—"An Ecomodernist Manifesto"[11]

This recently coined myth for a better world is born from the traditions of modernist thought. The ecomodernist doctrine of the Anthropocene draws a line from the ability of the scientific method to identify processes of environmental change to claiming the ability to control and shape them. The idea of piloting Spaceship Earth arose when modernism was at its peak, and the articulation of earth system processes was understood as the first step toward being able to "tweak the dials" of the global climate system. Although many of these early earth system scientists have rejected the idea of controlling the climate system for a range of reasons,[12] the myth of the good Anthropocene persists. For example, while stopping short of concrete policy proposals, E. O. Wilson's *Half-Earth* explores a world in which half the planet is put aside for conservation while the other half is allocated for human occupation and use. This doctrine, of course, is an explicit manifestation of the dualism that has characterized Western philosophy since at least the Enlightenment era. But this extreme solution is strongly motivated: decades of work on species conservation is culminating in a mass extinction event that, while not unprecedented, has not occurred during human history. Within the frame of nature-culture dualism, this solution springs forth as the goal: exclude humans from nature. Of course, we have not known a "natural" world since humans first spread across the continents. The ideas of unspoiled nature and terra nullius came with the Doctrine of Discovery, as settlers in the New World were ill-equipped to detect the omnipresent human signal in the carefully tended open woodlands of New England and New South Wales, in the forests of the Amazon and Papua New Guinea. Even as ecomodernists recommend that "our experience of transcendence in the outdoors should translate into the desire for all humans to benefit from the fruits of modernization and be able to experience similar transcendence,"[13] this transcendence in fact relies on continued care by the people who tended the landscapes of the past. Excluding people from nature across the New World has produced landscapes of impoverished biodiversity. But so too has unfettered occupation. Careful balance is incongruent with the dualist myth.

It is important to note that the ecomodernist approach acknowledges the problems raised by mobilizing a single myth to find a path through the transformative changes underway. Our view of the Anthropocene as a space of emergent coexistence is in line with the statement that "the politics of ecomodernism may come down to convening diverse views on what it means to be human in the Anthropocene."[14] The point at which we diverge with ecomodernism, however, is in the formulae that are predicated on the idea that "what it means to be human" is "not-nature." The ecomodernist formulae are underpinned by doctrine that the scientific method (i) can make special claims about knowledge, (ii) is sufficient for identifying both the problems and the solutions to challenges of the Anthropocene, and (iii) heralds a golden age of humanity on Earth. This creates a compelling theodicean[15] symbol of a "good Anthropocene." This raises a question, of course: What is good about this myth of the Anthropocene? As John Dewey observed, "The great problem concerning ends is to discriminate between those which are 'good' in a near-by and partial view, and those which are enduringly and inclusively good. The former are more obvious; the latter depend on the exercise of reflection and often can be discovered and sustained in thought only by reflection which is patient and thorough. Even so, it is notorious that things that are simply *judged* to be good are pallid and without power to move us compared with warmer and nearer goods which make a direct appeal to those impulses and desires that are already urgent."[16]

The transformations of earth systems, living systems, societies, and institutions implied by the ecomodernist doctrine cannot be adjudged "good" if they violate, for example, the criteria of the Universal Declaration of Human Rights. A global-scale implementation of decoupled human and natural spaces is problematic for an international human rights regime that supports freedom of movement and resists arbitrary detention and for an international order in which human dignity is fully realized for all peoples. Human suffering in this transformative moment matters, and the disregard for the dignity of people who would be moved from their land into cities to achieve the required intensification is troubling. Furthermore, the role of humans in global landscapes is so ingrained (except perhaps in Antarctica) that to remove humans completely may be akin to removing a keystone species, with unpredictable, cascading consequences for ecosystem structure and function.

Ecomodernism presents a powerful symbol of hope for many in the context of increasing Anthropocentric urgency. It represents a persuasive coherence of deep conservationism and technological optimism. Rather than reject the ecomodernist myth outright, the idea of coexistence would ask of those who share our misgivings to consider what opportunities the ecomodernist myth presents for exploring unimagined formulae. Innovations may be found in research on synthetic organic compounds as a human food source, or in a pragmatic focus on high-intensity energy sources. Ecomodernism has opened an important space for debate and discussion.

Environmental Justice and Difficult Conversations

The environmental justice movement seeks a fair distribution of benefits and burdens among populations. Since the 1990s, particularly in the United States, the movement and its scholarship have done much to make space for the disenfranchised and those disproportionately affected by industrial development and natural disaster. The field has highlighted the shortcomings of social and environmental impact assessment institutions since the National Environmental Policy Act of 1970 and has called for more equitable processes of emergency preparedness and response. This work has contributed to new policy and regulation in agriculture and urban planning, and elucidated important ideas such as chemical trespass and climate justice. Our purpose here is to consider what happens when efforts to shed light on the "shadow places of injustice"[17] are matched with deliberative efforts to understand the unjust, because therein lies the humanity of the seemingly profane other. This co-creation of deliberative political forums for conversations across the spectrums of disciplines, perspectives, and values is difficult to achieve. How might we better foster spaces of deliberation?

Some examples are appropriate at this juncture. At a Janus Forum lecture at Brown University in October 2013, a seemingly deliberative space was closed as we in the audience and those on the podium failed to listen carefully to the narrative of an energy industry actor. The lecture featured Bill McKibben of 350.org, who advocates divestment from coal; journalist and author Christian Parenti;[18] the former chief executive officer of Duke Energy, James Rogers;[19] and a student representative from Brown's coal-divestment campaign.[20] In Rogers's contributions, he portrayed the energy industry as a complex protagonist across the energy-production sector. He reflected on the 1970s during the oil embargo, when oil prices reached record highs and domestic production was decreasing in the United States. In response, President Nixon enacted a suite of bills, such as the Energy Supply and Environmental Coordination Act of 1974, which directed the Federal Energy Administration to support the use of coal for electricity generation where possible,[21] and the Energy Policy and Conservation Act of 1975, which made $750 million available for underground low-sulfur mines. Although Carter rolled back some of Nixon's energy reform acts through the 1978 National Energy Act, there were further coal-supporting bills passed in the late 1970s. For Duke Energy and other energy producers, this changing legislative landscape demanded considerable adaptation and innovation. Rogers made the point that as the government enacted, the energy sector responded—and it would do so again. The narrative of his copanelists and the audience (including author Siri Veland) discounted the significance of the observation that the coal industry is a subsidiary of the energy-production industry. Rogers stated explicitly that if government policy were enacted to target renewables, the energy sector would adapt.

We heard him, but we could not listen. It seems appropriate here to end with the quote that appears on the webpage of the Janus Forum lecture. The excerpt appears in a letter from Pierre-Joseph Proudhon to Karl Marx, from May 1846: "I applaud with all my heart your thought of bringing to light all opinions; let us give the world the example of a learned and far-sighted tolerance, but let us not, because we are the head of a movement, make ourselves the leaders of a new intolerance, let us not pose as the apostles of a new religion, even if it be the religion of logic, the religion of reason. Let us gather together and encourage all protests, let us brand all exclusiveness, all mysticism; let us never regard a question as exhausted, and when we have used our last argument, let us begin again, if necessary, with eloquence and irony."[22]

A second example concerns public health in Central Appalachia. The Clean Air Act Amendments of 1990 authorized new programs to permit and restrict sulfur emissions for the purposes of reducing acid rain. Other provisions included increased enforcement authority. The mining industry adapted to the new regulations by seeking sources of coal that were lower in sulfur. An unintended consequence of this was the incentive to engage in mountaintop removal mining: the coal reserves in the central Appalachians are of low sulfur content but situated in steep mountainous regions, often in multiple thin beds. These reserves had not been financially viable until the 1990 Clean Air Act Amendments increased the costs of using high sulfur coal. Mountaintop removal involves clear-cutting forests and often using explosives to expose coal reserves, with removed vegetation and excavated debris dumped in adjacent valleys. The important work of Rebecca Scott[23] and a host of other scholars has highlighted the ecological destruction caused by mountaintop-removal mining and the associated health impacts, including elevated mortality, in nearby Appalachian communities. Their stories are critical for highlighting the injustice embodied by the disregard for the well-being of workers, their families, and home communities. However, this scholarship offers few tools for Appalachian communities to find alternative, sustainable livelihoods. It is apparent in the political context of the United States in 2018 that these communities possess few alternative means to achieve dignity. In an adversarial democratic system, these means have proved challenging to identify, resulting in increased polarization and gridlock over time.

These two examples bring to light the importance of clarifying the potential for unintended trade-offs in addressing problems of environmental injustice. Compromise can be a challenging narrative in the context of inequity, but in fact "we are called to acknowledge that in the midst of all we cannot choose, we also make choices."[24] Judgments of appropriateness, validity, and equity are contestable, and politics are inevitable. Integration of multiple interests (that is, a win-win solution) is desirable, but more often compromise (a small lose-small lose solution) is necessary. These compromises may embody justice when participants have the resources to negotiate and are in a position to assess what is gained and what is lost. "It is difficult to compare gains in apples and losses in oranges, for example."[25] Importantly, trade-offs have to be assessed through space, through time, and, indeed, across species.[26] Herbert Simon coined the term *satisficing* to describe the search for this outcome: "Because real-world optimization ... is impossible, the real economic actor is a satisficer, a person who accepts 'good enough' alternatives, not because less is preferred to more but because there is no choice. Many economists ... have argued that the gap between satisfactory and best is of no great importance ... ; others, including myself, believe it does matter, and matters a great deal."[27] In the context of injustice, it does matter a great deal.

To make these kinds of difficult choices, Deborah Rose writes, is to write "a love story" of care "when all you love is being trashed."[28] She laments that "instead of the kiss of life, we humans too frequently offer a resounding no [that] ripples and reverberates across animals and trees, through photosynthesis and oxygen, even into the breath and into the heartbeat and rhythms of life itself." Our responsibility, then, is to go beyond shedding light on injustice, to offer alternative perspectives on the benefits of coexistence. In an effort to identify a mode of decision making that is explicit in this aspiration, the Elders[29] published a position statement entitled "Strengthening the United Nations" in 2015. This statement proposed that the right of veto in the United Nations Security Council only be exercised while "explaining, clearly and in public, what alternative course of action they propose, as a credible and efficient way to protect the populations in question." Democracy gives us the tools to shape deliberative and propositional processes.[30]

Indigenous Navigation

Indigenous and traditional cosmological myths enact myriad frames for negotiating the Anthropocene and continue to provide a frame of reference despite the wide-scale impacts of colonization.[31] Although the doctrines are stable, Indigenous formulae and symbols continue to evolve along with their changing context. In some regions, Indigenous governance systems are reasserting their commitment to human dignity in global forums, such as through the Cochabamba Peoples' Agreement and the Declaration on the Rights of Mother Earth. Sustainable management of landscapes goes hand in hand with self-determination in cases such as that of the Menominee of the Great Lakes Region or the Wampis of Peru. The recent recognition of legal personhood of the Whanganui River in New Zealand as an ancestor of the Whanganui iwi[32] radically reframes water governance. These achievements broaden the solution spaces for global environmental crises by mobilizing a range of concepts, time scales, and actors that offer alternatives within and between Indigenous communities and across broader global-knowledge networks.[33]

The proposition is not to take on Indigenous formulae and symbols in an act of "benign" appropriation. Indigenous communities worldwide suffer under a constant state of emergency due to the burden on health, culture, education, and community that is the colonial legacy. Furthermore, the diversity of Indigenous doctrines worldwide means that trade-offs between sustainability and other values will differ from one nation to another. For example, the 2,250-megawatt coal-fired Navajo Generating Station, built outside Page, Arizona, to provide water and electricity to consumers and an economic resource for the Navajo Nation, is likely to close in the next few years, due to the low cost of natural gas rather than to its impacts on local air quality and global climate. In another example, Greenlanders, seeking a sustainable independence from Denmark, opted out of the Paris Agreement in order to continue the economic development afforded by oil, gas, and mineral reserves.

The proposition is that the diversity of doctrines represented in Indigenous cosmological myths is not a fictional approximation for an objective earth that is the realm of Enlightenment knowing. Indeed, "what could at first glance seem like a far-fetched ancestral tradition actually showcases Indigenous peoples' ability to make useful and constructive observations on climate forecasting."[34] This decentering of science and technology in managing risks opens spaces for working within myths that offer different explanations for the place of humans in the world and the ways in which we might relate to rapid change. The works of Doreen Massey, Richie Howitt, Debbie Rose, Tim Ingold, Karen Barad, Donna Haraway, Bruno Latour, Jane Bennet, and Sarah Whatmore have done much to further these possibilities.

Managing Risk

Since the efforts of Henri Dunant to establish the International Federation of the Red Cross (IFRC), humanitarian response to disasters has involved training people in basic first-aid techniques, organizing response institutions, and supplying affected communities with emergency medicines, food, and shelter. Nations, corporations, and individuals support a growing cohort of humanitarian organizations, from the United Nations Office for Disaster Risk Reduction, the IFRC, Save the Children, and Doctors without Borders, to the smaller charities and even individual volunteers focused on direct aid to affected individuals. Indeed, that "tragedy is seductive," explains the poetics of disaster; "after all, it is beautiful."[35] As Levinas wrote, it is in the face of the other that the ability to understand and act emerges; this is what continues to encourage humanitarian aid institutions and the donations and volunteerism that support them. The case studies throughout this volume have sought to enable "a distinctive kind of empathy"[36] by situating the reader in a position of considering the experience of another. Studying "the structure of experience by exploring the kinds of change that it is susceptible to"[37] can provide insight into the sources and expressions of urgency in the face of emergencies.

The demands of the Anthropocene have seen exceptional events become chronic; for example, for every steady improvement in food security in Ethiopia and the Central African Republic, a new famine exacerbated by drought and conflict emerges, with concomitant demands for disaster aid. Inevitably, recurrent and urgent disasters vie with building resilience over the long term for limited time, attention, and resources. There is less seduction in the chronic disaster, and even less in the disaster that, through good planning, never was.[38] As a result, the calls for donations for chronic disasters as well disaster risk reduction make less urgent narratives. Nevertheless, even here the space is opening for new approaches. The Sendai Framework adopted in 2015 commits to focusing efforts on disaster risk reduction rather than only on disaster response.[39] The significance of this shift to long-term and contextual vulnerabilities is likely to improve our ability to maintain human dignity through extreme events. The next steps must acknowledge the procedural vulnerabilities inherent in the ways in which we approach the risk and its political drivers.[40]

Governing *Homo oeconomicus*

Neoliberalism has become a particularly problematic identification, particularly because its doctrines are fluid, and its characterization takes at least three forms. To some liberals in the United States and the United Kingdom, neoliberalism describes the center-ward shift of their mainstream parties that started four or more decades ago. To economists and journalists, the term describes a form of globalized market fundamentalism most often symbolized as the *Washington Consensus*, although this term as originally proposed embodied a narrower set of prescriptions for a specific vision of Latin American reform.[41] This evolving symbol has some foundation in the individualist thinking of Ayn Rand. Since *Atlas Shrugged*, Ayn Rand's philosophy has offered an ideological platform that promises celebration of strength, independence, and self-sufficiency. "Political freedom" was to Rand "an individual's freedom from physical compulsion, coercion or interference by the government."[42] Rand's philosophy was in many ways a response to the rise of totalitarian forms of government on the left and right—couched within a worldview that sees the government not as an arena but as an actor, and within dualist rationality that begs for the opposite as cure: no government at all. Surreptitiously, this formula reproduces the coercion it seeks to avert by imposing a new set of explicitly undemocratic structures.

The third characterization of the term neoliberalism concerns evolution from *Homo sapiens* to *Homo oeconomicus*[43]—in which all aspects of human interaction are increasingly being viewed through a transactional lens. This thread has stimulated debate across the discipline of economics on the linkages between environmental change and economic policy. Nevertheless, the possibility this episteme offers of empirically identifying the relationships between policy alternatives and the shape of the marginal damage and abatement cost functions[44] provides a useful space for promoting discourse on environmental policies. The economic lens further permits comparative studies among nations, on the impacts of extreme weather events such as windstorms and heatwaves, food and fiber productivity, human health, and the likelihood of conflict.[45] There is, of course, limited capacity for these approaches to assess the economic damages of unprecedented conditions, cross-border effects, or nonlinear responses.[46] For example, we would argue that the future is irrationally discounted[47] on the rationale that economic growth cannot be reconciled with the breadth and rate of

impacts as global average warming rises toward 4°C and beyond. Nevertheless, this characterization has provided a focus for the limited time and
attention of policymakers. As such, it serves to make an uncertain future
concrete.

Totalitarianism and China

Apart from some environmental interests, there are in fact few advocacy
organizations across the world today proposing a totalitarian model of
communism as a preferred system of governance of the future. Undeniably, there are few remaining states that claim to be dictatorships of the
proletariat: China, Cuba, Laos, Vietnam, and North Korea. Several other
states have or have had communist party rule in a multiparty system, such
as Nepal. One way in which these states have argued for their continuing
relevance has been in the model of redistribution, which even in inequitable manifestations of communism has depressed the upper tail of the
ecological footprint distribution.[48] Is it possible to achieve an adequate level
of human development at the lower end of the ecological footprint distribution under this kind of governance? It has been suggested that the only
nation that achieved this combination of high Human Development Index
(HDI) and low environmental footprint was Cuba.[49] And indeed, this could
be argued in 2003, when Cuba's HDI was 0.7 and its ecological footprint
was 96 percent of the available biocapacity.

Using the same data,[50] figure 5.1 shows this comparison for 2013, demon-
strating that as nations improve their HDI score, their per capita ecological
footprints typically rise. The "golden square" of sustainability was defined
by Daniel Moran and colleagues as an HDI over 0.8 and an ecological footprint that is less than the global average biocapacity. The ratio between the
per capita footprint and the biocapacity can be thought of as the "number
of earths" required for current consumption patterns. No countries reside
in this golden square at present, but five countries, including Cuba, are
close. These countries are characterized by small populations and small
geographic areas. They have different governance and different cultures,
different industries and different histories. What is clear is that a dictatorship of the proletariat is not a demonstrated path to sustainability by this
measure. Nevertheless, this measure, characterized as necessary but not sufficient to monitor pathways toward sustainability, was another step, similar
to the Yale Environmental Performance Index, toward the quantification of

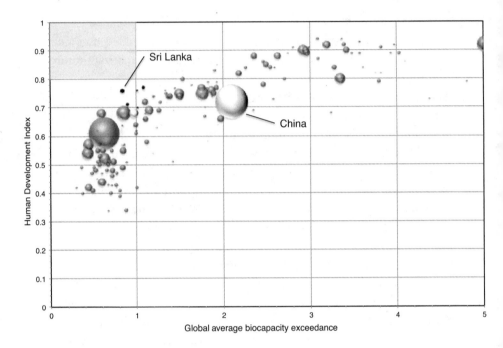

Figure 5.1
Graph showing the relationship between the Human Development Index and the fraction by which a nation exceeds the global average biocapacity per capita for 2013. The light gray box is the criterion for sustainability from Moran et al., "Sustainable Development": an HDI above 0.8 with an ecological footprint smaller than global average biocapacity. The bubble size corresponds to population. The communist countries are shown in white, apart from Cuba. The black bubbles indicate countries that meet the less strict criterion of HDI above 0.7 with biocapacity exceedance no more than 10 percent: Sri Lanka, Dominican Republic, Georgia, Moldova, and Cuba. Six countries are missing from the graph due to very high per capita biocapacity exceedance (Luxembourg, Qatar, Australia, Trinidad and Tobago, Canada, and the United States, in order from highest to lowest exceedance). North Korea is missing from the graph due to lack of data.

a more holistic type of progress than greenhouse gas emissions alone. Such approaches have spurred a deeper enquiry into the data needs (for both availability and reliability) engendered by this type of approach,[51] as well as the adequacy of the measures themselves.[52]

What about China, specifically? In 2013, China exceeded global average biocapacity per person by more than 100 percent and is still aspiring to an HDI of 0.8. On this measure, China offers few clear models. However, on the question of greenhouse gas emissions alone there is more potential. China's population of 1.35 billion people contribute just twice the carbon dioxide emissions of the 321 million inhabitants of the second-most-polluting nation, the United States. In 2017, the World Wildlife Fund published the following statement on its website: "In the coming decades China is predicted to become the world's largest economy, with pressure on the natural environment expected to grow. At the same time, China is becoming a major investor overseas and a global leader in renewable energy and clean technology—a huge opportunity for the world. The battle for the future of our planet will rely heavily on the path that China will take."[53] Some optimism might be founded upon the decoupling of energy and GDP growth in the 2005–2015 decade, which supported China's commitments in the Paris Agreement. China's nationally determined contributions to the global accord include a commitment to peak total national carbon dioxide emissions by 2030 and to increase the forest stock by 4.5 billion cubic meters. In parallel with these international commitments, China has released a variety of national energy plans, from the Strategic Energy Action Plan (2014–2020) to the thirteenth Five-Year Plan (2016–2020). These plans have called variously for an energy consumption cap of 4.8 GTCe[54] and 5 GTCe, whereas the actual emissions in 2015, according to official Chinese figures, was 4.3 GTCe. The reduction in emissions between 2014 and 2015, the first ever recorded for China, "was achieved through substantial increases in nuclear energy (29%), hydropower (5%) and other renewable energy such as wind and solar energy (21%).[55] In part, the motivation for this engagement with a national energy policy that aligns with the international climate change regime has come from dire air-quality problems in the major cities. Particulate matter pollution was linked to 1.23 million premature deaths in 2010, with associated damages estimated at 9.7 to 13.2 percent of China's GDP.[56] The ambitious emissions reduction target is also linked to an economic downturn from 2015 to 2016, with a resulting overcapacity in energy generation.[57] As discussed in chapter 4, hopes for a shift in doctrines in the Chinese government concerning Anthropocene responses have to be tempered by the many interests being served at every level of this complex government. As a result, rather than suggesting that centralized command and control has a proven track record in responding in the Anthropocene, this analysis opens the space for exploring "no regrets" strategies—that is, mitigation and adaptation policies that serve multiple interests and outcomes.[58] These strategies provide political cover through approaches such as building resilience to the risks of weather disasters and increasing efficiency through energy- and water-efficient infrastructure. The lesson of China in fact is less about centralized decisions than it is about integrating multiple interests.

Governing Intolerance

The realignment of democratic political ideologies over the last decade is a global phenomenon. The splintered variety of identifications, including nationalist populism of the left and right, conservative and progressive flavors of neoliberalism, civil libertarianism, globalism, managed democracy, democratic socialism, cognitive capitalism, and more, have coalesced into an identity-based conservative/liberal divide, whether social or fiscal. A particular facet of this evolving realignment is the apparent challenge of accommodating intolerance for alternative viewpoints within doctrines of tolerance. Indeed, Wendy Brown suggests, a universal doctrine of political tolerance does not exist, but rather there are "specific contexts, provocations and political formulations of tolerance, and tolerance is always nestled within larger political orders of power and meaning."[59] For instance, the use of tolerance and its repressive potential can be invoked as a symbol for the banning of headscarves in some European countries, the tacit acceptance of Southern slavery by antebellum Northern Americans, and the removal of light-skinned children from their Indigenous parents in Australia and Canada. The symbol is confounded at present by the emergence of a trade-off between liberty and security in response to international terrorist threats. Political tolerance as doctrine is demanding, yet tolerance is "an essential prerequisite to justice and democracy, an ethos and practice of coexistence required before it is even possible to inaugurate the project of sharing power and rule, settling law, and respecting all human beings as ends."[60] Thus, as increasingly polarized political factions grapple with the Anthropocene transformation, how will urgency shape the space for tolerance?

Transformation

"Do you know the way to Tipperary?"
"Yes, but I wouldn't start from here."
—Irish joke

A version of the old joke reproduced here might come up in any place the unwary visitor might encounter a local in the right mood. It might also come from Rebecca Solnit's comic Angel of Alternate History responding to a fervent advocate of communism, neoliberalism, ecomodernism, or environmentalism finding themselves too far from their utopia. Here is where we find ourselves, and our starting point thus cannot be otherwise. The provocation, then, is what transformative change might look like in an Anthropocene in which we struggle to envision a myth of a sustainable world and we cannot agree on a way to achieve it. Furthermore, we have argued, these challenges are linked: feeling agency to act on transformative potential requires secure narratives of the past, present, and future.

The *brutal fact* or the *abyss* of ontological insecurity results when the three pillars—the state, science, and the economy—fail to provide security.[61] This insecurity, we have argued, engenders urgent responses to the Anthropocene—populist nationalism, hyperseparated human and natural spaces, totalitarian chic, disaster colonialism,[62] and more. In each new myth, the idea of revolution is central. Once the old has been overthrown, the new, better world will rise from the ashes. Such fundamentalist notions work within a rationality in which there can only be one world, one solution, one doctrine.[63] Once all hindrances to that doctrine are overcome, formulae will emerge, and peace and prosperity will ensue.

And, yet, we know that "history is not an army," marching forward. "It is a crab scuttling sideways, a drip of soft water wearing away stone, an earthquake breaking centuries of tension."[64] Finding ways to nudge the crab, so to speak, in the general direction of ecological sustainability, to softly but implacably insist on human dignity, to break the centuries of tension of ingrained systems of injustice, requires a different kind of thinking. To illustrate such thinking, we take one more dip into history, into the guerilla

tactics of ancient Rome and their indirect influence on twentieth-century
European struggles against fundamentalism.

Quintus Fabius Maximus Verrucosus, Cuncator

An observer in 1932 might be forgiven for predicting that Sweden would
succumb to civil war before Spain.[65] Both nations teetered on the brink of
civil war as internal divisions were fueled by increasingly polarized Marxist-
Leninist and Fascist doctrines. The erasure of the middle ground, as now,
became a tactic. For example, German communists targeted left-wing social
democrats as a strategic enemy to their revolution in 1929 and opened the
door for similar moves across Europe.[66] This conflict between left and far
left "facilitated Franco's path to power"[67] in Spain. In 1937, when George
Orwell arrived to fight the fascist rule of Franco, he came as part of the
Worker's Party of Marxist Unification movement, a non-Stalinist militia. As
a social democrat, he wished to fight fascist rule, but found himself also targeted by pro-Stalinists. Orwell wished to publish reflections on his experience, but was denied by editors who worried his writings would weaken the
antifascist movement. As result, he was inspired to write *1984*.[68] In Spain,
for the expedience of tactical advantage, the Marxist movement acted to
galvanize the polarized factions of the far left and right, erasing the middle
ground.

Conversely, Sweden averted civil war in the late 1930s, albeit with the
ethical gray zones its subsequent neutrality presents. Swedish social democrats led by four-time prime minister Per Albin Hansson had appropriated the Fascist symbol of the *people's home*. Around the same time, the
social partnership between capital and labor ("social corporatism") led to
the Saltsjöbaden Agreement (Saltsjöbadsavtalet). By uniting ideas of home,
nationalism, and socialism, Hansson invoked a symbol in which "the caring home supports no privilege or discrimination ... where we do not know
slave owners or subordinates, where we can feel at home and comfortable
with 'one's own.'" The result was to hijack the Nazi understanding of the
people's home, preventing an extremist ideology from the left or the right
from taking hold.

This approach to reform had its roots in the Fabian Society, from which
the London School of Economics can claim its origins. This movement
has since come to symbolize the political left—but like Orwell, the Fabian
Society emerges as a more complex protagonist. The society owes its name

to General Quintus Fabius Maximus Verrucosus. His agnomen, Cunctator, signifies someone who tested the patience of his adversaries. His tactics against Hannibal during the Second Punic War avoided the traditional pitched battles in formation and instead used skilled and specialized bands of soldiers to target the vital supply lines of the enemy. In this way, Fabius prevailed against an enemy of far greater numbers. To his contemporaries, his tactics made him a "lingerer," but he won respect once his effectiveness became apparent.

The London society that took on his ideas two millennia later sought to work against the prevailing view of its time that the inhabitants of poor-houses were there because of their own moral misconduct. The society suggested that poverty had structural origins, and its members thought that by targeting the root causes of the condition, they might enable a more productive population. Working against the political currents of their time, they took on the tactics of Fabius to target key issues with indirect and specialized tools, such as a campaign to introduce sewage systems. Their Fellowship of the New Life became an alternative to the Marxist movement. They published the Minority Report of the Poor Law Commission, which became the foundational text for the Swedish model. Their goal was to make socialism moderate and the middle ground respectable. Their tactic was silver buckshot in place of the silver bullet.[69]

Similarly, the Swedish model successfully reclaimed the middle just as it was being erased elsewhere on the continent. This middle ground allowed interests to be integrated where possible and balanced where necessary to achieve outcomes that satisficed. Avoiding the worst case makes for an unheroic narrative: "Most environmental victories look like nothing happened; the land wasn't annexed by the army, the mine didn't open, the road didn't get cut through, the factory didn't spew effluents that didn't give asthma to the children who didn't wheeze and panic and stay indoors on beautiful days."[70] In this way, we may invoke the symbol of the Angel of Alternate History, whose "face is turned toward the futures that never come to pass."[71]

Reclaiming the Commons

The idea that the problems of the Anthropocene were amenable to silver buckshot was initially rejected. Garrett Hardin was famous for his striking symbol—tragedy—of his postulate that the degradation of common-pool resources was inevitable, unless privatization or government regulation was imposed.[72] Later reviews of this postulate suggested that though the tragedy of the commons was vivid, it was incomplete.[73] Nevertheless, the symbol continued to be an important tool for understanding the challenges of the Anthropocene. The fact that the atmosphere is a commons, for example, became a problem to be solved. The traditional means of regulation or privatization stimulated proposals such as extending tradeable and retireable permits to all limited natural resources. Others suggested that technological advances such as cheap renewable energy or carbon dioxide sequestration could avoid the commons problem altogether.[74] In many ways, the solution to the tragedy of the commons became not a means to govern the Anthropocene, but an end in itself.

By 2003, Thomas Dietz, Elinor Ostrom, and Paul Stern observed that Hardin had "missed the point that many social groups, including the herders on the commons that provided the metaphor for his analysis, have struggled successfully against threats of resource degradation by developing and maintaining self-governing institutions. Although these institutions have not always succeeded, neither have Hardin's preferred alternatives of private or state ownership."[75] Furthermore, the concept of the commons developed by Ostrom was differentiated from Hardin's property rights system of open access in which there is no social rivalry or interaction, no norms or values, and therefore no opportunity for the formation of rules (table 5.1). Hardin's tragedy of the commons is thus more correctly a tragedy of open access. Ostrom argues that so long as people can interact, even where they cannot exclude each other, and where the actions of each impact the ability of others to use a good, a set of rules for interaction can emerge—that is, an institution specialized to that case. Nevertheless, *tragedy of the commons* remains a tenacious phrase that continues to direct expectations for governance over shared resources.

Table 5.1
Property regimes dependent on excludability and rivalry

	Excludable	Not excludable
Rivalrous	Private property	Common pool
Nonrivalrous	Club goods	Open access

Source: Based on Ostrom et al., *Future of the Commons.*

The institutions that develop in common property regimes are based on the development and negotiation of shared concepts, coming from a set of symbols that then can "be used to analyze a wider diversity of problems."[76] Commons thinking, then, emerges as a foundation for enabling the transformation of institutions in the Anthropocene, encouraging negotiation. It is a means of elucidating productive tensions among diverse myths. Indeed, difficulties in common-pool management emerge not from incomplete knowledge or irrational beliefs, but from a rationality that is necessarily bounded.[77] Within this behavioral model, "one doesn't have to make choices that are infinitely deep in time, that encompass the whole range of human values, and in which each problem is interconnected with all the other problems in the world."[78] Rather, "persons are intendedly rational but only limitedly so," within the boundaries of the problem at hand and circumscribed by their own myths.[79] In many cases, decisions do not appear to be even approximately rational with respect to the myths of others.[80] As a result, the assumption that good decisions about natural resources emerge from axiomatic choice theory based on perfect information and utility maximization is ill-founded.[81] Instead, relational approaches that support self-organizing managers of the commons at a range of institutional levels have emerged in various ways in the manner of silver buckshot.

In this way, Ostrom's socioecological theories and observations were emergent from but also transformative of a myth that problematized the commons. This is a position, then, that is propositional:[82] that is, it is both "critical and constructive."[83] As a result, commons thinking supports the understanding of the ways in which the many myths of the Anthropocene do not only coexist with, but can contribute to, for example,

• the faith in human ingenuity and the hope for the future of ecomodernism,
• the difficult and painful trade-offs illuminated by environmental justice,
• the contextual and relational philosophies of Indigenous myths,
• the focus on resilience building of the disaster and risk community,
• the quantitative analysis of *Homo oeconomicus*, and
• the integration of multiple interests of the Chinese.

As the tolerance that symbolizes democracies is put under strain, the transformative potential of commons thinking can turn a tragedy into a benefit. Our proposition is that commons thinking encourages the discussions required to support more transparent, inclusive, and pluralist approaches to our Anthropocene. This is the logic of the included middle.[84]

Urgency in the Anthropocene

"Now if you'll just tell me where you're going, I can take you there."
"I'm going to find Alberto."
"Is Alberto another Eleutherodactylus portoricenis?"
"No. He is a poet."
"Where is he?"
Pepe looked at him in surprise. "I don't know."
It was the boy's turn to think for a moment before answering. Then he said in his cheerful way, "Well, the thing to do is to start out, isn't it?"
"Oh, yes," Pepe exclaimed.
He was glad to find that the boy was so sensible.
—Doris Troutman Plenn[85]

In this book, we have argued that the Anthropocene is one of innumerable myths that human beings use to explain their world. It is a myth that coexists with many others—myths of democracy, creation, sustainable development, the causes of typhoons, and the rationality of the market. As we have reiterated, a myth is a schema that helps us understand causation in the world, not a story that is either false or factual in any empirical sense. Most critically, these myths constrain our ability to see the present, to lay courses forward, and to imagine alternate futures. In the face of the Anthropocene, we see this as a coupled problem of phenomenon and discourse.

We know myths primarily through their symbols, such that shared symbols can give the impression of shared myth, whereas doctrines and formulae can turn out to be fundamentally different. This can be useful, as when the Swedish government appropriated the fascist symbol of the people's home, or problematic, as when Russ George annexed the concern for ocean acidification to justify ocean fertilization. The symbol of humans as wholly reliant on the integrity of the environment can take us on a path toward policies of separating human settlement and modes of production from nature in order to protect it. The same symbol can lead us to value intimate synchrony within locally evolving urban and rural production systems. As a result, powerful symbols of future aspirations, such as the total eradication of poverty or a zero-carbon economy, can paradoxically lead to

policy paralysis as stakeholders talk past each other or accuse one another
of misappropriation.

These concerns take on an urgent cast in the particular context of the
Anthropocene, a myth that promises to take us outside of our experience.
We have used the lessons of natural philosophy and human history throughout this book to shine a light on many aspects of the human-environment
relationship. Our time stands out as one of struggle not only to understand
and navigate social relations, but also to understand and navigate our relationships with earth systems. No epoch mirrors another, and if there are
lessons from history, we need to apply them to a new set of social relations,
economic conditions, and environmental crises. For this reason, urgency in
the Anthropocene is more than emergency, the response to unimaginable
material extremes; it is a case of ontological crisis. Geological strata do not
speak for themselves or for us. The urgency of the Anthropocene comes as
we respond to centuries of ongoing catastrophes while also narrating future
cataclysms: we are not in a calm time planning for a violent future, but in
a violent present, planning for an unshaped future.

Certainly, the current regimes are insufficient. The latest international
agreement will not forever remove our destructive potentialities: "the too-
big players in the too-big stories of capitalism and the Anthropos, both of
which invite odd apocalyptic panics and even odder disengaged denun-
ciations rather than attentive practices of thought, love, rage, and care."[86]
Democracy in and of itself, consensual, adversarial, or deliberative, is not
sufficient. The election of populist heads of state in response to chronic or
acute disasters, whether in the United States rustbelt or in the aftermath of
Typhoon Haiyan, eventuate in the context of ontological insecurities. In
the face of the unimaginable disasters of the future, the urgency to respond
could lead to further polarization and a retreat to totalitarianism, reproducing the injustices of the past. The role of the ideal is to envisage a better
world, but to act on principle, according to unquestioned myth or doctrine,
is the more dangerous path. The ideal is, by definition, abstract, and to act
on it ignores "not only consequences but also conditions," giving problems "unreal formulations which substitute artificial questions of principle
for the genuine issues of specific circumstance."[87] Whose knowledge traditions and social networks best trace out future pathways? What timescale of
thinking is needed? What innovations in governance and policy?

Although we may hope for a technological or political solution to any of the myriad challenges presented by the Anthropocene, it remains true that there is no remote, distant, or future wilderness capable of containing the externalities of our current choices; there never was.[88] All choices affect things that humans value. Human values and interests are multiple, changing and ubiquitous over spatial and temporal scales, challenging processes of governance. All choices are contingent. As such, "to some extent we are all blind and no doubt will remain so."[89] All choices are based on imperfect rationality, experienced from within a cosmological myth. Coexistence, if framed as a harmonious state of interaction among different peoples and their environments, might be understood as a propositional idea, one that we ought to pursue; one in which people ought to resolve these complexities and find consensus on a path forward. We put forward a proposition of coexistence that rejects such a monologue. Coexistence is a matter of fact that some dominant myths continue to ignore, marginalize, sideline, or render invisible. It is our urgent concern that as the Anthropocene urgency manifests, this precipitates responses precisely according to a singular framing of coexistence—one that prescribes responses according to one unifying narrative of earth systems—constraining the options we are able to imagine.[90]

The awkward spaces of coexistence[91] that constitute relations with Indigenous forms of governance, with marginalized minorities, with dynamic and increasingly unpredictable earth system processes, demand that we avoid treating "our values as beyond question, lest we be left without an answer."[92] To navigate these geographies of coexistence, myths must be approached as hypotheses to be tested and brought into context with other myths. To make the most of our limited rationality, not to mention our limited planet, engaging both constructively *and* antagonistically, by inviting and challenging debate[93] with multiple trains of thought and action, offers much to recommend it. As with the Fabian approach and the Swedish model, the success of any endeavor in working toward human dignity has not been achieved in the absence of conflict, protest, and political debate. On the contrary, the ability to reconsider and reform institutions depends on the capacity to deliberately argue the alternatives, rising above "naive ideas about which kinds of institutions are 'good' or 'bad.'"[94]

Thus, coexistence is not a matter of finding warm and comfortable consensus among bounded and defined actors. It is about grappling with the messy, fragile, and slippery,[95] where the middle ground is not an abstract compromise but the place that we inhabit; it is not a normative proposition but an observation of situatedness. This entails contending with the dynamic and unpredictable properties of the more-than-human; finding places of refuge in wind, water, sunlight, rock; "becoming with" earth systems.[96] This means pushing the boundaries into holistic perspectives on risk that consider in unison the intersections of political, natural, and anthropogenic hazards, climate change mitigation, global change adaptation, human development, and human dignity.

Moreover, no success in the face of the Anthropocene, be it a timely weather forecast, a thoughtful risk-reduction strategy, or a robust democratic model, is anything but conditional. Conducting many experiments at once, learning from success and failure, is an ongoing task. In this sense, as citizens, we should penalize only doing nothing. The result is not to seek to follow through on one line until it succeeds or fails definitely, but to explore several tentative paths, continuing to pursue a few that look most promising at a given moment and abandoning failures early and gracefully.[97] In a series of rural metaphors: don't put all the eggs in one basket, don't bet the farm, and harvest the experience.

Nevertheless, a normative commitment is unavoidable. Indeed, it is demanded of us. Nurturing the alternatives that avoid injustices requires an approach in which understanding the relationality of all social-justice issues comes to the fore. To stay with coexistence, to "stay with the trouble,"[98] our commitment is to nurturing connections, building relationships, co-constructing alternatives, reweaving the social and environmental fabric— to permit situated engagements among actors with a stake. This requires a robust form of coexistence. There are injustices, they emerge from unjust processes, and they require attention. Our commitment is to human dignity. This does not imply that we will arrive at some utopian future through a prescribed approach to utopian consensus. Rather, we do not shy away from the conflict, discomfort, or complexity that is inevitable in relational ways forward. The thing to do is to start out.

Notes

Preface

1. Frantz and Howitt, "Geography."

2. Machiavelli, *Discourses* I, 47, 47.

1 Whose Anthropocene?

1. Thoreau, *Walden*, 4.

2. Beck, "World at Risk."

3. Massey, *For Space*; Rose, *Wild Country*; Stoffle and Arnold, "Confronting the Angry Rock"; and Veland and Lynch, "Arctic Ice Edge Narratives."

4. Ginn, "Horses."

5. Haraway, *Staying with the Trouble*, 35.

6. Hajer, *Politics of Environmental Discourse.*

7. Beck, Giddens, and Lash, *Reflexive Modernization*, 3.

8. Because of his humble origins, this now-famous work was not acknowledged until the 1820s and 1830s.

9. Crutzen and Stoermer, "Anthropocene."

10. Crutzen, "Effects of Industrial and Agricultural Practices," 424.

11. Crutzen, "Anthropocene"; Zalasiewicz et al., "Stratigraphy of the Anthropocene"; and Waters et al., "Anthropocene Is Functionally and Stratigraphically Distinct."

12. Brondizio et al., "Re-conceptualizing the Anthropocene."

13. Steffen, Crutzen, and McNeill, "Anthropocene," 615: "Global change includes alterations in a wide range of global-scale phenomena land use and land cover,

urbanisation, globalisation, coastal ecosystems, atmospheric composition, riverine flow, nitrogen cycle, carbon cycle, physical climate, marine food chains, biological diversity, population, economy, resource use, energy, transport, communication, and so on. Interactions and linkages between the various changes listed above are also part of global change and are just as important as the individual changes themselves."

14. Steffen, Persson, et al., "Anthropocene"; and Waters et al., "Anthropocene Is Functionally and Stratigraphically Distinct."

15. Rittel and Webber, "Dilemmas in a General Theory."

16. Zalasiewicz et al., "Anthropocene," 838.

17. Veland and Lynch, "Scaling the Anthropocene."

18. Coates, *Between the World and Me.*

19. Waters et al., "Anthropocene Is Functionally and Stratigraphically Distinct," 2622.

20. Blay, "L'impossible Risque Zéro."

21. Vernadsky, *Scientific Thought,* 71.

22. Dewey, *Ethics.*

23. Chapin et al., "Ecosystem Stewardship."

24. Howitt, "Knowing/Doing."

25. Dalby, "Anthropocene Geopolitics," 104.

26. Schipper et al., "Linking Disaster Risk Reduction."

27. Brunner and Lynch, *Adaptive Governance,* 26.

28. United Nations International Strategy for Disaster Risk Reduction, "UNISDR Terminology."

29. Sillmann et al., "Climate Emergencies."

30. Kahan, "Cultural Cognition"; Kahan et al., "Culture and Identity-Protective Cognition"; Sjöberg, "Factors in Risk Perception"; and Slovic, "Perception of Risk."

31. Norgaard, "People Want to Protect Themselves."

32. Leiserowitz, "Climate Change Risk Perception"; and Kahan et al., "Polarizing Impact."

33. Veland et al., "Procedural Vulnerability"; Doohan, "Helping"; Bankoff, "Rendering the World Unsafe"; and Twigg, *Disaster Risk Reduction.*

34. Paris Agreement, "Adoption of the Paris Agreement," 1.

35. Rockström et al., "Planetary Boundaries."

36. See, for example, Campbell et al., "Responding to Health Impacts"; Barnosky et al., "Sixth Mass Extinction"; and Wake and Vredenburg, "Sixth Mass Extinction."

37. MEA, *Ecosystems and Human Well-Being*, fig. 4, p. 5.

38. See, for example, Wardle et al., "Terrestrial Ecosystem Responses."

39. Dirzo et al., "Defaunation in the Anthropocene."

40. Lippmann, *Public Opinion*, 236.

41. Dale Jamieson, professor of environmental studies, philosophy, and law at New York University and author of *Reason in a Dark Time*, quoted in Stehr, "Exceptional Circumstances."

42. Gilley, "Authoritarian Environmentalism," 288.

43. Beeson, "Coming of Environmental Authoritarianism"

44. Brunner and Ascher, "Science and Social Responsibility."

45. Dryzek, "Rhetoric in Democracy."

46. Lerner, Pool, and Lasswell, "Comparative Analysis," 733.

47. Dewey, *Ethics*; Lavine, "Interpretive Turn."

48. Whitehead, *Religion in the Making*.

49. Bohr, *Quantum Postulate*, 580.

50. Bohr, *Philosophical Writings*, 20.

51. Dalby, "Anthropocene Geopolitics," 111–112.

52. Gödel, "Über"; translated in van Heijenoort, *From Frege to Gödel*.

53. Foucault, *Archaeology of Knowledge*.

54. Hajer, *Politics of Environmental Discourse*.

55. In which it is found that subjective perception is a greater predictor of behavior than any objective risk assessment. See, for example, Kahan et al., "Polarizing Impact"; Kahan, "Culture and Identity-Protective Cognition"; and Sjöberg, "Factors in Risk Perception."

56. Mol, "Ontological Politics," 74, 75.

57. Ibid., 76.

58. Law, *After Method*.

59. Ibid.

60. Törzsök, "Nondualism."

61. O'Brien et al., "Interpretations of Vulnerability," 78.

62. Adger et al., "Cultural Dimensions," 113.

63. For two sides of this coin, see Dryzek, *Politics of the Earth*, and Mouffe, *Agnostics*: essentially at odds, but trying to solve the same problem.

64. Lasswell, Lerner, and Pool, *Comparative Study of Symbols*, 12.

65. Wilkinson, Clark, and Burch, *Other Voices*, 11.

66. For similar concepts, defined in more detail, see Thacker, *In the Dust*, 6.

67. Whitehead, *Function of Reason*, 31.

68. Ibid.

69. Ibid.

70. The following is discussed in Book III of Plato's *Republic*, written in 360 BCE. See, for example, http://www.gutenberg.org/ebooks/1497.

71. Mosca, Kahn, and Livingston, *Elementi Di Scienza Politica*, 71.

72. Lasswell, Lerner, and Pool, *Comparative Study of Symbols*, 1.

73. Lee, *Republic*.

74. Ibn Khaldūn's analysis of the Berber peoples, the famous *Muqaddimah*, has been misconstrued as racist, largely due to colonial-era translations of his work. See also Hannoum, "Translation and Colonial Imaginary."

75. See, for example, Lasswell and Kaplan, *Power and Society*.

76. Laski, *State*, 12.

77. See, for example, Combs, "Process Approach," 55.

78. Lippman, *Public Opinion*, 151.

79. Sapir, "Concept of Personality," 413.

80. Hutton, *Theory of the Earth*, 87–89.

81. See, for example, Gould, "Uniformitarianism." Gould's 1987 book, *Time's Arrow*, also provides an excellent summary of the doctrines of geology.

82. These problems include *falsificationism*, in which a consequence was validated but for the wrong reason, and *immunization*, in which a consequence that has been falsified is modified in such a way as to save its generating hypothesis.

83. Italian geologist Antonio Stoppani referred to an *Anthropozoic* era, considering humans to be a new physical force in the landscape.

84. Crutzen and Stoermer, "Anthropocene."

85. Hulme, "Conquering of Climate."

86. Note that this is not intended to be a definitive description of an abstract Indigenous Australian whole. Rather, by drawing on some key elements of Central and Northern Australian Indigenous myths, we aim both to assert that the theoretical framework we apply can shed light on some perspectives on Indigenous cultures and to give presence and space to cosmologies, complete with systems of governance, that coexist with those established within the discourses of such analyses.

87. Rose, "Indigenous Water Philosophy," 38.

88. Ibid., 40.

89. Bradley, *Yanyuwa Country*, xi.

90. Rose, "Indigenous Water Philosophy," 42.

91. For instance, Dreaming trails across Arnhem in Northern Australia follow an ice age geography into territories submerged more than ten thousand years ago. See, for example, Flood, *Archaeology of the Dreamtime*; Nunn and Reid, "Aboriginal Memories"; and Veland et al., "Procedural Vulnerability."

92. Quoted in Rose, "Indigenous Water Philosophy," 62.

93. Moisio et al., "Mapping the Political Geographies."

94. Shore, "Inventing."

95. From the Maastricht Treaty Title I: Common Provisions, Article F, and echoed in Title VI: Provisions on Cooperation in the Fields of Justice and Home Affairs, Article K.2. European Union, 1998–2017, http://eur-lex.europa.eu/.

96. Green, "Subsidiarity and European Union."

97. The Assembly of European Regions is an independent network of more than 270 regions in thirty-five countries and twenty-three interregional partner networks in Europe.

98. Millon-Delsol, *L'État subsidiaire*.

99. Ibid., 8; see also Carozza, "Subsidiarity as Structural Principle."

100. Spahn and Franz, "Consensus Democracy."

101. Follestad, "Rafting," 39.

102. Pålsson, "Principle of Subsidiarity," 6.

103. Whitehead, *Function of Reason*, 65–66.

104. Rogow and Lasswell, *Power, Corruption, and Rectitude*, 2.

105. Veland and Lynch, "Scaling the Anthropocene," 4.

106. Elvin, "Some Reflections."

107. Ibid.

108. Berndt and Berndt, *Arnhem Land*; Berndt and Berndt, *First Australians*; Berndt, *World of First Australians*; Verran, "Doing 'the Dreaming'"; and Rose, *Wild Country*.

109. Rigby, "Writing after Nature." See also Castree et al., "Changing the Intellectual Climate."

110. Rose, *Nourishing Terrains*, 41 (emphasis added). See also Rose, "Land Rights."

111. Rose, *Wild Country*.

112. Rose, *Nourishing Terrains*, x.

113. Bawaka Country et al., "Co-becoming Bawaka," 30.

114. Tedlock, *Popul Vuh*.

115. Beach et al., "Ancient Maya Impacts."

116. Ford and Nigh, "Origins of the Maya Forest Garden."

117. Beach et al., "Ancient Maya Impacts," x.

118. Pritchard, *Ancient Near East*.

119. Rigby, "Writing after Nature."

120. Eisenberg, *Ecology of Eden*, 124.

121. Ibid., 121.

122. Pritchard, *Ancient Near East*, 104–106.

123. Xenophon, "Memorabilia and Oeconomicus."

124. Wicksteed and Cornford, *Aristotle*; quoted in Kate Rigby, "Writing after Nature."

125. Geisinger, "Uncovering the Myth."

126. Known to the French-speaking world as the Siècle des Lumières, and to the German-speaking world as the Aufklärung, the Age of Enlightenment is dated variously as beginning between 1620 and 1715 and ending perhaps around 1800 or so. But this highly contested era reverberates through to the present day with its influence on science, politics, culture, and rationalism. It certainly contained the seeds of what is now termed the Late Modern Era, considered to have commenced with the Industrial Revolution. Like the Anthropocene, its boundaries are fuzzy and context-dependent.

127. From Merchant, *Death of Nature*, 69.

128. French mathematician credited with the invention of the probability calculus (1623–1662).

129. Foucault, *Birth of Biopolitics*; and Beck, "World at Risk."

130. Scott, *Seeing Like a State*, 3–4.

131. Scott, *Seeing Like a State*.

132. Robertson, *Future Work*, 92 (quoting John Locke, *Second Treatise of Government* [1690]). Marx held the same view and "regarded uncultivated land ... as 'not being of value' because no human labor has been incorporated in it" (ibid., 94).

133. Comte and Littré, *Principles De Philosophie Positive*, 32.

134. See, for example, de Groot, Wilson, and Boumans, "Typology."

135. Rigby, *Topographies of the Sacred*.

136. Geisinger, "Uncovering the Myth."

137. Merkle, "Scientific Management." Of course, the term *scientific management* is subject to various interpretations as it continues to evolve. See also Scott, *Seeing Like a State*; and Saul, *Voltaire's Bastards*.

138. Brunner, *Adaptive Governance*, 2. For more on scientific management, see also Brunner, *Finding Common Ground*.

139. Brand and Fischer, "Overcoming the Technophilia/Technophobia Split," 239.

140. Fleming, "Pathological History."

141. Brand and Fischer, "Overcoming the Technophilia/Technophobia Split."

2   Urgency Manifest

1. Associated Press, "Flaws Seen." Zhang Qiang, an expert on disaster mitigation at Beijing Normal University's Institute for Social Development and Public Policy, is quoted in the article.

2. Lippman, *Public Opinion*, 25.

3. Recall from chapter 1 that there is no implication that this myth is necessarily false.

4. Dunant, *Memory of Solferino*.

5. Ibid., xx.

6. Ibid., 51.

7. Ibid., 53.

8. Ibid., 62.

9. The International Federation of Red Cross and Red Crescent Societies, "Our Vision and Mission."

10. Cashman and Cronin, "Welcoming a Monster"; Howitt, Havnen, and Veland, "Natural and Unnatural Disasters"; de Jong, et al., "Process, Practice and Priorities"; and Fassin and Pandolfi, *Contemporary States of Emergency*.

11. The International Federation of Red Cross and Red Crescent Societies, "History."

12. Libæk, "Red Cross"; Libæk wrote this account, which appeared on the official website of the Nobel Prize, in 2003.

13. See Fassin and Pandolfi, *Contemporary States of Emergency*.

14. See chapter 3; see also Cashman and Cronin, "Welcoming a Monster"; Németh and Cronin, "Volcanic Structures"; Howitt, Havnen, and Veland, "Natural and Unnatural Disasters"; Veland et al., "Procedural Vulnerability"; Howitt et al., "Intercultural Capacity Deficits"; Fassin and Pandolfi, *Contemporary States of Emergency*; Coombes, Johnson, and Howitt, "Indigenous Geographies II"; Bankoff, Frerks, and Hilhorst, *Mapping Vulnerability*; Bankoff, "Rendering the World Unsafe"; and Doohan, "Helping."

15. Hewitt, "Power of Development."

16. Kauffman, "Death Rides the Forest."

17. Consider, for example, Stephens and Ruth, "Federal Forest-Fire Policy." The mechanisms that link fire, fuel, and climate change, however, are still actively debated in the scientific literature, as exemplified by contributions such as Littell et al., "Climate and Wildfire Area."

18. Steelman and McCaffrey, "Flexible Fire Management."

19. For instance, the Grain Storage and Marketing Project in Ethiopia—described in World Bank, "Project Completion Report"—aimed to "support the establishment of an orderly grain marketing and input distribution system," for which "the Government's agenda was quite different from the Bank's." "The Government's policy of socializing the grain trade and the emphasis on consumer interests conflicted with the principles established at appraisal" (iv–v). According to the neoliberal market doctrine, grain stores keep food prices low, and are therefore a hindrance to a healthy economy. As result, most nations do not keep stores "for a rainy day"—nor for a drought-stricken day.

20. See, for example, Levi-Strauss, *The Savage Mind*, for an early example of this articulation in Western thinking of traditional practices as effective adaptation.

21. World Bank, "Project Completion Report."

22. See also Benjaminsen, "Supply-Induced Scarcity," for a critique of the desertification discourse, where he shows that the Sahel region has been greening since the 1980s and that the conflicts some would ascribe to climate change are more accurately ascribed to policies that prevent pastoralists from accessing pastures.

23. Ibid.

24. Giddens, *Constitution of Society*.

25. Stoffle, Arnold, and Van Vlack, "Facing the Unimaginable," 13, referencing Giddens, *Consequences of Modernity*. See also Beck, *Risk Society*; and, with regard to climate change, Veland and Lynch, "Arctic Ice Edge Narratives."

26. Barnett, Dessai, and Jones, *Vulnerability to Climate Variability*.

27. David Jones was quoted in Macey, "This Drought."

28. Consider the symbols used by local political activist Craig Isherwood: "The tormented irrigators are family farmers of our national food bowl, the producers of the nation's food supply, who have barely held on through a decade of drought exacerbated by water restrictions for phony 'environmental flows,' but now when they finally have an opportunity to replenish their land and grow full crops, they are being blocked" (Isherwood, "Genocidalists").

29. As noted by Stephen Schneider in "Abrupt Non-linear Climate Change," and by many others.

30. See, for example, Levinas, "Revelation."

31. Arendt, in her classic book *Eichmann in Jerusalem*, which was collated from a series of articles published in the *New Yorker* magazine in 1963.

32. Howitt, "Knowing/Doing"; and Howitt, "Book Reviews"; see also Bergo, "Face in Levinas."

33. Edmund Husserl participated in debates on the crises in culture and values in interwar Germany, but rising fascist ideology prevented him from publishing from 1933 on, and he died in 1938. His incomplete but influential final book, *Crisis of European Sciences*, was published in 1954. See Carr, "Foreword."

34. Stanford economist Paul Romer said this in reference to a crisis in American education in November 2004 at a venture capitalist meeting in California, as reported in Rosenthal, "Terrible Thing." It has since been used widely by anyone looking for opportunity in a catastrophe, as happened in the case of Typhoon Haiyan.

35. Lagmay et al., "Devastating Storm Surges."

36. Esteban et al., "Storm Surge Awareness"; National Disaster Risk Reduction and Management Center, "Effects of Typhoon 'Yolanda'"; and Mas et al., "Field Survey Report."

37. Watson, "Typhoon Haiyan."

38. Throughout this section, we will use the WMO designation, *Haiyan*, to avoid confusion.

39. Lagmay et al., "Devastating Storm Surges."

40. Evans and Falvey, "Annual Tropical Cyclone Report."

41. Monserrat and Rabinovich, "Meteotsunamis."

42. Lin and Emanuel, "Grey Swan Tropical Cyclones."

43. Trenberth, Fasullo, and Shepherd, "Climate Extreme Events."

44. Stott et al., "Attribution of Extreme Weather."

45. For example, Cho et al., "Anthropogenic Footprint."

46. Walsh, "Climate Change."

47. Fisher, "Why the Philippines."

48. United Nations Office for Disaster Risk Reduction, "Super Typhoon Haiyan."

49. World Bank, "Damages from Extreme Weather."

50. Nixon, *Slow Violence*, 59.

51. Mangroves and forests are examples of effective "soft" protections against the impacts of extreme storms. Wide bands of mangrove forests dampen storm surges along coastal zones, and upland forests protect against mudslides during extreme precipitation. See Acosta et al., "Loss and Damage."

52. Gocotano et al., "Is the Response Over?"

53. The US government contributed US$87 million primarily through USAID and the Department of Defense. The American Red Cross independently contributed US$87 million raised through private donations, following their doctrine of nonpartisanship.

54. Lum and Margesson, "Typhoon Haiyan (Yolanda)," 8.

55. Global Humanitarian Assistance, *Global Humanitarian Assistance Report*, 43.

56. Ibid., 7.

57. Alcantara, "Lessons Learned."

58. Swithern, "Response to Typhoon Haiyan."

59. Gocotano et al., "Is the Response Over?"

60. Kitong and Calibo, "Guidelines and Training."

61. Salenga et al., "Medicines Management."

62. Veland et al., "Narrative Matters for Sustainability."

63. Poumadere et al., "2003 Heat Wave in France."

64. Curato, "Politics of Anxiety."

65. Francisco, "Analysis."

66. Curato, "In the Philippines."

67. Punzalan, "Duterte Blames Yolanda."

68. Lasswell, Lerner, and Pool, *Comparative Study of Symbols*, 11.

69. Gleick, "Wet Year," 1.

70. Nagourney, "When Is a Drought Over?"

71. Steinbeck, *Grapes of Wrath*, 34.

72. Wartzman, *Obscene in the Extreme*, 6.

73. Steinbeck, *Grapes of Wrath*, xi.

74. See, for example, the publications on migrant or undocumented farm workers by Sonia Nazario in the *Los Angeles Times*, republished and expanded in the book *Enrique's Journey*.

75. Osborn, "Native American Winters Doctrine."

76. Also called the Palmer Drought Severity Index.

77. Palmer, *Meteorological Drought*, 1.

78. Steinbeck, *Grapes of Wrath*, 161.

79. Scott, *Seeing Like a State*, 4.

80. United States Drought Monitor, "Drought Classification."

81. Van Loon et al., "Drought in the Anthropocene."

82. Grafton et al., "Global Insights."

83. Cohen, "Colorado River Basin."

84. Carman, "California Corporate Farms."

85. Developed by Bhuiyan at the Indian Institute of Technology in 2004.

86. See, for example, Chen et al., "Groundwater Storage Changes."

87. Bachmair et al., "Drought Indicators Revisited"; and Gleick, "Wet Year."

88. Heathcote, *Drought and Human Story*.

89. Griffin and Anchukaitis, "2012–2014 California Drought."

90. Ibid., 9022.

91. Gleick, "Wet Year."

92. Swain et al., "Extraordinary California Drought."

93. Griffin and Anchukaitis, "2012–2014 California Drought," 9017.

94. Turner et al., "Managing Drought."

95. Brunner and Lynch, *Adaptive Governance*, 84.

96. To the author's knowledge, this symbol was first invoked as *here and now* in Poumadere et al., "2003 Heat Wave in France."

97. A quote from Coelho posted to his Facebook page on November 7, 2011.

98. But with an aspirational 1.5°C target; see chapter 4 for a detailed discussion.

99. United Nations Framework Convention on Climate Change, Rio de Janeiro (United Nations, 1992). Text available at http://www.unfccc.int.

100. Schneider, "'Dangerous' Climate Change."

101. United Nations International Strategy for Disaster Risk Reduction, *Summer 2003 Heat Wave*. Later authors have revised the death toll up to as many as seventy thousand people.

102. Poumadere et al., "2003 Heat Wave in France," 1483.

103. Zielo and Matzarakis, "Heat Health Action Plans."

104. Hémon and Jougla, "Heat Wave in France."

105. Poumadere et al., "2003 Heat Wave in France," 1490.

106. Ibid.

107. BBC News, "'Over 11,000' Dead."

108. CRED and UNISDR, "Poverty and Death."

109. Stott, Stone, and Allen, "Human Contribution."

110. See, for example, articles such as Schar et al., "Increasing Temperature Variability"; and Meehl and Tebaldi, "More Intense."

111. Alexander, "Global Observed Long-Term Changes."

112. For example a ranger in Alice Springs, Australia, in 2009, in personal communication with S. Veland, said: "With so much variability, added variability is not so much the issue."

113. Caruth, *Trauma*.

114. Steffen et al., "Trajectory of the Anthropocene."

115. Kasperson et al., "Social Amplification of Risk."

3 Urgent Policy

1. Ribot, "Cause and Response," 667.

2. Stevens, "Water in the Atmosphere," 34.

3. Beck, *Risk Society*, 12.

4. Jacobs and Kelly, *Smogtown*.

5. Carson, *Silent Spring*; Mowat, *Never Cry Wolf*; Abbey, *Desert Solitaire*; and Bookchin, *Our Synthetic Environment*.

6. Carson met with President Kennedy and submitted to him the Pollution Committee report, "Resources for the People," recommending a Department of Environmental Health. For more information, see Lear, *Rachel Carson*; and Brinkley, *Rachel Carson and JFK*. In "The Birth of EPA," Lewis writes, "In fact, EPA today may be said without exaggeration to be the extended shadow of Rachel Carson."

7. Giddens, *Consequences of Modernity*.

8. Mahdi, "Los Angeles Air Quality."

9. For some more detail, see Veland and Lynch, "Arctic Ice Edge Narratives."

10. Leach, "Democracy in the Anthropocene?"

11. Rockström et al., "Planetary Boundaries," 475.

12. Hajer, *Politics of Environmental Discourse*.

13. Haraway, "Situated Knowledges"; and Howitt and Suchet-Pearson, "Changing Country, Telling Stories."

14. Leopold, *Sand County Almanac*, 132.

15. Shellenberger and Nordhaus, "Death of Environmentalism," 7. That is, *goal substitution*: a poorly defined problem mistakes means for ends.

16. Ibid.

17. Asafu-Adjaye et al., "Ecomodernist Manifesto." The founding signatories of the manifesto, along with Shellenberger and Nordhaus, are John Asafu-Adjaye, University of Queensland; Linus Blomqvist, Breakthrough Institute; Stewart Brand, Long Now Foundation; Barry Brook, University of Tasmania; Ruth DeFries, Columbia University; Erle Ellis, University of Maryland; Christopher Foreman, University of Maryland; David Keith, Harvard University; Martin Lewis, Stanford University; Mark Lynas, Cornell University; Roger Pielke Jr., University of Colorado; Rachel Pritzker, Pritzker Innovation Fund; Joyashree Roy, Jadavpur University; Mark Sagoff, George Mason University; Robert Stone, Filmmaker; and Peter Teague, Breakthrough Institute. Note that Shellenberger left the Breakthrough Institute in 2016.

18. Ibid., 23–24.

19. Ibid., 12.

20. This is the case also for the Ecomodernist Society of Finland, which focuses not on decoupling at home, but on overpopulation and worldwide resource use.

21. Thoreau, *Walden*.

22. See, for example, the works of Albert Bierstadt (1830–1902), such as *The Rocky Mountains, Lander's Peak*.

23. Thoreau, *Civil Disobedience*.

24. Hendrick, "Influence of 'Civil Disobedience.'"

25. King, *Pilgrimage to Nonviolence*.

26. Keller and Turek, *American Indians*.

27. Leopold, *Game Management*, xxxi (emphasis in original).

28. Leopold, "Why the Wilderness Society," 6.

29. The 1960s; see the introduction to this chapter.

30. Abbey, *Desert Solitaire*.

31. Abbey's eight instructions for an authoritarian government to succeed include the following: "Mechanize agriculture to the highest degree of refinement, thus forcing most of the scattered farm and ranching population into the cities ... because farmers, woodsmen, cowboys, Indians, fishermen, and other relatively self-sufficient types are difficult to manage unless displaced" (*Desert Solitaire*, 117).

32. Shellenberger and Nordhaus, "Death of Environmentalism," 7.

33. See, for example, Lewis, "On Human Connectedness."

34. Wilson, *Half-Earth*.

35. Recall from chapter 1 that the doctrine affirms the stable perspectives; the formula develops these perspectives into prescriptions or policies; and the symbol communicates the perspectives and prescriptions.

36. United Nations International Strategy for Disaster Risk Reduction, "World's Cities in 2016."

37. Asafu-Adjaye et al., "Ecomodernist Manifesto," 23.

38. Ibid., 16. The manifesto suggests that "as much as three-quarters of all deforestation globally occurred *before* the Industrial Revolution" (emphasis added).

39. Ibid., 20.

40. Shellenberger and Nordhaus, "Death of Environmentalism."

41. Indeed, the cowman in Aldo Leopold's quote, which introduces this section, does think like a mountain, realizing his role, and perhaps considers this the more humane and connected care for the world.

42. Berkes, Berkes, and Fast, "Collaborative Integrated Management"; Fitzpatrick and Kleegan, "Human Impacts"; King and Hood, "Ecosystem Health"; Walker and Schulze, "Sustainable Maize Production"; Lind et al., *Gammelnorsk*.

43. For example, in "The Big Conservation Lie," Mbaria and Ogada draw lines from colonial perspectives on Africans as part of the ecosystems (and themselves not, by consequence) and implicate the donations of left-leaning conservationists from across the West in right-wing military authoritarianism. The narrative that African communities also wish to conserve and have millennia of experience in coexistence, they say, is still denied in conservation discourse. In the United States, Michael Francis Turek and Robert H. Keller write of similar militarized and authoritarian dispossession in the implementation of national park policy; see Keller and Turek, *American Indians*.

44. Latour, *We Have Never Been Modern*.

45. Ibid., loc. 301 of 3230, Kindle.

46. United Nations Environment Programme, "ABC of SCP." The goals specify the parameters of decoupling as the relationship between (1) economic variables, such as Gross Domestic Product (GDP) or the Human Development Index (HDI), and (2) environmental variables, such as resource use or environmental indicators.

47. OECD Environment Programme, "Indicators to Measure Decoupling."

48. United Nations Environment Programme, "Sustainable Consumption and Production Indicators."

49. Rayner, "Planetary Boundaries"; Nordhaus, Shellenberger, and Blomqvist, *Planetary Boundaries Hypothesis*; and Breakthrough Staff, "'Numerous Drawbacks.'"

50. Kareiva, Marvier, and Lalasz, "Conservation in the Anthropocene."

51. See Latour, *Politics of Nature*.

52. Shellenberger and Nordhaus, "Death of Environmentalism."

53. Leach et al., "Transforming Innovation for Sustainability," 11.

54. UN General Assembly, "Transforming Our World," 14 and para. 54.

55. Ibid., 3.

56. Ibid., 2.

57. Hajer et al., "Beyond Cockpit-ism," 1652.

58. Shawki, "Norms and Normative Change."

59. Death and Gabay, "Doing Biopolitics Differently?"

60. UN General Assembly, "Transforming Our World."

61. Scott, *Seeing Like a State*.

62. Penn, "Patronage."

63. UN General Assembly, "Transforming Our World," 5.

64. UN General Assembly, "Transforming Our World," 5.

65. Gasalla and Gandini, "Loss of Fishing Territories"; Veland and Bryceson, *Building Houses on Sand*.

66. Shawki, "Norms and Normative Change," 263.

67. UN General Assembly, "Transforming Our World," 5.

68. UN General Assembly, "Transforming Our World," 13.

69. "The Sustainable Development Goals Report from the United Nations" (2016) reads, "As of 2015, over 23,000 species of plants, fungi and animals were known to face a high probability of extinction. Human Activities are causing species extinctions at rates three orders of magnitude higher than those normal throughout the Earth's history; the period from 2011 to 2015 was the hottest on record, with sea ice reaching its lowest level in history and coral bleaching coral reefs."

70. UN General Assembly, "Transforming Our World," 5.

71. See, for example, Penn, "Patronage"; Gabay, "Special Forum"; and Esquivel, "Power."

72. UN General Assembly, "Transforming Our World," 1.

73. United Nations, "Sustainable Development Goals Report," 26.

74. Weber, "Reproducing Inequalities through Development," referring to McMichael, "Changing the Subject."

75. Food and Agricultural Organization, "Voluntary Guidelines," also see Shawki, "Norms and Normative Change."

76. Scott, Hall, and Gossling, "Paris Climate Change Agreement."

77. Ibid., 943.

78. UN General Assembly, "Transforming Our World," 5.

79. An organization of retired world leaders, including Nelson Mandela, Gro Harlem Bruntland, Desmond Tutu, and Kofi Annan.

80. Schleussner et al., "Armed-Conflict Risks Enhanced."

81. The Office of Decolonization notwithstanding.

82. United Nations, "Sustainable Development Goals Report," 42.

83. UN General Assembly, "Transforming Our World," 5.

84. Leach et al., "Transforming Innovation for Sustainability."

85. Howitt, "Scales of Coexistence"; consider also the vertical capacity deficits embodied in the United Nations' Sustainable Development Goals.

86. Ribot, "Cause and Response."

87. Hajer et al., "Beyond Cockpit-ism."

88. Schipper et al., "Linking Disaster Risk Reduction."

89. Burton, Kates, and White, *Environment as Hazard*.

90. See, for example, Oliver-Smith, "Traditional Agriculture"; Oliver-Smith, "Post Disaster Consensus"; and Burton, Kates, and White, *Environment as Hazard*.

91. United Nations International Strategy for Disaster Risk Reduction (UNISDR) "Sendai Framework for Disaster Risk Reduction," 121. The Sendai Framework for Disaster Risk Reduction 2015–2030 was adopted at the third UN World Conference in Sendai, Japan, on March 18, 2015.

92. Kelman, "Climate Change." See chapter 4 for more details on the Paris Agreement of the Parties to the UN Framework Convention on Climate Change.

93. Kelman, "Linking Disaster Risk Reduction."

94. Ibid., 255.

95. Schipper et al., "Linking Disaster Risk Reduction," 225.

96. Kelman, "Linking Disaster Risk Reduction."

97. Ibid. Kelman draws attention to an example from Kobe, Japan, where the building codes that prescribed heavy roofs to withstand typhoons (a climatological hazard) failed to take into consideration the exacerbated risk of damage from heavy roofs during earthquakes (a geophysical hazard).

98. Leichenko and O'Brien, *Environmental Change and Globalisation*; Schipper et al., "Linking Disaster Risk Reduction"; and Thomalla, Smith, and Schipper, "Cultural Aspects of Risk."

99. The resilience framework includes a carefully defined discourse for describing how social-ecological systems across scales go through cycles of growth, conservation, release, and reorganization. Smaller, faster cycles affect the slower, larger cycles, and the latter sets conditions for the former. For instance, four yearly elections reorganize governance, while centuries of democracy set conditions; or a rare, large-scale forest fire will set conditions for the reproduction of species within the ecosystem. A transformation happens as the structure and function of the system changes—for instance, in going from productive agricultural land to saline, unproductive soils. Resilience can be positive or negative: soil salinity is highly resilient but unwanted. See Gundersen and Holling, *Panarchy*, for more information.

100. United Nations International Strategy for Disaster Risk Reduction, "UNISDR Terminology," 9.

101. Kelman, "Linking Disaster Risk Reduction."

102. Dalby, "Biopolitics and Climate Security," 184.

103. Beck, *Risk Society*. The world *similitude* describes the worldview of mediaeval Europe, in which observations of earth processes were interpreted as divine communications.

104. In hazards literature, the conventional approach has been to speak of vulnerability as a combination of exposure and sensitivity. In later years, *vulnerability* has taken over the meaning of *sensitivity*.

105. Gergan, "Living with Earthquakes"; Veland et al., "Procedural Vulnerability"; Németh and Cronin, "Volcanic Structures"; and Stoffle and Arnold, "Confronting the Angry Rock."

106. Stoffle and Arnold, "Confronting the Angry Rock"; Stoffle et al., "Timescapes in Conflict"; and Stoffle, Arnold, and Van Vlack, "Facing the Unimaginable."

107. Howitt, Havnen, and Veland, "Natural and Unnatural Disasters."

108. Hsu, Howitt, and Miller, "Procedural Vulnerability"; Hsu, "Lost Found and Troubled in Translation"; and Howitt et al., "Organisational Capacity."

109. Fassin and Pandolfi, *Contemporary States of Emergency*.

110. Krüger et al., *Cultures and Disasters*, 1, 10. The Krüger et al. book was the result of international conferences on cultures and disasters convened in 2011 in Bielefeld and 2013 in Erlangen, and an international conference on disaster risk reduction in London in 2014.

111. United Nations International Strategy for Disaster Risk Reduction (UNISDR), "Sendai Framework for Disaster Risk Reduction," 15; see also Kelman, "Climate Change."

112. International Federation of Red Cross and Red Crescent Societies, Cannon, and Schipper, *World Disasters Report 2014*.

113. Ibid., 206.

114. Mansuri and Rao, *Localizing Development*.

115. Bankoff, "Rendering the World Unsafe"; and Bankoff, Frerks, and Hilhorst, *Mapping Vulnerability*.

116. International Federation of Red Cross and Red Crescent Societies, Cannon, and Schipper, *World Disasters Report 2014*, 205.

117. White, "Geography and Public Policy," 104.

118. Roberts and Pelling, "Climate Change-Related Loss."

119. Jones, "Environmental Risk Assessment." See also Adger, Arnell, and Tompkins, "Successful Adaptation"; Eakin and Luers, "Assessing the Vulnerability"; and Weaver et al., "Improving the Contribution."

120. Lovelock et al., "Assessing the Risk."

121. Brondizio et al., "Re-conceptualizing the Anthropocene."

122. Landau, "Redundancy," 355.

123. See, for example, Rawls, "Idea of an Overlapping Consensus"; Mouffe, "Deliberative Democracy."

124. Landau, "Redundancy," 356.

4 Urgent Governance

1. Keynes, *The Collected Writings*, 409.

2. Dewey, *The Later Works*, 52.

3. Haida Gwaii are the islands of the Haida people, now part of Canada. The northern island is also called Graham Island.

4. Lukacs, "World's Biggest Geoengineering Experiment."

5. Ibid. "The Guardian has seen government correspondence which indicates that Environment Canada officers met with Disney's company in June and expressed their misgiving about any ocean fertilisation going forward, but appear to not have taken further action" (1).

6. The London Convention was adopted in 1972, and the associated London Protocol entered into force in 2006.

7. *Geoengineering* is defined as "a broad set of methods and technologies that aim to deliberately alter the climate system in order to alleviate the impacts of climate change" (Boucher, Gruber, and Blackstock, "Synthesis Session," 2).

8. Annex 1, XI/20.10, p. 221 from Decisions Adopted by the Conference of the Parties to the Convention on Biological Diversity at its Eleventh Meeting (Hyderabad, India, October 8–19, 2012), UNEP/CBD/COP/11/35.

9. Interview with Russ George, reported in Laumer, "Russ George's Geoengineering Experiment."

10. See, for example, Rogelj et al., "Energy System Transformations."

11. EarthData, "Giovanni."

12. *Eutrophication* is the process whereby dissolved oxygen in water is depleted through excessive growth of algae, causing die-off of aquatic fauna. It is most often caused by the presence of excessive nutrients in the water.

13. Crutzen, "Albedo Enhancement."

14. See National Research Council, *Climate Intervention.*

15. Hamilton, "Geoengineering."

16. Bellamy and Lezaun, "Crafting a Public."

17. Critical Global Discussions, "What Is Climate Engineering?," 1.

18. Dryzek, "Institutions," 951.

19. A partnership of the UK Royal Society, the World Academy of Sciences, and the Environmental Defense Fund to expand the discourse around SRM research governance.

20. A nonprofit think tank based in Washington, DC, founded by four former Senate Majority leaders—two Democrats and two Republicans.

21. A research collaboration among researchers from the Universities of Oxford and Sussex and University College London.

22. Critical Global Discussions, "What Is Climate Engineering?"

23. Rousseau, "Social Contract and Discourses," 184.

24. Jasanoff, "New Climate for Society," 236.

25. Turner et al., "Two Types."

26. See, for example, two important contributions to this discourse: Wilbanks and Kates, "Global Change"; and Cash et al., "Scale and Cross-Scale Dynamics."

27. Ferguson, "Changing Atmosphere," 292.

28. Ibid., 296.

29. Ibid., 304.

30. Ungar, "Social Scares," 445.

31. Clark and Westrum, "Paradigms and Ferrets."

32. Dryzek, "Institutions for the Anthropocene," 941.

33. https://unfccc.int/process/the-kyoto-protocol.

34. Grubb, "Kyoto Protocol."

35. *Bunker fuels* are defined loosely as fuels supplied to ships and aircraft that are conducting international trade and transportation.

36. The International Civil Aviation Organization and the International Maritime Organization, respectively.

37. See, for example, Victor, "Toward Effective International Cooperation."

38. Bailey and Tomlinson, "Post-Paris."

39. The increase as of 2016 is 0.85°C since 1850.

40. Understanding on Rules and Procedures Governing the Settlement of Disputes, WTO Agreement, Annex 2.

41. See, for example, Guzman, "Design of International Agreements"; and Blum, "Bilateralism."

42. See chapter 5 for further discussions on the benefit of the commons.

43. Dietz, Ostrom, and Stern, "Struggle."

44. Rogelj et al., "Paris Agreement."

45. Rockström et al., "Safe Operating Space."

46. Biermann, "Planetary Boundaries," 7.

47. Dryzek, "Institutions."

48. See, for example, Sabel and Victor, "Governing."

49. See Ostrom, "Polycentric"; see also literatures exemplified by, for example, Folke et al., "Problem of Fit."

50. See, for example, Biermann, "Planetary"; see also Biermann et al., "Transforming," 7: "In some cases, global interdependencies might require a global "grand bargain" and hence a strong global institution in one area, as in the case of climate change. In other cases, however, ... a network of focused institutions might be more effective."

51. The Earth System Governance Project was a ten-year research initiative under the auspices of the International Human Dimensions Programme on Global Environmental Change (IHDP) which concluded in 2014. There are many important contributions to the ideas of earth system governance. This discussion will not be exhaustive of the excellent scholarship embodied by these contributions, but we ask the reader to consider, as an example, Biermann, *Earth System Governance*.

52. Biermann et al., "Transforming," 57.

53. Biermann, "Rationale."

54. Blum, "Bilateralism," 350.

55. Sebenius, "Sequencing."

56. Vidal, "Copenhagen."

57. MRV stands for measurement, reporting, and verification.

58. Keohane and Victor, "Regime."

59. See, for example, Folke et al., "Adaptive"; Ostrom, "Polycentric"; Morgan, "Managing Carbon"; Brunner and Lynch, *Adaptive*.

60. Victor, "Effective International Cooperation," 99.

61. Victor, House, and Joy, "Madisonian."

62. Ibid., 1820.

63. Ostrom, "Polycentric."

64. Victor, "Effective International Cooperation."

65. See http://www.gutenberg.org/files/2680/2680-h/2680-h.htm.

66. Burton, "Modernising," 173.

67. Ginsburg and Melton, "Constitutional Amendment Rule."

68. See, for example, Lutz, "Theory of Constitutional Amendment."

69. See, for example, Rubin, "Environmental-Policy."

70. Ascher, "Resolving the Hidden Differences."

71. Lasswell, Lerner, and Pool, *Comparative Study*, 4.

72. Kareiva and Marvier, "Conservation for the People."

73. These schemes include fencing, altered and controlled use of rangelands/ wilderness areas, changing to alternative livestock breeds better adapted to depredation, shepherding, and altered timing of lambing and slaughtering, which each increase the costs to already economically pressured farmers and herders. See, for example, Swenson and Andrén, "Tale of Two Countries"; Linnell et al., "Sustainably Harvesting"; and Risvoll, Fedreheim, and Galafassi, "Trade-Offs."

74. Rose, *Wild Country*.

75. See, for example, Humphrey, *Preservation*.

76. Gilley, "Authoritarian Environmentalism."

77. Shearman and Smith, *Climate Change Challenge*, 4.

78. The following is a selection of recent polls with unexpected or at least inward-looking results: the large margin of defeat of the Scottish independence referendum in 2014, the success of the "leave" vote in the Brexit referendum in the United Kingdom in 2016, the election of Donald Trump as president of the United States in 2016, the narrow defeat in 2016 of the Colombian peace plebiscite, the near defeat of the conservative government in the United Kingdom in 2017, the election of Emmanuel Macron as president of France in 2017, the weakness of Angela Merkel's support in the German election of 2018, and the indecisive Italian election of 2018.

79. Moore, "Modernisation," 952.

80. Dreyer, "Only China."

81. Wang, "Sustainable Legitimacy."

82. Chao, "More Pollution Control."

83. Choi, "Shiyan City."

84. Moore, "Modernisation."

85. Zhang, "Carbon Emissions Trading."

86. Lo, "National Development."

87. For comparison, according to the International Energy Agency, China's total carbon dioxide emissions from fossil fuels alone in 2014 measured 9,135 million tons. That same year, the United States emissions from fossil fuels measured 5,176 million tons, OECD Europe's emissions measured 3,392 million tons, and India's emissions measured 2,020 million tons. Data obtained from www.iea.org.

88. Lo, "Challenges."

89. See, for example, Beeson, "Environmental Authoritarianism."

90. Ibid., 288.

91. Acharya, "Southeast Asia's Democratic Moment."

92. Arias-Maldonado, "Imaginary Solution?"

93. Prewitt, "Public Statistics," 114.

94. Liefferink and Andersen, "Strategies."

95. See, for example, the critique of Lijphart's theoretical approach in Barry, "Political Accommodation." It should be noted, however, that Arend Lijphart was explicit that he "merely discovered what political practitioners had repeatedly—and independently of both academic experts and one another—invented years earlier" (Lijphart, "Constitutional Design," 97).

96. Strictly speaking, *neocorporatism* refers to "a set of institutions in which the interest organizations of industrial capital and labor are brought together in a framework with the state" (Lash, "End of Neo-Corporatism?," 7). We are using the term a little more broadly here to include other nonstate actors, per Jones, *Routledge Encyclopedia*.

97. Lehmbruch and Schmitter, *Patterns*, 264. See also Schmitter, "Reflections."

98. Kaplan, "American Ethics," 36.

99. Dryzek and Stevenson, "Global Democracy"; see also Jahn, "Environmental Performance."

100. Arsenault, *Effects of Political Institutions*.

101. Lijphart and Crepaz, "Corporatism"; see also Lijphart, *Democracies*.

102. Arsenault, *Effects of Political Institutions*, 82.

103. Hsu and Zomer, "Environmental Performance Index."

104. Jahn, "Environmental Performance."

105. Dryzek et al., *Green States*.

106. Ibid.

107. Agamben, *State of Exception*; see also Klein, *Shock Doctrine*.

108. Schmitt, *Political Theology*.

109. Castree, "Geographers," 244.

110. Doremus, "Rhetoric and Reality."

111. Agamben, *State of Exception*.

112. Rossiter, *Constitutional Dictatorship*.

113. Smith, "Against Ecological Sovereignty," 105.

114. Rossiter, *Constitutional Dictatorship*.

115. Schmitt, *Political Theology*.

116. Smith, "Against Ecological Sovereignty," 106.

117. Agamben, *State of Exception*, 48.

118. Agamben, *Homo Sacer*.

119. Stevenson, "Psychic Life."

120. De Larrinaga and Doucet, "Sovereign Power," 517.

121. Agamben, *State of Exception*, 33.

122. Smith, "Against Ecological Sovereignty."

123. Ibid., 108.

124. Rossiter, *Constitutional Dictatorship*, 314.

125. Grubb, "Economics"; see chapter 1.

126. Dalby, "Biopolitics."

127. Smith, "Against Ecological Sovereignty," 114.

128. Of course, not all agree with Agamben's perspective that the state of exception is becoming prevalent today. For instance, Huysmans argues: "Biopolitics does not enact anomie but its contrary: an extremely detailed governance and self-governance of relations between humans and between humans and their environment." Biopolitics, according to Huysman, internally generates change and resistance, such that "political life is not simply imposition through governance but always also necessarily struggles over knowledge, technologies, living conditions, discriminations, etc." (Huysmans, "Jargon of Exception," 179). See also Smith, "Against Ecological Sovereignty"; and Dalby, "Biopolitics."

129. Smith, "Against Ecological Sovereignty," 110.

130. Cover, "Foreword"; nomos is our normative universe.

131. Agamben, *Homo Sacer*.

132. Ibid.

133. Ibid.

134. Huysmans, "Jargon of Exception," 179.

135. Morgensen, "Biopolitics," 69.

136. Howitt, "Sustainable Indigenous Futures."

137. Howitt, Havnen, and Veland, "Natural and Unnatural Disasters."

138. Stanner, *After the Dreaming.*

139. See, for example, Porter and Barry, *Planning for Coexistence.*

140. Howitt, "Scales of Coexistence."

141. Also termed arrivant or migrant; see Brathwaite, *The Arrivant.*

142. Bess, "New Zealand's Treaty."

143. Strelein, "Mabo to Yorta Yorta."

144. Ibid., 5.

145. The high court appeals are formally Matter No. B8 of 1996, the Wik Peoples, appellants, and the State of Queensland & ors, respondents; and matter No. B9 of 1996, the Thayorre People, appellants, and the State of Queensland & ors, respondents—otherwise known as the *pastoral leases* case.

146. Strelein, *Compromised Jurisprudence.*

147. The Native Title Amendment Act of 2008 was the governmental response to this decision. It took two years to pass the bill after the longest debate in the history of the Senate.

148. A representation of this literature in Australia includes works by Noel Pearson, Marcia Langton, Michael Dodson, Richard Howitt, and Elizabeth Povinelli.

149. Strelein, *Compromised Jurisprudence.*

150. Ibid.

151. Howitt, "Scales of Coexistence."

152. Porter and Barry, *Planning for Coexistence?*

153. Anaya, *Indigenous Peoples.*

154. For careful analyses of the declaration, see Anaya and Wiessner, "UN Declaration,"15; Shawki, "Norms"; Kingsbury, "'Indigenous Peoples'"; Errico, "Draft UN Declaration"; Barelli, "Role of Soft Law"; and Lennox and Short, *Handbook.*

155. Lennox and Short, *Handbook,* 39.

156. United Nations, *United Nations Declaration.*

157. United Nations, "Draft United Nations Declaration."

158. Errico, "Draft UN Declaration," 749 (emphasis added).

159. Compare Errico, "Draft UN Declaration," with United Nations, "Draft United Nations Declaration."

160. Rawls, *Political Liberalism*, 133. See also comments from Patton on philosophical justifications for Indigenous rights in Lennox and Short, *Handbook*.

161. Porter and Barry, *Planning for Coexistence?*, 192; citing Mouffe, "Deliberative Democracy."

162. Howitt, "Sustainable Indigenous Futures," 827.

163. Porter and Barry, *Planning for Coexistence?*, 190.

164. Lee Joachim is cited by Wilcock, Brierley, and Howitt, "Ethnogeomorphology," 581.

165. Stanner, "Aboriginal Religion."

166. Lynch et al., "Yorta Yorta People."

167. *Yorta Yorta v. Victoria and Others* (1998), para. 129.

168. Strelein, *Compromised Jurisprudence*.

169. Morgan, Strelein, and Weir, "Indigenous Rights."

170. Bischoff-Mattson and Lynch, "Justice, Science, or Collaboration."

171. Australia currently has sixty-five Ramsar wetlands that cover more than 8.3 million hectares. Ramsar wetlands are those that are representative, rare, or unique wetlands, or those important for conserving biological diversity. These are included on the List of Wetlands of International Importance developed under the Ramsar convention.

172. Lynch et al., "Yorta Yorta People," 115.

173. Weir, "Hope and Farce."

174. Jackson, Moggridge, and Robinson, *Effects of Changes*.

175. Morgan, Strelein, and Weir, "Indigenous Rights," 10.

176. Co-management schemes in Australian National Parks and areas of World Heritage are recognized internationally; see ibid.

177. The agreement was updated to include the newly formed Barmah National Park in 2010 under a successor Labor State government and Premier John Brumby.

178. Accessed from the Agreements, Treaties and Negotiated Settlements Project, at http://www.atns.net.au/agreement.asp?EntityID=2508.

179. John Thwaites, personal communication; Thwaites was the minister for water, among other portfolios, in the Bracks Government of 2002–2006.

180. Vidot, "Anger and Optimism." Interview with Nari Nari man Rene Woods, chair of the Murray Lower-Darling Rivers Indigenous Nations. The Cultural Flows Project "aims to secure a future where Indigenous water allocations are embedded within Australia's water planning and management regimes, delivering cultural, spiritual, social, environmental and economic benefit to communities in the Murray-Darling Basin and beyond" (http://www.mldrin.org.au/what-we-do/cultural-flows/).

181. Weir, *Murray River Country.*

182. Ibid.

183. This term has emerged as a more appropriate description of Indigenous interactions with land and water, as an alternative to the more restrictive idea of *environmental management* or *resource management*. See, for example, Altman and Whitehead, "Caring for Country."

184. Weir, "Hope and Farce."

185. Vidot, "Anger and Optimism."

186. van Dijk et al., "Millennium Drought."

187. Ibid.

188. Vidot, "Anger and Optimism."

189. Nadasdy, "Gift in the Animal," 26.

190. Mouffe, *Agnostics.* See also Porter and Barry, *Planning for Coexistence?*

191. Mouffe, *Democratic Paradox*, 131.

192. Porter and Barry, *Planning for Coexistence?*

193. Wiessner, "Indigenous Sovereignty," 58, in Pulitano, *Indigenous Rights.*

194. Howitt, "Sustainable Indigenous Futures," 818.

195. Porter and Barry, *Planning for Coexistence?*

196. Howitt, "Sustainable Indigenous Futures."

197. Porter and Barry, *Planning for Coexistence?*

198. Howitt, "Scales of Coexistence," 58.

199. Howitt and Suchet-Pearson, "Changing Country, Telling Stories."

200. Smith, *Decolonizing Methodologies.*

201. United Nations, "Assist Non-self-governing Territories." The United Nations Secretary General said, "Today, 17 Non-Self-Governing Territories across the globe remain under the purview of this Committee [Special Committee on Decoloniza-

tion]. I call on the international community to address the issue of self-government and find innovative and practical ways to implement the decolonization process. In this endeavour, we shall be guided by the principles enshrined in the United Nations Charter and the relevant General Assembly resolutions."

202. Ibid.

203. Rose, "Pattern, Connection, Desire."

204. McGinnis, "Political Economy."

205. Ibid.

206. Blum, "Bilateralism," 364; see also Anderson, "Ottawa Convention."

207. De Larrinaga and Doucet, "Sovereign Power."

208. Porter and Barry, *Planning for Coexistence.*

209. Smith, "Against Ecological Sovereignty," 113.

210. Ostrom, "Polycentric Systems."

211. Keohane and Victor, "Regime Complex."

212. Dryzek, "Institutions for the Anthropocene."

213. Ibid., 952.

214. In "Methodology of Transdisciplinarity," Basarab Nicolescu credited Stéphane Lupasco as formalizing this construction.

215. Bădescu and Nicolescu, *Stéphane Lupasco.*

216. Max-Neef, "Foundations of Transdisciplinarity."

5 Coexistence

1. Haraway, *Staying*, 35.

2. Lasswell, *Pre-View*, 40.

3. Veland et al., "Narrative Matters."

4. See, for instance, Hajer, *Politics.*

5. See chapter 4.

6. Boltanski, *On Critique*, 27.

7. Kaplan, *Conduct of Inquiry*, 11.

8. The Universal Declaration of Human Rights was proclaimed by the United Nations General Assembly in Paris on December 10, 1948.

9. The United Nations Declaration on the Rights of Indigenous Peoples made a first expression of group rights alongside individual rights; see Lennox and Short, *Handbook*, 39. See also chapter 4.

10. Strathern, *Reproducing the Future*.

11. Asafu-Adjaye et al., "Ecomodernist Manifesto."

12. For example, when asked whether we should consider geoengineering, Suki Manabe said, "I think it is a terrible idea, because the climate, even in the absence of global warming changes, can go up and down. ... People will blame you ... and there will likely be huge litigation costs, too. They will blame you for whatever happens to the climate from that point on" (Hickman, "Carbon Brief Interview"). Stephen Schneider wrote, "I would prefer to get slowly unhooked from our economic dependence on massive increases in carbon fuels than to try to cover the potential side effects of business-as-usual development with decades of sulphuric acid injections into the atmosphere or iron into the oceans or aerosols into the marine boundary layer, to say nothing of Buck Rogers schemes in space" (Schneider, "Geoengineering," 3859). Even earlier, Kellogg and Schneider wrote, "We believe that it would be dangerous to pursue any large-scale operational climate control schemes until we can predict their long-term effects on the weather patterns and the climate with some acceptable assurance. We cannot do so now, and it will be some time—if ever—before we can" (Kellogg and Schneider, "Climate Stabilization," 1170).

13. Shellenberger and Nordhaus, "Evolve," 246.

14. Breakthrough Staff, "Modern in Ecomodernism."

15. Theodicy holds that the current pain and suffering is tolerable because it will ultimately be vindicated. See also Hamilton, "Theodicy."

16. Dewey, *Theory of the Moral Life*, 52 (emphasis in original).

17. Plumwood, *Shadow Places*.

18. Parenti, *Tropic of Chaos*.

19. Brown University, "Colleges and Coal."

20. A student-led campaign for Brown University's endowment investments to divest from companies and funds that profit from the coal industry.

21. Miller, "Energy Policy." He further notes: "Energy policies to promote coal use were arguably partially offset by more stringent environmental policies adopted during the same period, including the Surface Mining. Control Act, 30 U.S.C. § 1201 (1988), and amendments to the Clean Air Act, 42 U.S.C. §§ 7401–7671 (1988 & Supp. V 1993), that restricted the use of tall stacks as a means of dispersing pollution. See Davis, supra note 2, at 39–57 (discussing the history of the relationship between government and the coal industry); see generally McBride and Pendergrass, 'Coal'" (717).

22. El_Dahdah and Proudhon, "Letter," 21.

23. Scott, *Removing Mountains*.

24. Rose, "Shimmer," 61.

25. Brunner and Lynch, *Adaptive Governance*, 24.

26. See, for example, Hodgson et al., "Climate Change."

27. Simon, *Sciences of the Artificial*, 28–29.

28. Rose, "Shimmer."

29. Proposal 2 of the Elders, "Strengthening the United Nations," 3. See also chapter 4 for further discussion.

30. Haraway, *Staying with the Trouble*.

31. Walker, Natcher, and Jojola, *Reclaiming Indigenous Planning*.

32. In the Māori language, Te Reo, the word *iwi* is roughly equivalent to the English word *tribe* or *nation*.

33. Houston, "Environmental Justice Storytelling"; Houston, "Crisis"; and Veland et al., "Narrative Matters."

34. Douglas Nakashima, head of the small islands and indigenous knowledge section at the UN Educational, Scientific and Cultural Organization (UNESCO), quoted in Tabary, "Indigenous Knowledge."

35. Here, Rebecca Solnit invokes Walter Benjamin's Angel of History to create an Angel of Alternate History, a comic angel that "can see atrocities not unfolding" (Solnit, *Hope in the Dark*, 71).

36. Ratcliffe, "Phenomenology," 473.

37. Ibid., 474.

38. Solnit, *Hope in the Dark*; Houston, "Environmental Justice Storytelling."

39. See chapter 3, under "We Have Always Been Humanitarian."

40. Schipper et al., "Linking"; and Veland et al., "Procedural"; see also chapter 3.

41. Williamson, "Strange History."

42. Rand, *Lexicon*, 5.

43. See Brown et al., "Theorizing Tolerance."

44. The *marginal damage function* in environmental economics describes the relationship between each unit of a damaging act (such as a ton of carbon dioxide emitted) and the damage in units of currency. The area under this function is the total damage, and the shape may change with time. The *marginal abatement cost function*

describes the additional cost of decreasing damage by one unit (e.g., emitting one less ton of carbon dioxide). This function varies in time and by industry.

45. See, for example, Schlenker, Hanemann, and Fisher, "Impact of Global Warming"; and Brohé and Greenstone, "Economic Impacts."

46. Dell, Jones, and Olken, "Learn from the Weather."

47. That is, the discount rate applied to future damage is large and may even increase over time rather than remaining constant or even declining. See, for example, Karp, "Global Warming."

48. The ecological footprint is measured using three factors as described in http://data.footprintnetwork.org/: "resource intensity in the production of goods and services; consumption of goods and services per person; and population size." Biocapacity is measured as "bioproductive area times the productivity of each hectare."

49. Moran et al., "Measuring Sustainable Development"; see also the Footprint Network's data portal at http://data.footprintnetwork.org/countryMetrics.html.

50. See http://www.footprintnetwork.org/.

51. See, for example, Selomane et al., "Sustainability Indicators."

52. Hamann, Biggs, and Reyers, "Exploration."

53. WWF, "China at a Crossroads."

54. GTCe is gigatons of "coal equivalent," which is not a measure typically used by international monitoring agencies and hence difficult to verify.

55. Olivier et al., *Trends*, 15.

56. For data, see ibid., as well as New Climate Economy, *Better Growth*; CCCPC, "Decision"; and World Bank and Development Research Center of the State Council, *Urban China*.

57. Climate Home, "Don't Celebrate Yet."

58. See, for example, Collins, "Climate Change Negotiations Polarize"; and, more recently, Hallegatte, "Strategies."

59. Brown et al., "Theorizing Tolerance," 161.

60. Ibid., 164.

61. Beck, *World at Risk*, 45.

62. Klein, *Shock Doctrine*.

63. Castree, "Geography and Global Change Science"; and Castree, "Geographers and Discourse."

64. Solnit, *Hope in the Dark*, 3.

65. Thorsen, *Fabianismen*; see also Brandal, Bratberg, and Thorsen, "Nordic Model."

66. Brandal, Bratberg, and Thorsen, "Nordic Model."

67. Ibid.; see also Beevor, *Battle for Spain*.

68. Aaronovitch, "*1984.*"

69. See, for example, Macfarlane, "Energy."

70. Solnit, *Hope in the Dark*, 71.

71. Ibid.

72. Hardin, "Tragedy of the Commons."

73. See, for example, Feeny et al., "Tragedy of the Commons."

74. See, for example, Rachlinski, "Psychology of Global Climate Change"; and Elliott and Hanson, "Discussion."

75. Dietz, Ostrom, and Stern, "Struggle," 1907.

76. Ostrom, "Institutional Rational Choice," 24.

77. Bounded rationality is a concept first introduced by Herbert A. Simon in "A Behavioral Model of Rational Choice."

78. Simon, *Reason in Human Affairs*, 20.

79. Ostrom and Ostrom, *Quest*, 119; Simon, *Reason*.

80. See Simon, *Models*.

81. Ostrom and Ostrom, "Quest for Meaning."

82. That is, it uses El Khoury's concept of a propositional space in which alternatives already coexist. See El Khoury, *Globalization Development*.

83. Dobbernack and Modood, "Tolerance," 171. The quotation in context is as follows: "Can we have a position, then, that is critical and constructive: that takes notice of, but does not turn regulatory effects into absolutes, at least not at the expense of political and interpretive struggles over the nature and meaning of tolerance? This would be a position that does not just problematize but can articulate and develop further the normative understandings expressed in institutions, by engaging citizens, and among oppositional movements."

84. The *principle of the excluded middle*—arising first with Aristotle but formalized by Alfred North Whitehead, and Bertrand Russell in the *Principia Mathematica*—holds that a statement cannot be both true and false at the same time. That is, *A* is false, or *not-A* is false. Cf. Walt Whitman, *Song of Myself*: "Do I contradict myself? Very well then I contradict myself, (I am large, I contain multitudes.)"

85. Plenn, *The Green Song (La Canción Verde)*, 57.

86. Haraway, *Staying with the Trouble*, 55.

87. Ibid., 44.

88. Indeed, the wilderness so carefully constructed in the American psyche can be more descriptively seen as either *quiet* or *wild* country; as country cared for by its human families; and country from which they have been expelled. See Rose, *Wild Country*.

89. Lasswell, *Pre-View*, 40.

90. Veland et al., "Narrative Matters."

91. Howitt, "Scales of Coexistence."

92. Kaplan, *American Ethics*, 49.

93. Frantz and Howitt, "Geography."

94. Ostrom, *Understanding Institutional Diversity*, 29.

95. Howitt, "Scales of Coexistence."

96. See also Veland, "Transcending."

97. Brunner and Lynch, *Adaptive Governance*.

98. Le Guin, *Dancing*; and Haraway, *Staying with the Trouble*.

Bibliography

Aaronovitch, D. "1984: George Orwell's Road to Dystopia." *British Broadcasting Corporation Magazine*, February 8, 2013. http://www.bbc.com/news/magazine-21337504.

Abbey, E. *Desert Solitaire: A Season in the Wilderness*. New York: Ballantine Books, 1988.

Acharya, Amitav. "Southeast Asia's Democratic Moment." *Asian Survey* 39, no. 3 (1999): 418–432.

Acosta, L. A., E. A. Eugenio, P. B. M. Macandog, D. B. Magcale-Macandog, E. K. H. Lin, E. R. Abucay, A. L. Cura, and M. G. Primavera. "Loss and Damage from Typhoon-Induced Floods and Landslides in the Philippines: Community Perceptions on Climate Impacts and Adaptation Options." *International Journal of Global Warming* 9, no. 1 (2016): 33–65.

Adger, W. Neil, Nigel W. Arnell, and Emma L. Tompkins. "Successful Adaptation to Climate Change across Scales." *Global Environmental Change* 15, no. 2 (2005): 77–86.

Adger, W. Neil, Jon Barnett, Katrina Brown, Nadine Marshall, and Karen O'Brien. "Cultural Dimensions of Climate Change Impacts and Adaptation." *Nature Climate Change* 3, no. 2 (2013): 112.

Agamben, G. *State of Exception*. Translated by K. Attell. Chicago: University of Chicago Press, 2008.

Agamben, Giorgio. *Homo Sacer: Sovereign Power and Bare Life*. Stanford: Stanford University Press, 1998.

Alcantara, Patrick. "Lessons Learned from the Philippine Government's Response to Typhoon Haiyan." *Journal of Business Continuity & Emergency Planning* 7, no. 4 (2014): 335.

Alexander, Lisa V. "Global Observed Long-Term Changes in Temperature and Precipitation Extremes: A Review of Progress and Limitations in IPCC Assessments and Beyond." *Weather and Climate Extremes* 11 (2016): 4–16.

Altman, Jon C., and Peter J. Whitehead. "Caring for Country and Sustainable Indigenous Development: Opportunities, Constraints and Innovation." ANU Research Publications, Technical/Working Paper, 2003. http://hdl.handle.net/1885/40996, http://digitalcollections.anu.edu.au/handle/1885/40996.

Anaya, S. James. *Indigenous Peoples in International Law*. New York: Oxford University Press, 2004.

Anaya, S. James, and Siegfried Wiessner. "The UN Declaration on the Rights of Indigenous Peoples: Towards Re-empowerment." *Third World Resurgence* 206 (2007). https://www.twn.my/title2/resurgence/206/cover3.doc (accessed March 19, 2018).

Anderson, Kenneth. "The Ottawa Convention Banning Landmines, the Role of International Non-governmental Organizations and the Idea of International Civil Society." *European Journal of International Law* 11, no. 1 (2000): 91–120.

Arendt, Hannah. *Eichmann in Jerusalem*. Penguin, 1963.

Arias-Maldonado, Manuel. "An Imaginary Solution? The Green Defence of Deliberative Democracy." *Environmental Values* 16, no. 2 (May 2007): 233–252.

Arsenault, M. P. *The Effects of Political Institutions on Varieties of Capitalism*. Cham, Switzerland: Palgrave Macmillan, 2017.

Asafu-Adjaye, J., L. Blomqvist, S. Brand, B. Brook, R. de Fries, E. Ellis, C. Foreman, D. Keith, M. Lewis, M. Lynas, T. Nordhaus, R. Pielke, R. Pritzker, J. Reeroy, M. Sagoff, M. Shellenberger, R. Stone, and P. Teague. "An Ecomodernist Manifesto." April 18, 2015. http://www.ecomodernism.org/manifesto-english/ (accessed March 22, 2017).

Ascher, William. "Resolving the Hidden Differences among Perspectives on Sustainable Development." *Policy Sciences* 32, no. 4 (1999): 351–377.

Associated Press. "Flaws Seen in Philippine Disaster Prep, Response." *The Jakarta Post*, November 12, 2013. http://www.pressreader.com/indonesia/the-jakarta-post/20131112/281775626924127 (accessed March 12, 2018).

Bachmair, Sophie, Kerstin Stahl, Kevin Collins, Jamie Hannaford, Mike Acreman, Mark Svoboda, Cody Knutson, et al. "Drought Indicators Revisited: The Need for a Wider Consideration of Environment and Society." *Wiley Interdisciplinary Reviews: Water* 3, no. 4 (2016): 516–536.

Bădescu, H., and B. Nicolescu. *Stéphane Lupasco: L'homme et l'oeuvre*. Monaco: Editions du Rocher, 1999.

Bailey, Rob, and Shane Tomlinson. "Post-Paris: Taking Forward the Global Climate Change Deal." April 21, 2016. London: The Royal Institute of International Affairs, Chatham House. https://www.chathamhouse.org/publication/post-paris-taking-forward-global-climate-change-deal (accessed March 12, 2018).

Bankoff, Gregory. "Rendering the World Unsafe: 'Vulnerability' as Western Discourse." *Disasters* 25, no. 1 (2001): 19–35.

Bankoff, Gregory, Georg Frerks, and Dorothea Hilhorst. *Mapping Vulnerability: Disasters, Development and People.* London: Earthscan, 2004.

Barelli, Mauro. "The Role of Soft Law in the International Legal System: The Case of the United Nations Declaration on the Rights of Indigenous Peoples." *International and Comparative Law Quarterly* 58, no. 4 (2009): 957–983.

Barnett, Jon, Suraje Dessai, and Roger N. Jones. *Vulnerability to Climate Variability and Change in East Timor.* Melbourne: Melbourne University Private, 2005.

Barnosky, A. D., N. Matzke, S. Tomiya, G. O. U. Wogan, B. Swartz, T. B. Quental, C. Marshall, et al. "Has the Earth's Sixth Mass Extinction Already Arrived?" *Nature* 471, no. 7336 (2011): 51–57.

Barry, Brian. "Political Accommodation and Consociational Democracy." *British Journal of Political Science* 5, no. 4 (1975): 477–505.

Bawaka Country, Sarah Wright, Sandie Suchet-Pearson, Kate Lloyd, Laklak Burarrwanga, Ritjilili Ganambarr, Merrkiyawuy Ganambarr-Stubbs, et al. "Co-becoming Bawaka: Towards a Relational Understanding of Place/Space." *Progress in Human Geography* 40, no. 4 (2015): 455–475. https://doi.org/10.1177/0309132515589437.

BBC News. "'Over 11,000' Dead in French Heat." *BBC News*, August 29, 2003.

Beach, Tim, Sheryl Luzzadder-Beach, Duncan Cook, Nicholas Dunning, Douglas J. Kennett, Samantha Krause, Richard Terry, Debora Trein, and Fred Valdez. "Ancient Maya Impacts on the Earth's Surface: An Early Anthropocene Analog?" *Quaternary Science Reviews* 124 (2015): 1–30.

Beck, U. *Risk Society: Towards a New Modernity.* London: Sage Publications, 1992.

Beck, U. *World at Risk. Cambridge*: Polity Press, 2009.

Beck, U., A. Giddens, and S. Lash. *Reflexive Modernization: Politics, Tradition and Aesthetics in the Modern Social Order.* Stanford, CA: Stanford University Press, 1994.

Beeson, M. "The Coming of Environmental Authoritarianism." *Environmental Politics* 19, no. 2 (2010): 276–294.

Beevor, A. *The Battle for Spain: The Spanish Civil War, 1936–1939.* New York: Penguin Books, 2006.

Bellamy, Rob, and Javier Lezaun. "Crafting a Public for Geoengineering." *Public Understanding of Science* 26, no. 4 (2017): 402–417.

Benjaminsen, Tor A. "Does Supply-Induced Scarcity Drive Violent Conflicts in the African Sahel? The Case of the Tuareg Rebellion in Northern Mali." *Journal of Peace Research* 45, no. 6 (2008): 819–836.

Bergo, Bettina. "The Face in Levinas: Toward a Phenomenology of Substitution." *Angelaki* 16, no. 1 (2011): 17–39.

Berkes, F., M. K. Berkes, and H. Fast. "Collaborative Integrated Management in Canada's North: The Role of Local and Traditional Knowledge and Community-Based Monitoring." *Coastal Management* 35, no. 1 (2007): 143–162.

Berndt, R. M., and C. H. Berndt. *Arnhem Land: Its History and Its People*. Melbourne: F. W. Cheshire, 1954.

Berndt, R. M., and C. H. Berndt. *The First Australians*. Canberra: Ure Smith, 1974.

Berndt, R. M. *The World of the First Australians: Aboriginal Traditional Life: Past and Present*. Canberra: Aboriginal Studies Press, 1988.

Bess, Randall. "New Zealand's Treaty of Waitangi and the Doctrine of Discovery: Implications for the Foreshore and Seabed." *Marine Policy* 35, no. 1 (2011): 85–94.

Biermann, F. *Earth System Governance: World Politics in the Anthropocene*. Cambridge, MA: MIT Press, 2014.

Biermann, F. "Planetary Boundaries and Earth System Governance: Exploring the Links." *Ecological Economics* 81 (2012): 4–9.

Biermann, F. "The Rationale for a World Environment Organization." In *A World Environment Organization: Solution or Threat for Effective International Environmental Governance*, edited by Frank Bierman and Steffen Bauer, 117–144. Farnham, UK: Ashgate Publishing, 2005.

Biermann, F., K. Abbott, S. Andresen, K. Backstrand, S. Bernstein, M. M. Betsill, H. Bulkeley, et al. "Transforming Governance and Institutions for Global Sustainability: Key Insights from the Earth System Governance Project." *Current Opinion in Environmental Sustainability* 4, no. 1 (2012): 51–60.

Bierstadt, Albert. *The Rocky Mountains, Lander's Peak, 1863*. Oil on canvas. 1895.

Bischoff-Mattson, Z., and A. H. Lynch. "Justice, Science, or Collaboration: Indigenous Cultural Water in Australia's Murray-Darling Basin." *Water Policy* (2018). doi: 10.2166/wp.2018.145.

Blay, Frédéric Le. "L'impossible Risque Zéro." *Choisir: Revue culturelle d'information et de réflexion*, no. 684 (July–Sept. 2017).

Blum, G. "Bilateralism, Multilateralism, and the Architecture of International Law." *Harvard International Law Journal* 49, no. 2 (2008): 323–379.

Bohr, Niels. *The Philosophical Writings of Niels Bohr*. Woodbridge, CT: Ox Bow Press, 1987.

Bohr, Niels. "The Quantum Postulate and the Recent Development of Atomic Theory." *Nature* 121 (1928): 580–590.

Boltanski, Luc. *On Critique: A Sociology of Emancipation*. Cambridge: Polity Press, 2011.

Bookchin, Murray. *Our Synthetic Environment*. New York: Harper & Row, 1974. Published under the pseudonym Lewis Herber.

Boucher, O., N. Gruber, and J. Blackstock. "Summary of the Synthesis Session." In *IPCC Expert Meeting Report on Geoengineering*, edited by O. Edenhofer, Ramón Pichs-Madruga, Youba Sokona, Christopher Field, Vicente Barros, Thomas F. Stocker, Qin Dahe et al., 1–7. Potsdam Institute for Climate Impact Research. Potsdam, Germany: IPCC Working Group III Technical Support Unit, Postdam Institute for Climate Impact Research, 2011.

Bradley, John. *Yanyuwa Country: The Yanyuwa People of Borroloola Tell the History of Their Land*. Cadillac, MI: Green House Press, 1988.

Brand, R., and J. Fischer. "Overcoming the Technophilia/Technophobia Split in Environmental Discourse." *Environmental Politics* 22, no. 2 (2013): 235–254.

Brandal, N., Ø. Bratberg, and D. Thorsen. *The Nordic Model of Social Democracy*. New York: Palgrave Macmillan, 2013.

Brathwaite, Kamau. *The Arrivant: A New World Trilogy*. Oxford: Oxford University Press, 1981.

Breakthrough Staff. "'Numerous Drawbacks' for 'Planetary Boundaries' Hypothesis: The Economist." *The Breakthrough*, June 14, 2012. https://thebreakthrough.org/archive/numerous_drawbacks_for_planetary_boundaries_economist (accessed March 17, 2018).

Breakthrough Staff. "What Is Modern in Ecomodernism? Nature, Technology, and Politics in the Anthropocene." *The Breakthrough*, July 14, 2015. https://thebreakthrough.org/index.php/dialogue/what-is-modern-in-ecomodernism.

Brinkley, Douglas. *Rachel Carson and JFK, an Environmental Tag Team*. Audubon Magazine, 2012.

Brohé, Arnaud, and Michael Greenstone. "The Economic Impacts of Climate Change: Evidence from Agricultural Output and Random Fluctuations in Weather." *American Economic Review* 97, no. 1 (2007): 354–385.

Brondizio, E. S., K. O'Brien, X. M. Bai, F. Biermann, W. Steffen, F. Berkhout, C. Cudennec, et al. "Re-conceptualizing the Anthropocene: A Call for Collaboration." *Global Environmental Change* 39 (2016): 318–327.

Brown University. "Colleges and Coal: Should Brown Divest?" News release, 2013.

Brown, W., J. Dobbernack, T. Modood, G. Newey, A. F. March, L. Tonder, and R. Forst. "What Is Important in Theorizing Tolerance Today?" *Contemporary Political Theory* 14, no. 2 (2015): 159–196.

Brunner, Ronald D. *Adaptive Governance: Integrating Science, Policy, and Decision Making*. New York: Columbia University Press, 2005.

Brunner, Ronald D. *Finding Common Ground: Governance and Natural Resources in the American West*. New Haven, CT: Yale University Press, 2002.

Brunner, Ronald D., and William Ascher. "Science and Social Responsibility." *Policy Sciences* 25, no. 3 (1992): 295–331.

Brunner, Ronald D., and Amanda H. Lynch. *Adaptive Governance and Climate Change*. Boston: American Meteorological Society; Chicago: University of Chicago Press, 2010.

Burton, Ian, Robert W. Kates, and Gilbert F. White. *The Environment as Hazard*. New York: Oxford University Press, 1978.

Burton, Paul. "Modernising the Policy Process: Making Policy Research More Significant?" *Policy Studies* 27, no. 3 (2006): 173–195.

Campbell, D., M. Stafford Smith, J. Davies, P. Kuipers, J. Wakerman, and M. McGregor. "Responding to Health Impacts of Climate Change in the Australian Desert." *Rural and Remote Health*, no. 1008 (2008): 1–9.

Carman, H. F. "California Corporate Farms: Myth and Reality." *Agricultural and Resource Economics Update* 12, no. 6 (2009): 9–11.

Carozza, Paolo G. "Subsidiarity as a Structural Principle of International Human Rights Law." *American Journal of International Law* 97, no. 1 (2003): 38–79.

Carr, David. "Foreword." In Edmund Husserl, *The Crisis of European Sciences and Transcendental Phenomenology: An Introduction to Phenomenological Philosophy*, xv–xliii. Evanston, Illinois: Northwestern University Press, 1970.

Carson, Rachel. *Silent Spring*. Boston: Houghton Mifflin Harcourt, 2002.

Caruth, Cathy. *Trauma: Explorations in Memory*. Baltimore: JHU Press, 1995.

Cash, David, W. Neil Adger, Fikret Berkes, Po Garden, Louis Lebel, Per Olsson, Lowell Pritchard, and Oran Young. "Scale and Cross-Scale Dynamics: Governance and Information in a Multilevel World." *Ecology and Society* 11, no. 2 (2006): article 8. https://www.ecologyandsociety.org/vol11/iss2/art8/ (accessed March 17, 2018).

Cashman, Katharine V., and Shane J. Cronin. "Welcoming a Monster to the World: Myths, Oral Tradition, and Modern Societal Response to Volcanic Disasters." *Journal of Volcanology and Geothermal Research* 176 (2008): 407–418.

Castree, Noel. "Geographers and the Discourse of an Earth Transformed: Influencing the Intellectual Weather or Changing the Intellectual Climate?" *Geographical Research* 53, no. 3 (2015): 244–254.

Castree, Noel. "Geography and Global Change Science: Relationships Necessary, Absent, and Possible." *Geographical Research* 53, no. 1 (2015): 1–15.

Castree, Noel, William M. Adams, John Barry, Daniel Brockington, Bram Buscher, Esteve Corbera, David Demeritt, et al. "Changing the Intellectual Climate." *Nature Climate Change* 4, no. 9 (2014): 763–768.

Committee of the Communist Party of China (CCCPC). "Decision on Major Issues Concerning Comprehensively Deepening Reforms." News release, 2013.

Chao, Liang. "More Pollution Control for Water Diversion Project." *China Daily*. November 29, 2011.

Chapin, F. Stuart, Stephen R. Carpenter, Gary P. Kofinas, Carl Folke, Nick Abel, William C. Clark, Per Olsson, et al. "Ecosystem Stewardship: Sustainability Strategies for a Rapidly Changing Planet." *Trends in Ecology & Evolution* 25, no. 4 (2010): 241–249.

Chen, Jianli, James S. Famigliett, Bridget R. Scanlon, and Matthew Rodell. "Groundwater Storage Changes: Present Status from Grace Observations." *Surveys in Geophysics* 37, no. 2 (2016): 397–417.

Cho, Changrae, Rong Li, S-Y Wang, Jin-Ho Yoon, and Robert R. Gillies. "Anthropogenic Footprint of Climate Change in the June 2013 Northern India Flood." *Climate Dynamics* 46, no. 3–4 (2016): 797–805.

Choi, Li Wen. "Shiyan City, Hubei Province Ecological Construction Assessment First in the Province." News release, June 9, 2017. http://www.nsbd.gov.cn/zx/sthj/201706/t20170609_484863.html.

Choy, J., and G. McGhee. "Groundwater: Ignore It, and It Might Go Away." *Water in the West*, December 19, 2014. http://waterinthewest.stanford.edu/groundwater/overview/ (accessed March 17, 2018).

Clark, Tim, and Ron Westrum. "Paradigms and Ferrets." *Social Studies of Science* 17, no. 1 (1987): 3–33.

Climate Home. "Don't Celebrate Yet: Why China's Green Shift Could Face Delays." *Climate Change News*, February 26, 2016. http://www.climatechangenews.com/2016/02/26/dont-celebrate-yet-why-chinas-green-shift-could-face-delays/.

Coates, Ta-Nehisi. *Between the World and Me*. New York: Random House, 2015.

Cohen, M. J. "The Colorado River Basin: Agenda for Use, Restoration, and Sustainability for the Next Generation." In *The 2012 Colorado College State of the Rockies Report Card*. State of the Rockies Project 2011–2012 Research Team, 2014.

Collins, C. P. "Climate Change Negotiations Polarize." *Ambio* 20, no. 7 (1991): 340–344.

Combs, James E. "A Process Approach." In *Handbook of Political Communication*, edited by Dan D. Nimmo and Keith R. Sanders, 39–65. Beverly Hills: Sage Publications, 1981.

Comte, Auguste, and Emile Littré. *Principes De Philosophie Positive*. JB Bailliere et fils, 1868.

Coombes, Brad, Jay T. Johnson, and Richard Howitt. "Indigenous Geographies II: The Aspirational Spaces in Postcolonial Politics—Reconciliation, Belonging and Social Provision." *Progress in Human Geography* 37, no. 5 (2012): 691–700.

Cover, Robert M. "Foreword: Nomos and Narrative." *Harvard Law Review* 97 (1983): 4.

CRED and UNISDR. "Poverty and Death: Disaster Mortality." 21. Brussels, Belgium: Center for Research on the Epidemiology of Disasters (CRED) and United Nations Office for Disaster Risk Reduction (UNISDR), 2016.

Critical Global Discussions. "What Is Climate Engineering?" http://www.ce -conference.org/what-climate-engineering.

Crutzen, Paul J. "Albedo Enhancement by Stratospheric Sulfur Injections: A Contribution to Resolve a Policy Dilemma?" *Climatic Change* 77, no. 3 (2006): 211.

Crutzen, Paul J. "The 'Anthropocene.'" In *Earth System Science in the Anthropocene*, edited by Eckart Ehlers and Thomas Krafft, 13–18. Berlin: Springer, 2006.

Crutzen, Paul J. "The Effects of Industrial and Agricultural Practices on Atmospheric Chemistry and Climate during the Anthropocene." *Journal of Environmental Science and Health, Part A* 37, no. 4 (2002): 423–424.

Crutzen, Paul J., and Eugene F. Stoermer. "The 'Anthropocene.'" *The International Geosphere—Biosphere Programme (IGBP) Newsletter* 41, May 2000.

Curato, Nicole. "Politics of Anxiety, Politics of Hope: Penal Populism and Duterte's Rise to Power." *Journal of Current Southeast Asian Affairs* 35, no. 3 (2017): 91–109.

Curato, Nicole. "In the Philippines, All the President's People." *New York Times*, May 31, 2017.

Dalby, Simon. "Anthropocene Geopolitics: Globalisation, Empire, Environment and Critique." *Geography Compass* 1, no. 1 (2007): 103–118.

Dalby, Simon. "Biopolitics and Climate Security in the Anthropocene." *Geoforum* 49 (2013): 184–192.

Dalby, Simon. "Geoengineering: The Next Era of Geopolitics?" *Geography Compass* 9, no. 4 (2015): 190–201.

Death, Carl, and Clive Gabay. "Doing Biopolitics Differently? Radical Potential in the Post-2015 Mdg and Sdg Debates." *Globalizations* 12, no. 4 (2015): 597–612.

de Groot, R. S., M. A. Wilson, and R. M. J. Boumans. "A Typology for the Classification, Description and Valuation of Ecosystem Functions, Goods and Services." *Ecological Economics* 41, no. 3 (2002): 393–408.

de Jong, Shona L. van Zijll, Dale Dominey-Howes, Carolina E. Roman, Emma Calgaro, Anna Gero, Siri Veland, Deanne K. Bird, et al. "Process, Practice and Priorities—Key Lessons Learnt Undertaking Sensitive Social Reconnaissance Research as Part of an (Unesco-Ioc) International Tsunami Survey Team." *Earth-Science Reviews* 107 (2011): 174–192.

De Larrinaga, Miguel, and Marc G. Doucet. "Sovereign Power and the Biopolitics of Human Security." *Security Dialogue* 39, no. 5 (2008): 517–537.

Dell, M., B. F. Jones, and B. A. Olken. "What Do We Learn from the Weather? The New Climate-Economy Literature." *Journal of Economic Literature* 52, no. 3 (2014): 740–798.

Dewey, John. *The Later Works, 1925–1953. Volume 7: 1932, Ethics.* Carbondale: Southern Illinois University Press, [1985], 2008.

Dewey, John. *Theory of the Moral Life.* New York: Holt, Rinehart and Winston, 1960.

Dietz, T., E. Ostrom, and P. C. Stern. "The Struggle to Govern the Commons." *Science* 302, no. 5652 (2003): 1907–1912.

Dirzo, R., H. S. Young, M. Galetti, G. Ceballos, N. J. B. Isaac, and B. Collen. "Defaunation in the Anthropocene." *Science* 345, no. 6195 (2014): 401–406.

Dobbernack, J., and T. Modood. "Tolerance in Critical and Political Theory: Coexistence or Parts of Something Bigger?" In *Undoing the Demos: Neoliberalism's Stealth Revolution,* edited by Wendy Brown, 164–168. Cambridge, MA: MIT Press, 2015.

Doohan, Kim. "Helping Whitefellas to See: Community Engagement and Cultural Pracices in Emergency Situations in Remote Regions (the Kimberley)." PhD thesis, Macquarie University, 2004.

Doremus, Holly. "The Rhetoric and Reality of Nature Protection: Toward a New Discourse." *Washington and Lee Law Review* 57 (2000): 11–73.

Dreyer, Jacob. "Only China Can Save the Planet." *Foreign Policy,* February 24, 2017, 24.

Dryzek, John S. "Institutions for the Anthropocene: Governance in a Changing Earth System." *British Journal of Political Science* 46, no. 4 (2016): 937–956.

Dryzek, John S. *The Politics of the Earth: Environmental Discourses.* Oxford: Oxford University Press, 1997.

Dryzek, John S. "Rhetoric in Democracy: A Systemic Appreciation." *Political Theory* 38, no. 3 (2010): 319–339.

Dryzek, John S., and Hayley Stevenson. "Global Democracy and Earth System Governance." *Ecological Economics* 70, no. 11 (2011): 1865–1874.

Dryzek, John S., David Downes, Christian Hunold, David Schlosberg, and Hans-Kristian Hernes. *Green States and Social Movements: Environmentalism in the*

United States, United Kingdom, Germany, and Norway. Oxford: Oxford University Press, 2003.

Dunant, Henri. *A Memory of Solferino*. Geneva: International Committee of the Red Cross, [1939] 1959.

Eakin, Hallie, and Amy Lynd Luers. "Assessing the Vulnerability of Social-Environmental Systems." *Annual Review of Environment and Resources* 31, no. 1 (2006): 365–394.

EarthData. "Giovanni: The Bridge between Data and Science." Version 4.24. NASA Earth Data, 2017.

Eisenberg, Evan. *The Ecology of Eden: Humans, Nature and Human Nature*. New York: Knopf, 1998.

El-Dahdah, Farès, and P. Proudhon. "Letter from Pierre-Joseph Proudhon to Karl Marx." *Assemblage* 41 (2000): 21. doi:10.2307/3171281.

Elders, The. "Strengthening the United Nations." News release, February 2015. https://theelders.org/sites/default/files/2015-04-22_elders-statement-strengthenin g-the-un.pdf (accessed March 19, 2018).

El Khoury, Ann. *Globalization Development and Social Justice: A Propositional Political Approach*. London: Routledge, 2015.

Elliott, S. M., and H. P. Hanson. "Discussion—Syndication of the Earth System: The Future of Geoscience?" *Environmental Science & Policy* 6, no. 5 (2003): 457–463.

Elvin, J. Mark. "Some Reflections on the Use of Styles of Scientific Thinking to Disaggregate and Sharpen Comparisons between China and Europe from S Ng to Mid-Qing Times (960 1850 Ce)." *History and Technology* 25 (2004): 53–103.

Errico, Stefania. "The Draft UN Declaration on the Rights of Indigenous Peoples: An Overview." *Human Rights Law Review* 7, no. 4 (2007): 741–755.

Esquivel, Valeria. "Power and the Sustainable Development Goals: A Feminist Analysis." *Gender and Development* 24, no. 1 (2016): 9–23.

Esteban, M., V. P. Valenzuela, R. Matsumaru, T. Mikami, T. Shibayama, H. Takagi, N. D. Thao, and M. De Leon. "Storm Surge Awareness in the Philippines Prior to Typhoon Haiyan: A Comparative Analysis with Tsunami Awareness in Recent Times." *Coastal Engineering Journal* 58, no. 1 (2016): 28.

Evans, A. D., and R. J. G. Falvey. "Annual Tropical Cyclone Report." News release, 2013. http://www.usno.navy.mil/NOOC/nmfc-ph/RSS/jtwc/atcr/2013atcr.pdf.

Fassin, Didier, and Mariella Pandolfi. *Contemporary States of Emergency: The Politics of Military and Humanitarian Interventions*. Cambridge, MA: Zone Books, 2010.

Feeny, D., F. Berkes, B. J. McCay, and J. M. Acheson. "The Tragedy of the Commons—22 Years Later." *Human Ecology* 18, no. 1 (1990): 1–19.

Ferguson, H. L. "The Changing Atmosphere: Implications for Global Security" In *Challenge of Global Warming*, edited by Dean E. Abrahamson, 44–62. Washington, DC: Island Press, 1988.

Fisher, Max. "Why the Philippines Wasn't Ready for Typhoon Haiyan." *Washington Post*, November 11, 2013. https://www.washingtonpost.com/news/worldviews/wp/2013/11/11/why-the-philippines-wasnt-ready-for-typhoon-haiyan/?utm_term =.8af4142006dd (accessed March 9, 2018).

Fitzpatrick, S. M., and W. F. Kleegan. "Human Impacts and Adaptations in the Caribbean Islands: An Historical Ecology Approach." *Earth and Environmental Science Transactions of the Royal Society of Edinburgh* 98 (2007): 29–45.

Fleming, James Rodger. "The Pathological History of Weather and Climate Modification: Three Cycles of Promise and Hype." *Historical Studies in the Physical and Biological Sciences* 37, no. 1 (2006): 3–25.

Flood, J. *Archaeology of the Dreamtime*. Honolulu: University of Hawaii Press, 1983.

Folke, C., L. Pritchard, F. Berkes, J. Colding, and U. Svedin. "The Problem of Fit between Ecosystems and Institutions: Ten Years Later." *Ecology and Society* 12, no. 1 (2007): article 30. https://www.ecologyandsociety.org/vol12/iss1/art30/ (accessed March 17, 2018).

Folke, Carl, Thomas Hahn, Per Olsson, and Jon Norberg. "Adaptive Governance of Social-Ecological Systems." *Annual Review of Environment and Resources* 30 (2005): 441–473.

Follestad, Marianne Solberg. "Bedre Enn Rafting I Sjoa!: En Studie Av Musikalsk Teambygging Med Korslaget Som Redskap." 2013.

Ford, Anabel, and Ronald Nigh. "Origins of the Maya Forest Garden: Maya Resource Management." *Journal of Ethnobiology* 29, no. 2 (2009): 213–236.

Foucault, Michel. *The Archaeology of Knowledge & the Discourse on Language*. New York: Pantheon Books, 1972.

Foucault, Michel. *The Birth of Biopolitics: Lectures at the Collège De France, 1978–1979*. Edited by Michel Senellart, Arnold I. Davidson, Alessandro Fontana, and François Ewald and translated by Graham Burchell. New York: Palgrave Macmillan, 2008.

Francisco, Rosemarie. "Analysis: Hero to Zero? Philippine President Feels Typhoon Backlash." *Reuters*, November 14, 2013. https://www.reuters.com/article/us-philippines-typhoon-aquino-analysis/analysis-hero-to-zero-philippine-president -feels-typhoon-backlash-idUSBRE9AE07U20131115.

Frantz, K., and R. Howitt. "Geography for and with Indigenous Peoples: Indigenous Geographies as Challenge and Invitation." *GeoJournal* 77, no. 6 (2012): 727–731.

Gabay, Clive. "Special Forum on the Millennium Development Goals: Introduction." *Globalizations* 12, no. 4 (2015): 576–580.

Gasalla, Maria A., and Fabricio C. Gandini. "The Loss of Fishing Territories in Coastal Areas: The Case of Seabob-Shrimp Small-Scale Fisheries in São Paulo, Brazil." *Maritime Studies* 15, no. 1 (2016): 9.

Geisinger, Alex. "Uncovering the Myth of a Jobs/Nature Trade-Off." *Syracuse Law Review* 51 (2001): 115.

Gergan, Mabel Denzin. "Living with Earthquakes and Angry Deities at the Himalayan Borderlands." *Annals of the Association of American Geographers* 107, no. 2 (2017): 490–498.

Giddens, A. *The Consequences of Modernity*. Cambridge: Polity Press, [1990] 2013.

Giddens, A. *The Constitution of Society: Outline of the Theory of Structuration*. Berkeley: University of California Press, 1984.

Gilley, B. "Authoritarian Environmentalism and China's Response to Climate Change." *Environmental Politics* 21, no. 2 (2012): 287–307.

Ginn, F. "When Horses Won't Eat: Apocalypse and the Anthropocene." *Annals of the Association of American Geographers* 105, no. 2 (2015): 351–359.

Ginsburg, Tom, and James Melton. "Does the Constitutional Amendment Rule Matter at All? Amendment Cultures and the Challenges of Measuring Amendment Difficulty." *International Journal of Constitutional Law* 13, no. 3 (2015): 686–713.

Gleick, Peter. "A Wet Year Won't Beat California's Never-Ending Drought." *WIRED*, January 22, 2017.

Global Humanitarian Assistance. *Global Humanitarian Assistance Report*. Bristol: Development Initiatives, 2014.

Gocotano, Allison, Lester Sam Geroy, Ma Rowena Alcido, Miguel Manuel Dorotan, Gloria Balboa, and Julie Lyn Hall. "Is the Response Over? The Transition from Response to Recovery in the Health Sector Post-Haiyan." *Western Pacific Surveillance and Response Journal: WPSAR* 6, no. S1 (2015): 5–9.

Gödel, Kurt. "Über Formal Unentscheidbare Sätze Der Principia Mathematica Und Verwandter Systeme I." *Monatshefte für mathematik und physik* 38, no. 1 (1931): 173–198.

Gould, Stephen Jay. "Is Uniformitarianism Necessary?" *American Journal of Science* 263, no. 3 (1965): 223–228.

Gould, Stephen Jay. *Time's Arrow, Time's Cycle: Myth and Metaphor in the Discovery of Geological Time*. Cambridge, MA: Harvard University Press, 1987.

Grafton, R. Quentin, Jamie Pittock, Richard Davis, John Williams, Guobin Fu, Michele Warburton, Bradley Udall, et al. "Global Insights into Water Resources, Climate Change and Governance." *Nature Climate Change* 3, no. 4 (2013): 315–321.

Green, Paul. "Subsidiarity and European Union: Beyond the Ideological Impasse? An Analysis of the Origins and Impact of the Principle of Subsidiarity within the Politics of the European Community." *Policy and Politics* 22, no. 4 (1994): 287–300.

Griffin, Daniel, and Kevin J. Anchukaitis. "How Unusual Is the 2012–2014 California Drought?" *Geophysical Research Letters* 41, no. 24 (2014): 9017–9023.

Grubb, Michael. "The Economics of the Kyoto Protocol." *World Economics Journal* 4, no. 3 (2003): 143–190.

Gunderson, L. H., and C. S. Holling. *Panarchy: Understanding Transformations in Human and Natural Systems*. Washington, DC: Island Press, 2002.

Guzman, Andrew T. "The Design of International Agreements." *European Journal of International Law* 16, no. 4 (2005): 579–612.

Hajer, Maarten A. *The Politics of Environmental Discourse: Ecological Modernization and the Policy Process*. New York: Clarendon Press, 1995.

Hajer, Maarten, Måns Nilsson, Kate Raworth, Peter Bakker, Frans Berkhout, Yvo de Boer, Johan Rockström, Kathrin Ludwig, and Marcel Kok. "Beyond Cockpit-ism: Four Insights to Enhance the Transformative Potential of the Sustainable Development Goals." *Sustainability* 7, no. 2 (2015): 1651–1660.

Hallegatte, S. "Strategies to Adapt to an Uncertain Climate Change." *Global Environmental Change* 19, no. 2 (2009): 240–247.

Hamann, Maike, Reinette Biggs, and Belinda Reyers. "An Exploration of Human Well-Being Bundles as Identifiers of Ecosystem Service Use Patterns." *PLoS One* 11, no. 10 (2016): e0163476.

Hamilton, Clive. "Geoengineering Is Not a Solution to Climate Change." *Scientific American*, March 10, 2015.

Hamilton, Clive. "The Theodicy of the 'Good Anthropocene.'" *Environmental Humanities* 7, no. 1 (2015): 233–238.

Hannoum, Abdelmajid. "Translation and the Colonial Imaginary: Ibn Khaldun Orientalist." *History and Theory* 42, no. 1 (2003): 61–81.

Haraway, Donna J. "Situated Knowledges: The Science Question in Feminism and the Privilege of Partial Perspective." *Feminist Studies* 14, no. 3 (1988): 575–599.

Haraway, Donna J. *Staying with the Trouble: Making Kin in the Chthulucene*. Durham, NC: Duke University Press, 2016.

Hardin, Garrett. "The Tragedy of the Commons." *Science* 162, no. 3859 (1968): 1243–1248.

Heathcote, Ronald Leslie. *Drought and the Human Story: Braving the Bull of Heaven*. Farnham, UK: Routledge, 2016.

Hémon, Denis, and Eric Jougla. "The Heat Wave in France in August 2003." *Epidemiology and Public Health/Revue d'Epidemiologie et de Sante Publique* 52, no. 1 (2004): 3–5.

Hendrick, George. "The Influence of Thoreau's 'Civil Disobedience' on Gandhi's Satyagraha." *New England Quarterly* 29, no. 4 (1956): 462–471.

Hewitt, Kenneth. "Power of Development." In *Sustainable Disasters? Perspectives and Powers in the Discourse of Calamity*, edited by J. Crush, 115–128. London: Routledge, 1995.

Hickman, Leo. "The Carbon Brief Interview: Syukuro Manabe." *Carbon Brief: Clear on Climate*, July 7, 2015.

Hodgson, Jenny A., Chris D. Thomas, Brendan A. Wintle, and Atte Moilanen. "Climate Change, Connectivity and Conservation Decision Making: Back to Basics." *Journal of Applied Ecology* 46, no. 5 (2009): 964–969.

Houston, Donna. "Crisis Is Where We Live: Environmental Justice for the Anthropocene." *Globalizations* 10, no. 3 (2013): 439–450.

Houston, Donna. "Environmental Justice Storytelling: Angels and Isotopes at Yucca Mountain, Nevada." *Antipode* 45, no. 2 (2013): 417–435.

Howitt, Richard. "Book Reviews: Murray River Country by Jessica Weir." *Australian Geographer* 42, no. 3 (2011): 343–349.

Howitt, Richard. "Knowing/Doing: A Manifesto for 'Radical Contextualist' Approaches to Social Geography." In *A Companion to Social Geography*, edited by V. J. Del Casino Jr., M. Thomas, P. Cloke, and R. Panelli, 131–145. Oxford: Blackwell, 2011.

Howitt, Richard. "Scales of Coexistence: Tackling the Tension between Legal and Cultural Landscapes in Post-Mabo Australia." *Macquarie Law Journal* 6 (2006): 49–64.

Howitt, Richard. "Sustainable Indigenous Futures in Remote Indigenous Areas: Relationships, Processes and Failed State Approaches." *GeoJournal* 77 (6) (2012): 817–828.

Howitt, Richard, Claire Colyer, Mitchell R. Hammer, Olga Havnen, Karen Huchendorf, and Carol Hubert. "Organisational Capacity for Engaging with Indigenous Australians." *Geographical Research* 52, no. 3 (2014): 250–262.

Howitt, Richard, and Sandra Suchet-Pearson. "Changing Country, Telling Stories: Research Ethics, Methods and Empowerment Working with Aboriginal Women." In *Fluid Bonds: Views on Gender and Water*, edited by Kuntala Lahiri-Dutt, 48–63. Kolkata: Stree Books, 2006.

Howitt, Richard, Kim Doohan, Sandie Suchet-Pearson, Sherrie Cross, Rebecca Lawrence, Gaim James Lunkapis, Samantha Muller, Sarah Prout, and Siri Veland.

"Intercultural Capacity Deficits: Contested Geographies of Coexistence in Natural Resource Management." *Asia Pacific Viewpoint* 54, no. 2 (2013): 126–140.

Howitt, Richard, Olga Havnen, and Siri Veland. "Natural and Unnatural Disasters: Responding with Respect for Indigenous Rights and Knowledges." *Geographical Research* 50, no. 1 (2012): 47–59.

Hsu, Angel, and Alisa Zomer. "Environmental Performance Index." *Wiley StatsRef: Statistics Reference Online*, 2016.

Hsu, M. "Lost, Found and Troubled in Translation: Reconsidering Imagined Indigenous 'Communities' in Post- Disaster Taiwan Settings." *AlterNative: An International Journal of Indigenous Peoples* 12, no. 1 (2016): 71–85.

Hsu, Minna, Richard Howitt, and Fiona Miller. "Procedural Vulnerability and Institutional Capacity Deficits in Post-Disaster Recovery and Reconstruction: Insights from Wutai Rukai Experiences of Typhoon Morakot." *Human Organization*, no. 2015 (2015): 308–318.

Hu, Dapeng. "Trade, Rural-Urban Migration, and Regional Income Disparity in Developing Countries: A Spatial General Equilibrium Model Inspired by the Case of China." *Regional Science and Urban Economics* 32, no. 3 (2002): 311–338.

Hulme, Mike. "The Conquering of Climate: Discourses of Fear and Their Dissolution." *Geographical Journal* 174, no. 1 (2008): 5–16.

Humphrey, Mathew. *Preservation versus the People? Nature, Humanity, and Political Philosophy*. Oxford: Oxford University Press, 2002.

Husserl, Edmund. *The Crisis of European Sciences and Transcendental Phenomenology: An Introduction to Phenomenological Philosophy*. Evanston, IL: Northwestern University Press, 1970.

Hutton, James. *Theory of the Earth: With Proofs and Illustrations*. London: Geological Society, 1899.

Huysmans, Jef. "The Jargon of Exception—on Schmitt, Agamben and the Absence of Political Society." *International Political Sociology* 2, no. 2 (2008): 165–183.

International Federation of Red Cross and Red Crescent Societies. "History." http://www.ifrc.org/en/who-we-are/history/ (accessed February 12, 2018).

International Federation of Red Cross and Red Crescent Societies. "Our Vision and Mission." http://www.ifrc.org/en/who-we-are/vision-and-mission/ (accessed November 29, 2017).

International Federation of Red Cross and Red Crescent Societies, Terry Cannon, and Lisa Schipper, eds. *World Disasters Report 2014: Focus on Culture and Risk*. Geneva, 2014. http://www.ifrc.org/en/publications-and-reports/world-disasters-report/world-disasters-report-2014/ (accessed November 29, 2017).

Isherwood, Craig. "Genocidalists Impose Water Restrictions on Food Producers during Flood." Citizens Electoral Council of Australia, January 7, 2011. http://cecaust.com.au/main.asp?sub=releases&id=2011_01_07_Block_Farmers.html (accessed March 12, 2018).

Jackson, Sue, Brad Moggridge, and Cathy J. Robinson. *Effects of Changes in Water Availability on Indigenous People of the Murray-Darling Basin: A Scoping Study*. Melbourne: CSIRO Melbourne, 2010. http://www.clw.csiro.au/publications/waterforahealthycountry/FactSheets/wfhc-MDB5-Indigenous-2010.pdf.

Jacobs, Chip, and William J. Kelly. *Smogtown: The Lung-Burning History of Pollution in Los Angeles*. New York: Overlook Press, 2008.

Jahn, Detlef. "Environmental Performance and Policy Regimes: Explaining Variations in 18 OECD-Countries." *Policy Sciences* 31, no. 2 (1998): 107–131.

Jamieson, Dale. *Reason in a Dark Time: Why the Struggle against Climate Change Failed—and What It Means for Our Future*. Oxford: Oxford University Press, 2014.

Jasanoff, Sheila. "A New Climate for Society." *Theory, Culture & Society* 27, no. 2–3 (2010): 233–253.

Jones, R. J. Barry. *Routledge Encyclopedia of International Political Economy*. London: Taylor & Francis, 2001.

Jones, Roger N. "An Environmental Risk Assessment/Management Framework for Climate Change Impact Assessments." *Natural Hazards* 23, no. 2 (2001): 197–230.

Kahan, Dan M. "Cultural Cognition as a Conception of the Cultural Theory of Risk." In *Handbook of Risk Theory*, edited by Sabine Roeser, Rafaela Hillerbrand, Per Sandin, and Martin Peterson, 725–759. Dordrecht, the Netherlands: Springer, 2012.

Kahan, Dan M., Donald Braman, John Gastil, Paul Slovic, and C. K. Mertz. "Culture and Identity-Protective Cognition: Explaining the White-Male Effect in Risk Perception." *Journal of Empirical Legal Studies* 4, no. 3 (2007): 465–505.

Kahan, Dan M., Ellen Peters, Maggie Wittlin, Paul Slovic, Lisa Larrimore Ouellette, Donald Braman, and Gregory Mandel. "The Polarizing Impact of Science Literacy and Numeracy on Perceived Climate Change Risks." *Nature Climate Change* 2, no. 10 (2012): 732–735.

Kaplan, Abraham. *American Ethics and Public Policy*. Westport, CT: Greenwood Press, 1963.

Kaplan, Abraham. *The Conduct of Inquiry: Methodology for Behavioral Science*. San Francisco: Chandler Publishing Company, 1964.

Kareiva, Peter, and Michelle Marvier. "Conservation for the People." *Scientific American* 297, no. 4 (2007): 50–57.

Kareiva, Peter, Michelle Marvier, and Robert Lalasz. "Conservation in the Anthropocene." *Breakthrough Journal*, no. 2 (Winter 2012). https://thebreakthrough.org/index.php/journal/past-issues/issue-2/conservation-in-the-anthropocene.

Karp, L. "Global Warming and Hyperbolic Discounting." *Journal of Public Economics* 89, no. 2–3 (2005): 261–282.

Kasperson, Roger E., Ortwin Renn, Paul Slovic, Halina S. Brown, Jacque Emel, Robert Goble, Jeanne X. Kasperson, and Samuel Ratick. "The Social Amplification of Risk: A Conceptual Framework." *Risk Analysis* 8, no. 2 (1988): 177–187.

Kauffman, J. B. "Death Rides the Forest: Perceptions of Fire, Land Use, and Ecological Restoration of Western Forests." *Conservation Biology* 18, no. 4 (2004): 878–882.

Keller, Robert H., and Michael F. Turek. *American Indians and National Parks*. Tucson: University of Arizona Press, 1999.

Kellogg, William W., and Stephen H. Schneider. "Climate Stabilization: For Better or for Worse." *Science* 186, no. 4170 (1974): 1163–1172.

Kelman, Ilan. "Linking Disaster Risk Reduction, Climate Change, and the Sustainable Development Goals." *Disaster Prevention and Management: An International Journal* 26, no. 3 (2017): 254–258.

Kelman, Ilan. "Climate Change and the Sendai Framework for Disaster Risk Reduction." *International Journal of Disaster Risk Science* 6, no. 2 (2015): 117–127.

Keohane, Robert O., and David G. Victor. "The Regime Complex for Climate Change." *Perspectives on Politics* 9, no. 1 (2011): 7–23.

Keynes, J. M. *The Collected Writings of John Maynard Keynes*. Vol. 21, *Activities 1931–1939: World Crises and Policies in Britain and America*, edited by Elizabeth Johnson and Donald Moggridge. Cambridge, UK: Royal Economic Society, 1978. doi:10.1017/UPO9781139524209.

King, L. A., and V. L. Hood. "Ecosystem Health and Sustainable Communities: North and South." *Ecosystem Health* 5, no. 1 (1999): 49–57.

King, Martin Luther. *Pilgrimage to Nonviolence*. New York: Fellowship Publications, 1960.

Kingsbury, Benedict. "'Indigenous Peoples' in International Law: A Constructivist Approach to the Asian Controversy." *American Journal of International Law* 92, no. 3 (2017): 414–457.

Kitong, Jacqueline, and Anthony Calibo. "Guidelines and Training for Maternal and Newborn Care Post-Haiyan." *Western Pacific Surveillance and Response Journal* 6, no. S1 (2015): 15–17.

Klein, Naomi. *The Shock Doctrine*. London: Penguin Books, 2008.

Krüger, Fred, Greg Bankoff, Terry Cannon, Benedikt Orlowski, and E. Lisa F. Schipper. *Cultures and Disasters: Understanding Cultural Framings in Disaster Risk Reduction.* London: Routledge, 2015.

Lagmay, Alfredo Mahar Francisco, Rojelee P. Agaton, Mark Allen C. Bahala, Jo Brianne Louise T. Briones, Krichi May C. Cabacaba, Carl Vincent C. Caro, Lea L. Dasallas, et al. "Devastating Storm Surges of Typhoon Haiyan." *International Journal of Disaster Risk Reduction* 11 (2015): 1–12.

Landau, Martin. "Redundancy, Rationality, and the Problem of Duplication and Overlap." *Public Administration Review* 29, no. 4 (1969): 346–358.

Lash, Scott. "The End of Neo-Corporatism? The Breakdown of Centralised Bargaining in Sweden." *British Journal of Industrial Relations* 23, no. 2 (1985): 215–239.

Laski, Harold Joseph. *The State in Theory and Practice.* New Brunswick: Transaction Publishers, 2008.

Lasswell, Harold D. *A Pre-View of Policy Sciences.* New York: Elsevier, 1971.

Lasswell, Harold D., and Abraham Kaplan. *Power and Society: A Framework for Political Inquiry.* New Haven, CT: Yale University Press, 1950.

Lasswell, Harold D., Daniel Lerner, and Ithiel de Sola Pool. *The Comparative Study of Symbols: An Introduction.* Stanford, CA: Stanford University Press, 1952.

Latour, Bruno. *Politics of Nature.* Cambridge, MA: Harvard University Press, 2009.

Latour, Bruno. *We Have Never Been Modern.* Cambridge, MA: Harvard University Press, 1993.

Laumer, John. "Did Russ George's Geoengineering Experiment Actually Work?" *Treehugger*, April 28, 2014.

Lavine, Thelma Z. "The Interpretive Turn from Kant to Derrida: A Critique." In *History and Anti-History in Philosophy*, edited by Thelma Z. Lavine and Victoria Tejera, 32–121. Dordrecht, the Netherlands: Springer, 1989.

Law, John. *After Method: Mess in Social Science Research.* London, New York: Routledge, 2004.

Leach, Melissa. "Democracy in the Anthropocene? Science and Sustainable Development Goals at the UN." *Huffington Post*, March 28, 2013.

Leach, Melissa, Johan Rockström, Paul Raskin, Ian Scoones, Andy C. Stirling, Adrian Smith, John Thompson, et al. "Transforming Innovation for Sustainability." *Ecology and Society* 17, no. 2 (2012): article 11. https://www.ecologyandsociety.org/vol17/iss2/art11/ (accessed March 19, 2018).

Lear, Linda. *Rachel Carson: Witness for Nature.* Boston: Houghton Mufflin Harcourt, 1998.

Lee, Henry Desmond Pritchard. *The Republic*. London: Penguin, [1955] 2003.

Le Guin, *Ursula K. Dancing at the Edge of the World: Thoughts on Words, Women, Places*. New York: Grove Press, 2017.

Lehmbruch, G., and P. C. Schmitter. *Patterns of Corporatist Policy-Making*. New Delhi: Sage Publications, 1982.

Leichenko, R., and K. O'Brien. *Environmental Change and Globalisation: Double Exposures*. Oxford: Oxford University Press, 2008.

Leiserowitz, Anthony. "Climate Change Risk Perception and Policy Preferences: The Role of Affect, Imagery, and Values." *Climatic Change* 77, no. 1 (2006): 45–72.

Lennox, Corinne, and Damien Short. *Handbook of Indigenous Peoples' Rights*. New York: Routledge, 2016.

Leopold, Aldo. *Game Management*. Madison: University of Wisconsin Press, 1987.

Leopold, Aldo. "Why the Wilderness Society." *Living Wilderness* 1, no. 6 (1935): 31–34.

Lerner, Daniel, Ithiel Pool, and Harold D. Lasswell. "Comparative Analysis of Political Ideologies: A Preliminary Statement." *Public Opinion Quarterly* 15, no. 4 (1951): 715–733.

Levinas, Emmanuel. "Revelation in the Jewish Tradition." In *The Levinas Reader*, edited by Sean Hand, 190–210. Oxford: Blackwell, 1989.

Levi-Strauss, Claude. *The Savage Mind*. Chicago: University of Chicago Press, 1966.

Lewis, Jack. "The Birth of EPA." *EPA Journal* 11 (1985): 6.

Lewis, Martin W. "On Human Connectedness with Nature." *New Literary History* 24, no. 4 (1993): 797–809.

Libæk, Ivar. "The Red Cross: Three-Time Recipient of the Peace Prize." *Nobelprize.org*, October 30, 2003. https://www.nobelprize.org/nobel_prizes/themes/peace/libaek/.

Liefferink, Duncan, and Mikael Skou Andersen. "Strategies of the 'Green' Member States in EU Environmental Policy-Making." *Journal of European Public Policy* 5, no. 2 (1998): 254–270.

Lijphart, Arend. "Constitutional Design for Divided Societies." *Journal of Democracy* 15, no. 2 (2004): 96–109.

Lijphart, Arend. *Democracies: Patterns of Majoritarian and Consensus Government in Twenty-One Countries*. New Haven, CT: Yale University Press, 1984.

Lijphart, Arend, and Markus M. L. Crepaz. "Corporatism and Consensus Democracy in Eighteen Countries: Conceptual and Empirical Linkages." *British Journal of Political Science* 21, no. 2 (1991): 235–246.

Lin, N., and K. Emanuel. "Grey Swan Tropical Cyclones." *Nature Climate Change* 6, no. 1 (2016): 106.

Lind, Vibeke, Annette Bär, Lise Aanensen, Pål Thorvaldsen, Kjell-Arne Augustsen, Marit Dyrhaug, and Inger Hansen. *Gammelnorsk Sau I Unike Kulturlandskap. Dyrevelferd Og Skjøtsel Av Kystlynghei Sett I Sammenheng.* Bioforsk Rapport, 2015.

Linnell, John D. C., Henrik Broseth, John Odden, and Erlend Birkeland Nilsen. "Sustainably Harvesting a Large Carnivore? Development of Eurasian Lynx Populations in Norway During 160 Years of Shifting Policy." *Environmental Management* 45, no. 5 (2010): 1142–1154.

Lippmann, Walter. *Public Opinion.* New York: Free Press, [1922] 1965.

Littell, J. S., D. McKenzie, D. L. Peterson, and A. L. Westerling. "Climate and Wildfire Area Burned in Western U. S. Ecoprovinces, 1916–2003." *Ecological Applications* 19, no. 4 (2009): 1003–1021.

Lo, A. Y. "Challenges to the Development of Carbon Markets in China." *Climate Policy* 16, no. 1 (2016): 109–124.

Lo, A. Y. "National Development and Carbon Trading: The Symbolism of Chinese Climate Capitalism." *Eurasian Geography and Economics* 56, no. 2 (2015): 111–126.

Lovelock, Catherine E., Trisha Atwood, Jeff Baldock, Carlos M. Duarte, Sharyn Hickey, Paul S. Lavery, Pere Masque, et al. "Assessing the Risk of Carbon Dioxide Emissions from Blue Carbon Ecosystems." *Frontiers in Ecology and the Environment* 15, no. 5 (2017): 257–265.

Lukacs, Martin. "World's Biggest Geoengineering Experiment 'Violates' UN Rules." *Guardian,* October 15, 2012.

Lum, Thomas, and Rhoda Margesson. "Typhoon Haiyan (Yolanda): US and International Response to Philippines Disaster." *Current Politics and Economics of South, Southeastern, and Central Asia* 23, no. 2 (2014): 1–209.

Lutz, Donald S. "Toward a Theory of Constitutional Amendment." *American Political Science Review* 88, no. 2 (1994): 355–370.

Lynch, Amanda H., David Griggs, Lee Joachim, and Jackie Walker. "The Role of the Yorta Yorta People in Clarifying the Common Interest in Sustainable Management of the Murray–Darling Basin, Australia." *Policy Sciences* 46, no. 2 (2013): 109–123.

Macey, Richard. "This Drought May Never Break." *Sydney Morning Herald,* January 4, 2008. https://www.smh.com.au/news/environment/this-drought-may-never-break/2008/01/03/1198949986473.html (accessed March 12, 2018).

Macfarlane, A. M. "Energy: The Issue of the 21st Century." *Elements* 3, no. 3 (2007): 165–170.

Machiavelli, Niccolo. *The Discourses*. London: Penguin, [1517] 1970.

Mahdi, Asma. "Los Angeles County's Energy and Air Quality Earn a C on UCLA Environmental Report Card." *UCLA Newsroom*, April 27, 2017.

Mann, Michael E., Raymond S. Bradley, and Malcolm K. Hughes. "Northern Hemisphere Temperatures during the Past Millennium: Inferences, Uncertainties, and Limitations." *Geophysical Research Letters* 26, no. 6 (1999): 759–762.

Mansuri, Ghazala, and Vijayendra Rao. *Localizing Development: Does Participation Work?* Washington, DC: World Bank Publications, 2012.

Mas, Erick, J. Bricker, Shuichi Kure, Bruno Adriano, Carine Yi, Anawat Suppasri, and Shunichi Koshimura. "Field Survey Report and Satellite Image Interpretation of the 2013 Super Typhoon Haiyan in the Philippines." *Natural Hazards and Earth System Sciences* 15 (2015): 805–816.

Massey, D. *For Space*. Thousand Oaks, CA: Sage Publications, 2005.

Max-Neef, Manfred. "Foundations of Transdisciplinarity." *Ecological Economics* 53 (2005): 5–16.

Mbaria, John, and Mordecai Ogada. *The Big Conservation Lie: The Untold Story of Wildlife Conservation in Kenya*. Auburn, WA: Lens & Pens Publishing, 2017.

McBride, Larry, and John Pendergrass. "Coal." In *Sustainable Environmental Law: Integrating Natural Resources and Pollution Abatement Law from Resources to Recovery*, edited by C. Campbell-Mohn, B. Breen, and J. W. Futrell, 993–1042. Washington, DC: West Publishing Co., 1993.

McGinnis, John O. "The Political Economy of Global Multilateralism." *Chicago Journal of International Law* 1, no. 2 (2000): 381.

McMichael, P. "Changing the Subject of Development." In *Contesting Development: Critical Struggles for Social Change*, edited by P. McMichael, 1–13. New York: Routledge, 2010.

MEA (Millennium Ecosystem Assessment). *Ecosystems and Human Well-Being: Synthesis*. Washington, DC: Island Press, 2005.

Meehl, G. A., and C. Tebaldi. "More Intense, More Frequent, and Longer Lasting Heat Waves in the 21st Century." *Science* 305, no. 5686 (2004): 994–997.

Merchant, Carolyn. *The Death of Nature: Women, Ecology, and the Scientific Revolution*. San Francisco: Harper & Row, 1989.

Merkle, Judith A. "Scientific Management." *International Encyclopedia of Public Policy and Administration* 3 (1998): 2036–2040.

Miller, Alan S. "Energy Policy from Nixon to Clinton: From Grand Provider to Market Facilitator." *Environmental Law* 25 (1995): 715–731.

Millon-Delsol, Chantal. *L'État subsidiaire: Ingérence et non-ingérence de l'État: le principe de subsidiarité aux fondements de l'histoire européenne.* Paris: Presses Universitaires de France-PUF, 1992.

Moisio, Sami, Veit Bachmann, Luiza Bialasiewicz, Elena dell'Agnese, Jason Dittmer, and Virginie Mamadouh. "Mapping the Political Geographies of Europeanization: National Discourses, External Perceptions and the Question of Popular Culture." *Progress in Human Geography* 37, no. 6 (2013): 737–761.

Mol, Annemarie. "Ontological Politics: A Word and Some Questions." *Sociological Review* 47, no. S1 (1999): 74–89.

Monserrat, Sebastià, and A. B. Rabinovich. "Meteotsunamis: Atmospherically Induced Destructive Ocean Waves in the Tsunami Frequency Band." *Natural Hazards and Earth System Sciences* 6, no. 6 (2006): 1035–1051.

Moore, S. M. "Modernisation, Authoritarianism, and the Environment: The Politics of China's South-North Water Transfer Project." *Environmental Politics* 23, no. 6 (2014): 947–964.

Moran, Daniel D., Mathis Wackernagel, Justin A. Kitzes, Steven H. Goldfinger, and Aurélien Boutaud. "Measuring Sustainable Development—Nation by Nation." *Ecological Economics* 64, no. 3 (2008): 470–474.

Morgan, M. Granger. "Managing Carbon from the Bottom Up." *Science* 289, no. 5488 (2000): 2285.

Morgan, Monica, Lisa Strelein, and Jessica Weir. "Indigenous Rights to Water in the Murray Darling Basin: In Support of the Indigenous Final Report to the Living Murray Initiative." AIATSIS Research Discussion Paper Series 14. Canberra, Australia 2004.

Morgensen, Scott Lauria. "The Biopolitics of Settler Colonialism: Right Here, Right Now." *Settler Colonial Studies* 1, no. 1 (2011): 52–76.

Mosca, Gaetano, Hannah D. Kahn, and Arthur Livingston. *Elementi Di Scienza Politica.* New York: McGraw-Hill, 1939.

Mouffe, Chantal. *Agonistics: Thinking the World Politically.* New York: Verso Books, 2013.

Mouffe, Chantal. "Deliberative Democracy or Agonistic Pluralism?" *Social Research* 66, no. 3 (Fall 1999): 745–758.

Mouffe, Chantal. *The Democratic Paradox.* New York: Verso Books, 2000.

Mowat, Farley. *Never Cry Wolf: The Amazing True Story of Life among Arctic Wolves.* Boston: Little, Brown, 1963.

Nadasdy, Paul. "The Gift in the Animal: The Ontology of Hunting and Human–Animal Sociality." *American Ethnologist* 34, no. 1 (2007): 25–43.

Nagourney, Adam. "When Is a Drought Over? A Wet California Wants to Know." *New York Times*, March 10, 2017. https://www.nytimes.com/2017/03/10/us/california-drought-snowpack.html (accessed March 19, 2018).

National Disaster Risk Reduction and Management Center, Philippines. "Effects of Typhoon 'Yolanda'(Haiyan)." *National Disaster Risk Reduction and Management Council (NDRRMC) Update*, April 3, 2014.

National Research Council. *Climate Intervention: Reflecting Sunlight to Cool Earth*. Washington, DC: National Academies Press, 2015.

Nazario, Sonia. *Enrique's Journey: The Story of a Boy's Dangerous Odyssey to Reunite with His Mother*. New York: Random House, 2007.

Németh, Károly, and Shane J. Cronin. "Volcanic Structures and Oral Traditions of Volcanism of Western Samoa (SW Pacific) and Their Implications for Hazard Education." *Journal of Volcanology and Geothermal Research* 186 (2009): 223–237.

New Climate Economy. *Better Growth, Better Climate: The New Climate Economy Report*. Washington, DC: Global Commission on the Economy and Climate, 2014.

Nicolescu, Basarab. "Methodology of Transdisciplinarity: Levels of Reality, Logic of the Included Middle and Complexity." *Transdisciplinary Journal of Engineering & Science* 1 (2010): 19.

Nixon, Rob. *Slow Violence and the Environmentalism of the Poor*. Cambridge, MA: Harvard University Press, 2011.

Nordhaus, Ted, Michael Shellenberger, and Linus Blomqvist. *The Planetary Boundaries Hypothesis: A Review of the Evidence*. 2012. https://thebreakthrough.org/blog/Planetary%20Boundaries%20web.pdf (accessed March 17, 2018).

Norgaard, Kari Marie. "'People Want to Protect Themselves a Little Bit': Emotions, Denial, and Social Movement Nonparticipation." *Sociological Inquiry* 76, no. 3 (2006): 372–396.

Nunn, Patrick D., and Nicholas J. Reid. "Aboriginal Memories of Inundation of the Australian Coast Dating from More Than 7,000 Years Ago." *Australian Geographer* 47 (2015): 1–37.

O'Brien, Karen, Siri Eriksen, Lynn Nygaard, and Ane Schjolden. "Why Different Interpretations of Vulnerability Matter in Climate Change Discourses." *Climate Policy* 7 (2007): 73–88.

OECD Environment Programme. "Indicators to Measure Decoupling of Environmental Pressure from Economic Growth: Executive Summary." White paper, 2002.

Oliver-Smith, Anthony. "Post Disaster Consensus and Conflict in a Traditional Society: The 1970 Avalanche of Yungay, Peru." *Mass Emergencies* 4 (1979): 39–52.

Oliver-Smith, Anthony. "Traditional Agriculture, Central Places, and Postdisaster Urban Relocation in Peru." *American Ethnologist* 4, no. 1 (1977): 102–116.

Olivier, J. G. J., Greet Janssens-Maenhout, Marilena Muntean, and Jeroen A. H. W. Peters. *Trends in Global Co2 Emissions: 2016 Report*. The Hague: PBL Netherlands Environmental Assessment Agency, 2016.

Osborn, B. P. "Native American Winters Doctrine and Stevens Treaty Water Rights: Recognition, Quantification, Management." *Journal of Water Law* 20, no. 5–6 (2009): 224–235.

Ostrom, Elinor. "Institutional Rational Choice: An Assessment of the Institutional Analysis and Development Framework." In *Theories of the Policy Process*, edited by Paul A. Sabatier, 21–64. Boulder, CO: Westview Press, 2007.

Ostrom, Elinor. "Polycentric Systems for Coping with Collective Action and Global Environmental Change." *Global Environmental Change* 20, no. 4 (2010): 550–557.

Ostrom, Elinor. *Understanding Institutional Diversity*. Princeton, NJ: Princeton University Press, 2009.

Ostrom, Elinor, Christina Chang, Mark Pennington, and Vlad Tarko. *Future of the Commons: Beyond Market Failure and Government Regulations*. London: Institute of Economic Affairs, 2012.

Ostrom, Elinor, and Vincent Ostrom. "The Quest for Meaning in Public Choice." *American Journal of Economics and Sociology* 63, no. 1 (2004): 105–147.

Palmer, Wayne C. "Meteorological Drought." US Department of Commerce Research Paper No. 45. Washington, DC, 1965.

Pålsson, Anne-Marie. "The EU's Principle of Subsidiarity: An Empty Promise." EUD Alliance for a Europe of Democracies. Belgium: EU Democrats, 2013.

Parenti, C. *Tropic of Chaos: Climate Change and the New Geography of Violence*. New York: Nation Books, 2011.

Paris Agreement. "Adoption of the Paris Agreement." FCCC/CP/2015/L. 9/Rev. 1, 2015.

Penn, Helen. "Patronage, Welfare, Tenders, Private Consultancies, and Expert Measurement: The Example of SDG 4.2." *Global Social Policy* 17, no. 2 (2017): 217–223.

Plenn, D. T. *The Green Song (La Canción Verde)*. New York: D. McKay Co., 1954.

Plumwood, V. *Shadow Places and the Politics of Dwelling*. Australian Humanities Review, no. 44 (2008), http://www.australianhumanitiesreview.org/archive/Issue -March-2008/plumwood.html.

Porter, L., and J. Barry. *Planning for Coexistence? Recognizing Indigenous Rights through Land-Use Planning in Canada and Australia*. New York: Taylor & Francis, 2016.

Poumadere, Marc, Claire Mays, Sophie Le Mer, and Russell Blong. "The 2003 Heat Wave in France: Dangerous Climate Change Here and Now." *Risk Analysis* 25, no. 6 (2005): 1483–1494.

Prewitt, Kenneth. "Public Statistics and Democratic Politics." In *Behavioral and Social Science: 50 Years of Discovery*, edited by Neil J. Smelser and Dean R. Gerstein, 113–128. Washington, DC: National Academies Press, 1986.

Pritchard, James Bennett. *The Ancient Near East: Supplementary Texts and Pictures Relating to the Old Testament*. Princeton: Princeton University Press, 1969.

Pulitano, Elvira. *Indigenous Rights in the Age of the UN Declaration*. Cambridge: Cambridge University Press, 2012.

Punzalan, Jamaine. "Duterte Blames Yolanda on Industrialized Nations, Belittles Us Aid." ABS-CBN News, October 17, 2016. http://news.abs-cbn.com/news/10/17/16/duterte-blames-yolanda-on-industrialized-nations-belittles-us-aid (accessed March 10, 2018).

Rachlinski, J. J. "The Psychology of Global Climate Change." *University of Illinois Law Review*, no. 1 (2000): 299–319.

Rand, Ayn. *The Ayn Rand Lexicon: Objectivism from A to Z*. Edited by. H. Binswanger. New York: Penguin, 1988.

Ratcliffe, Matthew. "Phenomenology as a Form of Empathy." *Inquiry* 55, no. 5 (2012): 473–495.

Rawls, John. "The Idea of an Overlapping Consensus." *Oxford Journal of Legal Studies* 7 (1987): 1.

Rawls, John. *Political Liberalism*. New York: Columbia University Press, 2005.

Rayner, Steve. *"Planetary Boundaries as Millenarian Prophesies: Malthusian Echoes."* Breakthrough, April 17, 2013.

Ribot, Jesse. "Cause and Response: Vulnerability and Climate in the Anthropocene." *Journal of Peasant Studies* 41, no. 5 (2014): 667–705.

Rigby, Kate. *Topographies of the Sacred: The Poetics of Place in European Romanticism*. Charlottesville: University of Virginia Press, 2004.

Rigby, Kate. "Writing after Nature." *Australian Humanities Review*, no. 39–40 (September 2006). http://australianhumanitiesreview.org/2006/09/01/writing-after-nature/.

Risvoll, Camilla, Gunn Elin Fedreheim, and Diego Galafassi. "Trade-offs in Pastoral Governance in Norway: Challenges for Biodiversity and Adaptation." *Pastoralism* 6, no. 1 (2016): 4.

Rittel, Horst W. J., and Melvin M. Webber. "Dilemmas in a General Theory of Planning." *Policy Sciences* 4, no. 2 (1973): 155–169.

Roberts, Erin, and Mark Pelling. "Climate Change-Related Loss and Damage: Translating the Global Policy Agenda for National Policy Processes." *Climate and Development* 10 (2016): 1–14.

Robertson, James. *Future Work: Jobs, Self-Employment, and Leisure after the Industrial Age.* London: Gower/Maurice Temple Smith Universe Pub, 1985.

Rockström, Johan, Will Steffen, Kevin Noone, Åsa Persson, F. Stuart III Chapin, Eric F. Lambin, Timothy M. Lenton, et al. "Planetary Boundaries: Exploring the Safe Operating Space for Humanity." *Ecology and Society* 14, no. 2 (2009): article 32. http://www.ecologyandsociety.org/vol14/iss2/art32/ (accessed March 19, 2018).

Rockström, Johan, Will Steffen, Kevin Noone, Åsa Persson, F. Stuart Chapin, Eric F. Lambin, Timothy M. Lenton, et al. "A Safe Operating Space for Humanity." *Nature* 461, no. 7263 (2009): 472–475.

Rogelj, J., M. den Elzen, N. Hohne, T. Fransen, H. Fekete, H. Winkler, R. S. Chaeffer, et al. "Paris Agreement Climate Proposals Need a Boost to Keep Warming Well Below 2 Degrees C." *Nature* 534, no. 7609 (2016): 631–639.

Rogelj, J., G. Luderer, R. C. Pietzcker, E. Kriegler, M. Schaeffer, V. Krey, and K. Riahi. "Energy System Transformations for Limiting End-of-Century Warming to Below 1.5 Degrees C." *Nature Climate Change* 5, no. 6 (2015): 519.

Rogow, Arnold A., and Harold Dwight Lasswell. *Power, Corruption, and Rectitude.* Englewood Cliffs, NJ: Prentice-Hall, 1963.

Rose, Deborah Bird. "Indigenous Water Philosophy in an Uncertain Land." In *From Disaster Response to Risk Management: Australia's National Drought Policy*, edited by Linda Courtenay Botterill and Donald A. Wilhite, 37–50. Dordrecht, the Netherlands: Springer, 2005.

Rose, Deborah Bird. "Land Rights and Deep Colonising: The Erasure of Women." *Indigenous Law Bulletin* 28 (1996): 6–13.

Rose, Deborah Bird. *Nourishing Terrains: Australian Aboriginal Views of Landscape and Wilderness.* Canberra: Australian Heritage Commission, 1996.

Rose, Deborah Bird. "Pattern, Connection, Desire: In Honour of Gregory Bateson." *Australian Humanities Review*, no. 35 (June 2005). http://australianhumanitiesreview .org/2005/06/01/pattern-connection-desire-in-honour-of-gregory-bateson/ (accessed March 19, 2018).

Rose, Deborah Bird. *Reports from a Wild Country: Ethics for Decolonisation.* Sydney: UNSW Press, 2004.

Rose, Deborah Bird. "Shimmer: When All You Love Is Being Trashed." In *Arts of Living on a Damaged Planet: Ghosts and Monsters of the Anthropocene*, edited by A. L. Tsing and N. Bubandt, 51–63. Minneapolis: University of Minnesota Press, 2017.

Rosenthal, Jack. "A Terrible Thing to Waste." *New York Times Magazine*, July 31, 2009. http://www.nytimes.com/2009/08/02/magazine/02FOB-onlanguage-t.html (accessed March 12, 2018).

Rossiter, Clinton L. *Constitutional Dictatorship: Crisis Government in the Modern Democracies*. New York: Harcourt Brace, 1948.

Rousseau, J. J. "Social Contract and Discourses." *The Social Contract or Principles of Political Right, Book 1*. Translated and with an introduction by G. D. H. Cole. New York: Bartelby, 2010.

Rubin, C. T. "Environmental-Policy and Environmental Thought—Ruckelshaus and Commoner." *Environmental Ethics* 11, no. 1 (1989): 27–51.

Sabel, C. F., and D. G. Victor. "Governing Global Problems under Uncertainty: Making Bottom-Up Climate Policy Work." *Climatic Change* 144 (2017): 15.

Salenga, Roderick, Yolanda Robles, Monet Loquias, Francis Capule, and Anna Melissa Guerrero. "Medicines Management in the Philippine Public Sector during the Response to Haiyan." *Western Pacific Surveillance and Response Journal* 6, no. S1 (2015): 82–85. doi:10.5365/wpsar.2015.6.2.HYN_012.

Sapir, Edward. "The Emergence of the Concept of Personality in a Study of Cultures." *Journal of Social Psychology* 5, no. 3 (1934): 408–415.

Saul, John Ralston. *Voltaire's Bastards: The Dictatorship of Reason in the West*. New York: Vintage Books, 1992.

Schar, C., P. L. Vidale, D. Luthi, C. Frei, C. Haberli, M. A. Liniger, and C. Appenzeller. "The Role of Increasing Temperature Variability in European Summer Heatwaves." *Nature* 427, no. 6972 (2004): 332–336.

Schipper, E. Lisa F., Thomalla Frank, Vulturius Gregor, Davis Marion, and Johnson Karlee. "Linking Disaster Risk Reduction, Climate Change and Development." *International Journal of Disaster Resilience in the Built Environment* 7, no. 2 (2016): 216–228.

Schlenker, Wolfram, W. Michael Hanemann, and Anthony C. Fisher. "The Impact of Global Warming on US Agriculture: An Econometric Analysis of Optimal Growing Conditions." *Review of Economics and Statistics* 88, no. 1 (2006): 113–125.

Schleussner, Carl-Friedrich, Jonathan F. Donges, Reik V. Donner, and Hans Joachim Schellnhuber. "Armed-Conflict Risks Enhanced by Climate-Related Disasters in Ethnically Fractionalized Countries." *Proceedings of the National Academy of Sciences of the United States of America* 113, no. 33 (2016): 9216–9221.

Schmitt, Carl. *Political Theology: Four Chapters on the Concept of Sovereignty*. Chicago: University of Chicago Press, 1985. First published as *Politische Theologie: Vier Kapitel Zur Lehre Von Der Souveränität*. Munchen: Duncker & Humblot, 1922.

Schmitter, P. C. "Reflections on Where the Theory of Neo-Corporatism Has Gone and Where the Praxis of Neo-Corporatism May Be Going." In *Patterns of Corporatist Policy-Making*, edited by G. Lehmbruch and P. C. Schmitter, 259–279. London: Sage, 1982.

Schneider, Stephen H. "Abrupt Non-linear Climate Change, Irreversibility and Surprise." *Global Environmental Change* 14, no. 3 (2004): 245–258.

Schneider, Stephen H. "Geoengineering: Could We or Should We Make It Work?" *Philosophical Transactions of the Royal Society of London A: Mathematical, Physical and Engineering Sciences* 366, no. 1882 (2008): 3843–3862.

Schneider, Stephen H. "What Is 'Dangerous' Climate Change?" *Nature* 411, no. 6833 (2001): 17–19.

Scott, D., C. M. Hall, and S. Gossling. "A Report on the Paris Climate Change Agreement and Its Implications for Tourism: Why We Will Always Have Paris." *Journal of Sustainable Tourism* 24, no. 7 (2016): 933–948.

Scott, James C. *Seeing Like a State: How Certain Schemes to Improve the Human Condition Have Failed*. New Haven, CT: Yale University Press, 1998.

Scott, Rebecca R. *Removing Mountains: Extracting Nature and Identity in the Appalachian Coalfields*. Minneapolis: University of Minnesota Press, 2010.

Sebenius, James K. "Sequencing to Build Coalitions: With Whom I Should I Talk First?" In *Wise Choices: Decisions, Games, and Negotiations*, edited by Richard Zeckhauser, Ralph Keeney, and James Sebenius, 324–348. Boston: Harvard Business School Press, 1996.

Selomane, Odirilwe, Belinda Reyers, Reinette Biggs, Heather Tallis, and Stephen Polasky. "Towards Integrated Social–Ecological Sustainability Indicators: Exploring the Contribution and Gaps in Existing Global Data." *Ecological Economics* 118 (2015): 140–146.

Shawki, Noha. "Norms and Normative Change in World Politics: An Analysis of Land Rights and the Sustainable Development Goals." *Global Change, Peace & Security* 28, no. 3 (2016): 249–269.

Shearman, David J. C., and Joseph Wayne Smith. *The Climate Change Challenge and the Failure of Democracy*. Westport, CT: Greenwood Publishing Group, 2007.

Shellenberger, Michael, and Ted Nordhaus. "The Death of Environmentalism." *Geopolitics, History and International Relations* 1, no. 1 (2009): 121.

Shellenberger, Michael, and Ted Nordhaus. "Evolve: Modernization as the Road to Salvation." In *Protecting Nature, Saving Creation*, edited by Pasquale Gagliardi, Anne Marie Reijnen, and Philipp Valentini, 241–247. New York: Palgrave Macmillan.

Shore, Cris. "Inventing the 'People's Europe': Critical Approaches to European Community 'Cultural Policy.'" *Man* 28, no. 4 (1993): 779–800.

Sillmann, Jana, Timothy M. Lenton, Anders Levermann, Konrad Ott, Mike Hulme, François Benduhn, and Joshua Horton. "Climate Emergencies Do Not Justify Engineering the Climate." *Nature Climate Change* 5 (2015): 290–292.

Simon, H. A. "A Behavioral Model of Rational Choice." *Quarterly Journal of Economics* 69, no. 1 (1955): 99–118.

Simon, H. A. *Models of Man: Social and Rational; Mathematical Essays on Rational Human Behavior in Society Setting.* New York: Wiley, 1957.

Simon, H. A. *Reason in Human Affairs.* Stanford: Stanford University Press, 1990.

Simon, H. A. *The Sciences of the Artificial.* Cambridge, MA: MIT Press, 1996.

Sjöberg, Lennart. "Factors in Risk Perception." *Risk Analysis* 20, no. 1 (2000): 1–12.

Slovic, P. "Perception of Risk." *Science* 236 (1987): 280–285.

Smith, Linda Tuhiwai. *Decolonizing Methodologies: Research and Indigenous Peoples.* London: Zed Books Ltd.; Dunedin: University of Otago Press, 1999.

Smith, Mick. "Against Ecological Sovereignty: Agamben, Politics and Globalisation." *Environmental Politics* 18, no. 1 (2009): 99–116.

Solnit, Rebecca. *Hope in the Dark: Untold Histories, Wild Possibilities.* New York: Nation Books, 2006.

Spahn, Paul Bernd, and Oliver Franz. "Consensus Democracy and Interjurisdictional Fiscal Solidarity in Germany." In *Managing Fiscal Decentralization*, edited by Ehtisham Ahmad and Vito Tanzi, 122–143. London: Routledge, 2000.

Stanner, William Edward Hanley. *After the Dreaming: Black and White Australians—an Anthropologist's View.* The Boyer Lectures 1968. Canberra: Australian Broadcasting Commission, 1969.

Stanner, William Edward Hanley. "On Aboriginal Religion: A Concluding Note." *Oceania* 34 (1964): 56–58.

Steelman, T. A., and S. M. McCaffrey. "What Is Limiting More Flexible Fire Management—Public or Agency Pressure?" *Journal of Forestry* 109, no. 8 (2011): 454–461.

Steffen, Will, Wendy Broadgate, Lisa Deutsch, Owen Gaffney, and Cornelia Ludwig. "The Trajectory of the Anthropocene: The Great Acceleration." *The Anthropocene Review* 2, no. 1 (2015): 81–98.

Steffen, Will, Paul J. Crutzen, and John R. McNeill. "The Anthropocene: Are Humans Now Overwhelming the Great Forces of Nature?" *Ambio* 36, no. 8 (2007): 614–621.

Steffen, Will, Åsa Persson, Lisa Deutsch, Jan Zalasiewicz, Mark Williams, Katherine Richardson, Carole Crumley, et al. "The Anthropocene: From Global Change to Planetary Stewardship." *Ambio* 40, no. 7 (2011): 739–761.

Stehr, Nico. "Exceptional Circumstances: Does Climate Change Trump Democracy?" *Issues in Science and Technology* 32, no. 2 (2016): 30.

Steinbeck, John. *The Grapes of Wrath*. London: Penguin, 2006.

Stephens, S. L., and L. W. Ruth. "Federal Forest-Fire Policy in the United States." *Ecological Applications* 15, no. 2 (2005): 532–542.

Stevens, Bjorn. "Water in the Atmosphere." *Physics Today* 66, no. 6 (2013): 29.

Stevenson, Lisa. "The Psychic Life of Biopolitics: Survival, Cooperation, and Inuit Community." *American Ethnologist* 39, no. 3 (2012): 592–613.

Stoffle, Richard W., and Richard Arnold. "Confronting the Angry Rock: American Indians' Situated Risks from Radioactivity." *Ethnos* 68, no. 2 (2003): 230–248.

Stoffle, Richard W., Richard Arnold, and Kathleen Van Vlack. "Facing the Unimaginable: Hopi and Southern Paiute Respond to Massive Risk Events." *Applied Anthropology* 35, no. 1 (2015): 13–21.

Stoffle, Richard W., Glen Rogers, Ferman Grayman, Gloria Bulletts Benson, Kathleen Van Vlack, and Jessica Medwied-Savage. "Timescapes in Conflict: Cumulative Impacts on a Solar Calendar." *Impact Assessment and Project Appraisal* 26, no. 3 (2008): 209–218.

Stott, P. A., N. Christidis, F. E. L. Otto, Y. Sun, J. P. Vanderlinden, G. J. van Oldenborgh, R. Vautard, et al. "Attribution of Extreme Weather and Climate-Related Events." *Wiley Interdisciplinary Reviews: Climate Change* 7, no. 1 (2016): 23–41.

Stott, P. A., D. A. Stone, and M. R. Allen. "Human Contribution to the European Heatwave of 2003." *Nature* 432, no. 7017 (2004): 610–614.

Strathern, M. *Reproducing the Future: Essays on Anthropology, Kinship and the New Reproductive Technologies*. Manchester: Manchester University Press, 1992.

Strelein, Lisa. *Compromised Jurisprudence: Native Title Cases since Mabo*. Canberra: Aboriginal Studies Press, 2009.

Strelein, Lisa. "From Mabo to Yorta Yorta: Native Title Law in Australia." *Washington University Journal of Law and Policy* 19 (2005): 225–271.

Swain, Daniel L., Michael Tsiang, Matz Haugen, Deepti Singh, Allison Charland, Bala Rajaratnam, and S. Noah Diffenbaugh. "The Extraordinary California Drought of 2013/2014: Character, Context, and the Role of Climate Change." *Bulletin of the American Meteorological Society* 95, no. 9 (2014): S3–S7.

Swenson, J. E., and Henrik Andrén. "A Tale of Two Countries: Large Carnivore Depredation and Compensation Schemes in Sweden and Norway." In *People and*

Wildlife, Conflict or Co-existence?, edited by Rosie Woodroffe, Simon Thirgood, and Alan Rabinowitz, 323–339. Cambridge: Cambridge University Press, 2005.

Swithern, Sophia. "How Does the Response to Typhoon Haiyan Compare with Other Recent Natural Disasters?" *Development Initiatives*, November 22, 2013. http://devinit.org/post/response-typhoon-haiyan-comparison/.

Tabary, Zoe. "Indigenous Knowledge Crucial to Tackling Climate Change, Experts Say." *Thompson Reuters Foundation*, June 28, 2017. http://news.trust.org/item/20170628160402-cblk8/?source=spotlight (accessed March 19, 2018).

Takagi, Hiroshi, M. Esteban, Tomoya Shibayama, Takahito Mikami, Ryo Matsumaru, Mario De Leon, Nguyen Danh Thao, Takahiro Oyama, and Ryota Nakamura. "Track Analysis, Simulation, and Field Survey of the 2013 Typhoon Haiyan Storm Surge." *Journal of Flood Risk Management* 10, no. 1 (2017): 42–52.

Tedlock, Dennis. *Popol Vuh: The Definitive Edition of the Mayan Book of the Dawn of Life and the Glories of Gods and Kings*. New York: Simon and Schuster, 1996.

Thacker, Eugene. *In the Dust of This Planet—Horror of Philosophy*. Vol. 1. Washington, DC: Zero Books, 2011.

Thomalla, Frank, Rebecca Smith, and E. Lisa F. Schipper. "Cultural Aspects of Risk to Environmental Changes and Hazards: A Review of Perspectives." In *Disaster's Impact on Livelihood and Cultural Survival: Losses, Opportunities, and Mitigation*, edited by Michele Companion, 3–18. Boca Raton, FL: CRC Press, 2015.

Thoreau, Henry David. *Civil Disobedience and Other Essays*. Mineola, NY: Dover Publications, 2012.

Thoreau, Henry David. *Walden, or, Life in the Woods*. New York: Vintage Books, 2011.

Thorsen, D. "Fabianismen—Derfor Fikk Norden Verdens Mest Solide Velferdsstater." *Verdibørsen*. Podcast audio. Oslo: Norwegian Broadcasting Association, 2017.

Törzsök, Judit. "Nondualism in Early Śākta Tantras: Transgressive Rites and Their Ontological Justification in a Historical Perspective." *Journal of Indian Philosophy* 42, no. 1 (2014): 195–223.

Trenberth, K. E., J. T. Fasullo, and T. G. Shepherd. "Attribution of Climate Extreme Events." *Nature Climate Change* 5, no. 8 (2015): 725–730.

Turner, A., S. White, J. Chong, M. A. Dickinson, H. Cooley, and K. Donnelly. "Managing Drought: Learning from Australia." White paper. Alliance for Water Efficiency, Institute for Sustainable Futures, University of Technology Sydney, Pacific Institute for the Metropolitan Water District of Southern California, San Francisco Public Utilities Commission, and Water Research Foundation, February 2016.

Turner, B. L., and Roger E. Kasperson, William B. Meyer, Kirstin M. Dow, Dominic Golding, Jeanne X. Kasperson, Robert C. Mitchell, and Samuel J. Ratick. "Two Types of Global Environmental Change: Definitional and Spatial-Scale Issues in Their Human Dimensions." *Global Environmental Change* 1, no. 1 (1990): 14–22.

Twigg, John. *Disaster Risk Reduction: Mitigation and Preparedness in Development and Emergency Programming.* London: Humanitarian Practice Network, Overseas Development Institute, 2004.

Uemura, R., V. Masson-Delmotte, J. Jouzel, A. Landais, H. Motoyama, and B. Stenni. "Ranges of Moisture-Source Temperature Estimated from Antarctic Ice Cores Stable Isotope Records over Glacial-Interglacial Cycles." *Climate of the Past* 8, no. 3 (2012): 1109–1125.

Ungar, Sheldon. "Social Scares and Global Warming: Beyond the Rio Convention." *Society & Natural Resources* 8, no. 5 (1995): 443–456.

UN General Assembly. "Transforming Our World: The 2030 Agenda for Sustainable Development." A/RES/70/1, October 21, 2015.

United Nations. "Draft United Nations Declaration on the Rights of Indigenous Peoples." *The Sub-Commission on Prevention of Discrimination and Protection of Minorities* (1994) 1994/45.

United Nations. "History of the United Nations." n.d. http://www.un.org/en/sections/history/history-united-nations/index.html (accessed March 12, 2018).

United Nations. "Draft United Nations Declaration on the Rights of Indigenous Peoples." *International Journal of Cultural Property* 8, no. 1 (1999): 307.

United Nations. "The Sustainable Development Goals Report." United Nations, 2016.

United Nations. "United Nations Declaration on the Rights of Indigenous Peoples." United Nations, 2007.

United Nations. "What the UN Can Do to Assist Non-self-governing Territories." United Nations Department of Public Information and United Nations Department of Political Affairs, 2015.

United Nations Environment Programme. "ABC of SCP: Clarifying Concepts on Sustainable Consumption and Production." United Nations, 2010.

United Nations Environment Programme. "Sustainable Consumption and Production Indicators for the Future SDGs." United Nations, 2015.

United Nations International Strategy for Disaster Risk Reduction. *Impacts of Summer 2003 Heat Wave in Europe.* Environmental Alert Bulletin, United Nations Environment Programme, 2004. https://www.unisdr.org/files/1145_ewheatwave.en.pdf (accessed March 19, 2018).

United Nations Office for Disaster Risk Reduction (UNISDR). "Sendai Framework for Disaster Risk Reduction 2015–2030." Geneva, Switzerland, March 18, 2015. https:// www.unisdr.org/we/coordinate/sendai-framework (accessed March 19, 2018).

United Nations International Strategy for Disaster Risk Reduction. "UNISDR Terminology on Disaster Risk Reduction." UNISDR, 2009.

United Nations International Strategy for Disaster Risk Reduction. "The World's Cities in 2016." Data booklet. UNISDR Department of Economic and Social Affairs, Population Division, 2016.

United Nations Office for Disaster Risk Reduction. "Super Typhoon Haiyan 'a Turning Point' for Disaster Risk Management." News release, November 12, 2013.

United States Drought Monitor. "Drought Classification." USDM, n.d.

van Dijk, Albert I. J. M., Hylke E. Beck, Russell S. Crosbie, Richard A. M. de Jeu, Yi Y. Liu, Geoff M. Podger, Bertrand Timbal, and Neil R. Viney. "The Millennium Drought in Southeast Australia (2001–2009): Natural and Human Causes and Implications for Water Resources, Ecosystems, Economy, and Society." *Water Resources Research* 49, no. 2 (2013): 1040–1057.

van Heijenoort, Jean. *From Frege to Gödel: A Source Book in Mathematical Logic, 1879–1931*. Cambridge, MA: Harvard University Press, 1967.

Van Loon, Anne F., Tom Gleeson, Julian Clark, Albert I. J. M. van Dijk, Kerstin Stahl, Jamie Hannaford, Giuliano Di Baldassarre, et al. "Drought in the Anthropocene." *Nature Geoscience* 9, no. 2 (2016): 89–91.

Veland, Siri. "Transcending Ontological Schisms in Relationships with Earth, Water, Air, and Ice." Special issue, "Thinking the Earth: Ways of Knowing, Modes of Care," edited by Lenore Manderson, *Weather Climate and Society* (July 2017): 607–619.

Veland, Siri, and Ian Bryceson. *Building Houses on Sand: Resilience Analysis of Erosion, Sedimentation and Coastal Management in Msasani Bay, Tanzania*. Ås, Norway: University of Life Sciences, 2005.

Veland, Siri, Richard Howitt, Dale Dominey-Howes, Frank Thomalla, and Donna Houston. "Procedural Vulnerability: Understanding Environmental Change in a Remote Indigenous Community." *Global Environmental Change* 23, no. 1 (2013): 314–326.

Veland, Siri, and Amanda H. Lynch. "Arctic Ice Edge Narratives: Scale, Discourse and Ontological Security." *Area* 49, no. 1 (2016): 9–17.

Veland, Siri, and Amanda H. Lynch. "Scaling the Anthropocene: How the Stories We Tell Matter." *Geoforum* 72 (2016): 1–5.

Veland, Siri, M. Scoville-Simonds, I. Gram-Hanssen, A. El Khoury, A. K. Schorre, A. H. Lynch, G. Hochachka, M. J. Nordbø, and M. Bjørkan. "Narrative Matters for

Sustainability: Transforming the Role of Storytelling to Realize 1.5°C Futures." Special issue, "Sustainability Governance and Transformation," edited by Bronwyn Hayward and Linda Sygnal, *Current Opinion in Environmental Sustainability* 31 (2018): 41–47.

Vernadsky, Vladimir Ivanovitch. *Scientific Thought as a Planetary Phenomenon.* Moscow: Nongovernmental Ecological V. I. Vernadsky Foundation, 1997.

Verran, Helen. "A Story about Doing 'the Dreaming.'" *Postcolonial Studies* 7, no. 2 (2004): 149–164.

Victor, David G. "Toward Effective International Cooperation on Climate Change: Numbers, Interests and Institutions." *Global Environmental Politics* 6, no. 3 (2006): 90.

Victor, David G., Joshua C. House, and Sarah Joy. "A Madisonian Approach to Climate Policy." *Science* 309, no. 5742 (2005): 1820–1821.

Vidal, John. "Copenhagen Climate Summit in Disarray after 'Danish Text' Leak." *Guardian*, December 8, 2009.

Vidot, Anna. "Anger and Optimism amongst Griffith Farmers Post MDBP." *ABC News Australia*, June 28, 2017.

Wake, David B., and Vance T. Vredenburg. "Are We in the Midst of the Sixth Mass Extinction? A View from the World of Amphibians." *Proceedings of the National Academy of Sciences* 105, no. S1 (2008): 11466–11473.

Walker, N. J., and R. E. Schulze. "An Assessment of Sustainable Maize Production under Different Management and Climate Scenarios for Smallholder Agro-Ecosystems in Kwazulu-Natal, South Africa." *Physics and Chemistry of the Earth, Parts A/B/C* 31, no. 15–16 (2006): 995–1002.

Walker, Ryan, David Natcher, and Ted Jojola. *Reclaiming Indigenous Planning.* Montreal: McGill-Queen's Press-MQUP, 2013.

Walsh, Bryan. "Climate Change Didn't Cause Supertyphoon Haiyan. But the Storm Is Still a Reason to Fight Warming." *TIME Magazine*, November 11, 2013. http://science.time.com/2013/11/11/climate-change-didnt-cause-supertyphoon-haiyan-but-the-storm-is-still-a-reason-to-fight-warming/ (accessed March 19, 2018).

Wang, Alex. "The Search for Sustainable Legitimacy: Environmental Law and Bureaucracy in China." *Harvard Environmental Law Review* 37 (2013): 365–440.

Wardle, David A., Richard D. Bardgett, Ragan M. Callaway, and Wim H. Van der Putten. "Terrestrial Ecosystem Responses to Species Gains and Losses." *Science* 332, no. 6035 (2011): 1273–1277.

Wartzman, R. *Obscene in the Extreme: The Burning and Banning of John Steinbeck's The Grapes of Wrath.* New York: PublicAffairs, 2009.

Waters, Colin N., Jan Zalasiewicz, Colin Summerhayes, Anthony D. Barnosky, Clément Poirier, Agnieszka Gałuszka, Alejandro Cearreta, et al. "The Anthropocene Is Functionally and Stratigraphically Distinct from the Holocene." *Science* 351, no. 6269 (2016): aad2622-1–aad2622-10.

Watson, Ivan. "Typhoon Haiyan Crushed Town 'Like Giant Hand from the Sky.'" *CNN*, November 11, 2013.

Weaver, Christopher P., Robert J. Lempert, Casey Brown, John A. Hall, David Revell, and Daniel Sarewitz. "Improving the Contribution of Climate Model Information to Decision Making: The Value and Demands of Robust Decision Frameworks." *Wiley Interdisciplinary Reviews: Climate Change* 4, no. 1 (2013): 39–60.

Weber, Heloise. "Reproducing Inequalities through Development: The MDGs and the Politics of Method." *Globalizations* 12, no. 4 (2015): 660–676.

Weir, J. K. "Hope and Farce: Indigenous Peoples' Water Reforms During the Millennium Drought." In *Unstable Relations: Indigenous People and Environmentalism in Contemporary Australia*, edited by E. Vincent and T. Neale, 122–167. Perth: UWA Publishing, 2016.

Weir, J. K. *Murray River Country: An Ecological Dialogue with Traditional Owners.* Canberra, Australia: Aboriginal Studies Press, 2009.

White, Gilbert F. "Geography and Public Policy." *Professional Geographer* 24, no. 2 (1972): 101–105.

Whitehead, Alfred North. *The Function of Reason.* Princeton, NJ: Princeton University Press, 1929.

Whitehead, Alfred North. *Religion in the Making.* New York: Macmillan Company, 1926.

Whitman, W. *Song of Myself.* Mineola, NY: Dover, 2001.

Wicksteed, P. H., and F. M. Cornford. *Aristotle, the Physics.* Cambridge, MA: Harvard University Press, 1957.

Wiessner, Siegfried. "Indigenous Sovereignty: A Reassessment in Light of the UN Declaration on the Rights of Indigenous People." *Journal of Transnational Law* 41 (2008): 1141–1176.

Wilbanks, Thomas J., and W. Robert Kates. "Global Change in Local Places: How Scale Matters." *Climatic Change* 43, no. 3 (1999): 601–628.

Wilcock, Deirdre, Gary Brierley, and Richard Howitt. "Ethnogeomorphology." *Progress in Physical Geography* 37, no. 5 (2013): 573–600.

Wilkinson, Kim M., Susan G. Clark, and William R. Burch. *Other Voices, Other Ways, Better Practices: Bridging Local and Professional Environmental Knowledge.* New Haven, CT: Yale School of Forestry & Environmental Studies, 2007.

Williamson, John. "The Strange History of the Washington Consensus." *Journal of Post Keynesian Economics* 27, no. 2 (2004): 195–206.

Wilson, Edward O. *Half-Earth: Our Planet's Fight for Life.* New York: W. W. Norton & Company, 2016.

Woods, Rene. "Murray-Darling: Cultural Flows and Economy for Indigenous Community Members." *ABC News*, June 27, 2017.

World Bank. "Damages from Extreme Weather Mount as Climate Warms." News release, November 18, 2013. http://www.worldbank.org/en/news/press-release/2013/11/18/damages-extreme-weather-mount-climate-warms (accessed March 10, 2018).

World Bank. "Project Completion Report, Ethiopia. Grain Storage and Marketing Project." World Bank Agriculture Operations Division, Country Department II Africa Regional Office, 1990.

World Bank, and Development Research Center of the State Council. *Urban China: Toward Efficient, Inclusive, and Sustainable Urbanization.* Washington, DC: World Bank Publications, 2014.

WWF. "China at a Crossroads." WWF, 2017. http://wwf.panda.org/what_we_do/footprint/transforming_china/ (accessed June 30, 2017).

Xenophon. *Memorabilia and Oeconomicus, with an English Translation by E. C. Marchant.* London: William Heinemann, 1923.

Young, O. R. "Arctic Environmental Issues: Prospects for International Cooperation." *Current Research on Peace and Violence* 12, no. 3 (1989): 105–110.

Zalasiewicz, Jan, Mark Williams, Richard Fortey, Alan Smith, Tiffany L. Barry, Angela L. Coe, Paul R. Bown, et al. "Stratigraphy of the Anthropocene." *Philosophical Transactions of the Royal Society of London A: Mathematical, Physical and Engineering Sciences* 369, no. 1938 (2011): 1036–1055.

Zalasiewicz, Jan, Mark Williams, Alan Haywood, and Michael Ellis. "The Anthropocene: A New Epoch of Geological Time?" Special issue, "Anthropocene: A New Epoch of Geological Time?," edited by Mark Williams, Jan Zalasiewicz, Alan Haywood, and Mike Ellis. *Philosophical Transactions of the Royal Society* 369, no. 1938 (2011): 835–841.

Zhang, Z. X. "Carbon Emissions Trading in China: The Evolution from Pilots to a Nationwide Scheme." *Climate Policy* 15 (2015): S104–S126.

Zielo, B., and A. Matzarakis. "Relevance of Heat Health Actions Plans for Preventive Public Health in Germany" (German title "Bedeutung von Hitzeaktionspläne für den präventiven Gesundheitsschutz in Deutschland"). *Gesundheitswesen*, June 17, 2017. doi: 10.1055/s-0043-107874.

Index